P9-DEI-130

# CROSSROADS
## *of the*
# CONTINENT

### A HISTORY OF THE FORKS
### OF THE RED AND ASSINIBOINE RIVERS

Edited by Barbara Huck

Heartland Associates Inc.
Winnipeg, Canada

Printed in Manitoba, Canada

*With its columns of Tyndall stone and circular shape, the entrance to The Forks National Historic Site, opposite, is not only visually appealing, but historically relevant, for it incorporates materials and ideas from some of the site's most significant periods.*

IAN WARD

*The Winnipeg Male Voice Choir posed for this photograph at Union Station just prior to leaving for a tour of the United States in March 1922.*

National Library of Canada Cataloguing in Publication Data

Main entry under title:

Crossroads of the continent:
A history of the Forks
of the Red and Assiniboine Rivers
/ Barbara Huck, editor.

Co-published by: Forks North Portage Partnership.
Includes bibliographical references.
ISBN 1-896150-34-9 (bound)
— ISBN 1-896150-38-1 (pbk.)

1. Forks, The (Winnipeg, Man.)—History.
2. Winnipeg (Man.)—History.
3. The Forks National Historic Site (Winnipeg, Man.)
I. Huck, Barbara.
II. Forks North Portage Partnership (Project)
FC3396.4.C76 2003      971.27'43      C2003-910506-7
F1064.5.W7C76 2003

DEPARTURE OF THE WINNIPEG MALE VOICE CHOIR FOR THE

7574-1

FOOTE 1951 / PROVINCIAL ARCHIVES OF MANITOBA 38

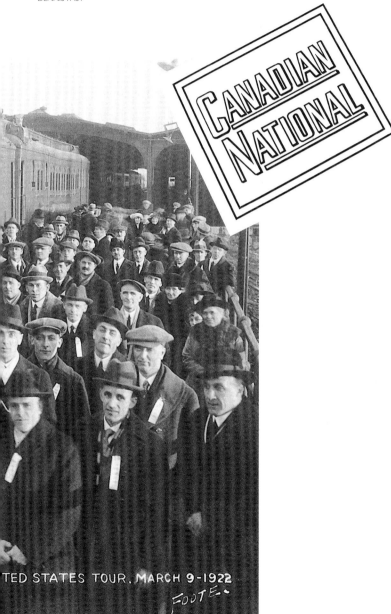

*Below right: the logo on one of CN's rail cars.*
DENNIS FAST

TED STATES TOUR. MARCH 9-1922
FOOTE.

# CREDITS

EDITOR
Barbara Huck

DESIGN
Dawn Huck

AUTHORS
Sarah Burton, Catherine Flynn, Marjorie Gillies, Frances Russell, Eleanor Stardom, Peter St. John, Harvey Thorleifson

COVER AND CHAPTER TITLE PAGE ART
Linda Fairfield

THE FORKS NORTH PORTAGE PARTNERSHIP BOARD
Bill Norrie – Chair, Daniel Boucher, Rosemary Chambers, Jerry Cianflone, Elaine Cowan, Leonard Harapiak, Wayne Onchulenko, Piara Sharma, Philip Sheps, Diana Regehr

THE FORKS HERITAGE ADVISORY COMMITTEE
Daniel Boucher – Chair, Karen Botting, Giles Bugailiskis, Barbara Ford, Jim Kacki, David McDowell, Clarence Nepinak, Bill Norrie, Dr. Leigh Syms, Lilian Tankard, Greg Thomas, Marilyn Williams

PREPRODUCTION
Avenue 4 Communications, Winnipeg, Canada

PRINTING
Friesens, Altona, Canada

*Neither this book, nor The Forks and The Forks National Historic Site would have been possible without the significant commitments and prolonged collaboration of the Government of Canada, the Province of Manitoba and the City of Winnipeg.*

*The Forks North Portage Partnership wishes to express its gratitude to Manitoba Culture, Heritage and Tourism's Heritage Grants Program, and to the Asper Foundation for their assistance in the creation of this history of The Forks.*

*Front cover images: fireworks by Dennis Fast; harbour light by Peter St. John*

# ACKNOWLEDGEMENTS

First and foremost, we would like to thank Harvey Thorleifson, senior scientist at the Geological Survey of Canada and the newly-elected president of the Geological Association of Canada, who took the time from a very busy schedule of research, travel and public speaking to write the first two chapters of this book. The Foundation of The Forks and Laying Down the Landscape give readers fascinating insights into Manitoba's ancient history.

Also of enormous help was Gaywood Matile, Quaternary geologist with the Manitoba Geological Survey, who provided a host of illustrations and computer models and was endlessly patient with our many questions. Others at the MGS assisted in many ways, including Greg Keller, GIS technologist, who helped to produce many of the graphic images and geologist Ruth Bezys, who answered queries and dug out information. Scott St. George, who works in Manitoba with the GSC, provided fascinating background information on the ancient Red River and the cycles of flooding in the region.

We had invaluable help throughout the creation of this book from the members of The Forks Heritage Advisory Committee, all of whom are listed on the previous page. They reviewed every chapter, offered information, assistance with sourcing images and provided a vitally important external perspective on the whole production.

Provincial archaeologist Leigh Syms and Forks site archaeologist Sid Kroker were particularly helpful over the Aboriginal chapter, as was Lilian Tankard over the fur trade chapter, while David McDowell proved to be a fount of information about the railway period. Barbara Ford and Greg Thomas of Parks Canada assisted in many ways, reading each section with care and offering suggestions on a number of occasions. Committee chair Daniel Boucher helped to keep the whole project on schedule.

At the Manitoba Museum, provincial geologist Graham Young vetted manuscripts and spent time with our artist, Linda Fairfield, as she created the paintings that open each chapter. Linda also received valuable advice on palaeontology from Betsy Thorsteinson, on nineteenth-century costumes from Barry and Judy McPherson and on the railway and steamship eras from historian Bob Coutts.

Our thanks, too, to Mary Anne Nylen of Neepawa, who sent us heritage seeds to photograph, as well as University of Manitoba historian Ed Rea, who read and commented on the fur trade chapter. Provincial historian Henry Trachtenberg made valuable suggestions for both the immigration and steamships sections and Hnausa educator and artist Nelson Gerrard, who is an expert on Icelandic history, vetted sections of the immigration chapter and allowed us to use one of his drawings. Randy Rostecki also assisted with the chapter on steamships, as did the staff at the Provincial Archives and Provincial Library in Winnipeg, and at the Brandon Chamber of Commerce.

Several people contributed to the railway section: Doug Whiteway, assistant editor at The Beaver, went over the manuscript with a fine eye; the volunteers at the Winnipeg Railway Museum offered both assistance and enthusiasm, and Raphael Leung at VIA Rail provided photographs and information and as well as access to the Countess of Dufferin.

The final section, The Forks Today, required the time and recollections of many people: Bill Norrie, former Winnipeg mayor and now chair of The Forks board; Nick Diakiw, former Winnipeg chief commissioner and later CEO of The Forks; former federal minister Jake Epp; Deputy Premier Jean Friesen and former MP Dorothy Dobbie, both members of the original Forks board; Al Baronas, vice-president and secretary to The Forks Task Force; current CEO Jim August, who has been involved with The Forks for many years; columnist and social activist Val Werier, and a trio of architects who continue to be involved with The Forks, Steve Cohlmeyer, Etienne Gaboury and Garry Hilderman. Thanks, too, to Gary Filmon, former premier of Manitoba, who proof read several sections with an eagle eye for detail, and saved us from a number of embarrassing errors.

Throughout, the members of The Forks staff – Paul Jordan, Toby Chase and Paul Webster, along with Michelle Du and Jeff Palmer – solved problems, provided contacts and illustrations and were tremendously supportive and helpful. And horticulturalist Gina Nickle provided both information and samples of dried plants for the sidebars on plant life at The Forks that are featured in every section.

For those of us who were intimately involved, this was an illuminating and enjoyable project. We learned a great deal about the long history of The Forks – the real heartland of Winnipeg – and I hope we have conveyed this fascinating information in a way that will engage and educate.


Barbara Huck
April 2003

*The Forks Plaza, decked out in late summer beauty.*

PETER ST. JOHN

PROVINCIAL ARCHIVES OF MANITOBA / N12509

A HORSE-DRAWN CARIOLE WHISKS A PASSENGER UP THE FROZEN ASSINIBOINE RIVER PAST UPPER FORT GARRY DURING THE WINTER OF 1840.

# TABLE OF CONTENTS

# PREFACE

This history of The Forks is very much the story of Winnipeg – how it was settled, how it developed, and how it grew and prospered through the vision of individuals and cooperation between and amongst governments. As mayor of the City of Winnipeg during the 1980s, I feel very privileged to have been part of a team of extraordinary individuals – administrators, politicians and citizen volunteers – all deeply committed to the vision of The Forks. You will read about them in the pages that follow.

The Forks has a unique and special place in the history of our city. It is still considered so today. Indeed, its very creation honoured those characteristics, and the cooperation needed to bring this vision to reality was in itself rare and perhaps unprecedented. The 1980s was a time of urban renewal in Winnipeg and the Core Area Initiative was the main vehicle in this renewal. As a tri-level government agreement, it was truly unique, in that it was the first time in Canada that a municipal government had signed an agreement as an equal partner with the federal government. One of the many programs under the agreement was the development we know as The Forks.

The vision of many helped to transform an abandoned railyard at the junction of the Red and Assiniboine Rivers into The Forks we know today. In the mid-'80s, following the political decision to undertake a major waterfront development, I recall the energy and enthusiasm as I, along with elected officials from the federal and provincial governments, received some very passionate presentations from citizens and planners. They presented ideas for converting the former Canadian National Railway's East Yards into a waterfront development for leisure and enjoyment.

The Forks has become Winnipeg's premiere "meeting place", combining commerce and recreation with numerous events, large and small, that capture the character of our multicultural community. We have seen the personality of our city reflected in such major events as the 1997 Red River Flood benefit concert, the 1999 Pan American Games cultural festivities, and the North American Indigenous Games of 2002. We have attended Winnipeg Symphony concerts and the Spiritfest Concerts for Causes.

The Forks Board is respectful of the public trust and the expectations that come with preserving The Forks as a "Meeting Place" of historic significance. We appreciate the support of the members of The Forks Heritage Advisory Committee, who lend their advice, views and expertise on matters of heritage integrity. I would also thank each of our three shareholders and the two ministers and mayor who represent them, for their active interest on behalf of the citizens of Canada, Manitoba and Winnipeg. The accomplishments from the early days of the redevelopment of The Forks to the present have been made possible through their full support and cooperation.

It is a very real pleasure to be part of this history book project, which gives the public the complete story of The Forks, where artifacts from Aboriginal encampments dating back some 6,000 years have been recovered. Future generations will add to this history. For the present, it is our hope that readers will come away with a better understanding of the rich history in the heart of our city at The Forks.

William Norrie, C.M., O.M., Q.C.
Chairman, The Forks North Portage Partnership

# FOREWORD

For most Manitobans and certainly for visitors, it now seems hard to imagine a Winnipeg without The Forks. It's the place we are drawn to for festivals, for celebrations great and small, for medal ceremonies in international games, or for a quiet evening stroll.

It has, in fact, become our prime public space, our town square, our piazza. The Forks is where we gather to celebrate Canada Day or to commemorate the tragedy of 9/11, and it was, most recently, where Manitobans welcomed the Queen.

More than fifteen years ago I was a part of the first Forks Board of Directors. I remember my first impressions of this windswept cinder strewn industrial site at the junction of the Red and Assiniboine Rivers. We had viewed it from afar, from the high buildings at Portage and Main, and had been struck by the sheer scale of the 100-acre site and by the task of reclamation that lay before us.

Later I walked the site and talked to CN workers in the Roundhouse (now the Children's Museum), hearing of the many springs they had spent ankle deep in mud as the ice floors of the workshop alternately thawed and froze in unsettled weather. Yet apart from this generation of railway workers and some dedicated riverbank fishermen, this was an unknown landscape – simply not part of the mental map of our own city.

The intervening years of work by successive boards of directors and the staff of three levels of government have created a meeting place that is valued by young and old. It is a destination for Manitobans and tourists in all seasons and has achieved a special place in our hearts.

Public advisory committees on heritage, and our Forks neighbours Parks Canada, helped to ensure that public archaeology and history had a prominent place in the early years of development. Advice from First Nations elders and others had made certain that the history of Aboriginal peoples and their long presence at the site has been prominent in our interpretations. Through public hearings, frequent open houses, and annual public meetings citizen interest has continued to grow. Public debate about the nature and future of The Forks is testimony to the sense of ownership that has come to characterize Winnipeg's sense of this special place.

The cooperation of three levels of government, the support of public and private sectors and the vision of many volunteers have returned to us our riverbanks. Together we have built a place of celebration and recreation, and The Forks has become one of the symbols of a New Winnipeg.

Jean Friesen, Ph.D.
Minister of Intergovernmental Affairs
Deputy Premier of Manitoba

NATIONAL ARCHIVES OF CANADA / C10513

*Artist William Armstrong entitled this painting "Setting up Camp on the Prairies". Similar camps would have been a familiar sight at The Forks between 1780 and 1870.*

*These lovely dart or atlatl points were among those found at The Forks. From top to bottom, they are a broken Hanna point of Tongue River silicified sediment, and two Shield Archaic points of quartzite; the second of these is similar in shape to Pelican Lake points found on the plains.*

# INTRODUCTION

From ancient Babylon on the Euphrates River in Mesopotamia, to London on the Thames, Paris on the Seine and Cairo on the Nile, many of the world's great cities were built on its major rivers. And following the European settlement of North America, almost every major city that predated the coming of the railways was built on the sea-coasts, on the Great Lakes or on one or more rivers. Like Montreal, New York, New Orleans and St. Louis, Winnipeg owes its existence to its waterways. Growing from an ancient meeting and trading place at the confluence of the Red and Assiniboine Rivers, its history stretches back millennia.

This is the story of The Forks, how it came to be and what gives it, in the words of geologist Harvey Thorleifson, its "immaculately featureless landscape". It is also a tale of human evolution and transformation, a chronicle of how a favoured meeting place grew into a continental crossroads, metamorphosed into a hub of the fur trade and became, for a time, the funnel through which all Western Canadian immigration and development passed. It's a saga of changing times and changing cultures, and ultimately it's a story of rediscovery.

It's the story of Winnipeg, but it's also Canada's story in microcosm. And it's a tale The Forks North Portage Partnership has been wanting to tell since the very first meeting of the board.

On behalf of everyone who worked long and hard to bring it to you, I hope it's a history that will enlighten and inform, bringing with it a greater appreciation of the treasure that lies at the heart of Winnipeg.

Barbara Huck

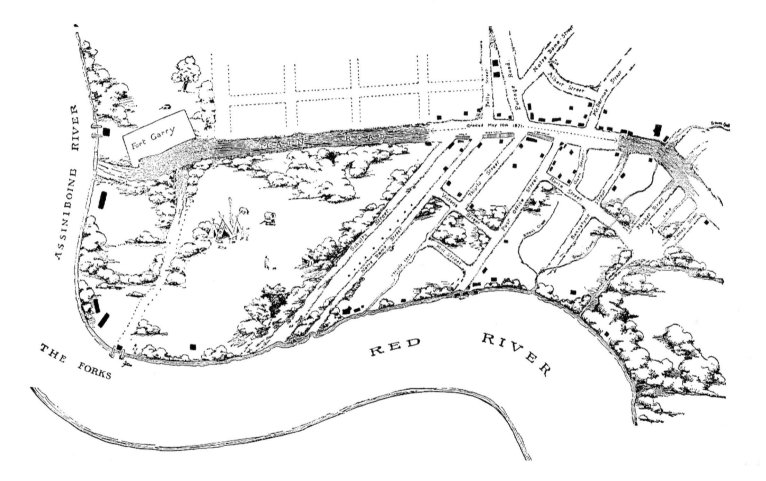

MANITOBA FREE PRESS FIFTIETH ANNIVERSARY NUMBER, NOVEMBER 9, 1922

*This lovely hand-drawn map of "the Flats", as they called it then, appeared in the* Manitoba Free Press *in November 1872. It shows The Forks as it looked on the eve of the creation of the City of Winnipeg, with Upper Fort Garry on the Assiniboine, an Aboriginal encampment near the trail to the Red River and a scattering of businesses and homes around the junction of "Main Road" and "Portage Road". In less than five years, this pastoral scene would be gone, as Winnipeg became the fastest-growing city in Canada.*

The Foundation

Life in Manitoba's Ordovician seas probably looked much like this. Fossils of chain coral, seen at the centre left and at the bottom of the painting; receptaculitids, the balloon-like plants on the sea floor; trilobites, such as the one furrowing the sand at the centre and a cephalopod, with dinner in its clutches, can all be seen in the Tyndall stone of the Manitoba legislature. Also shown are kelp-like crinoids and a nautilus floating at the centre of the opposite page.

# of The Forks

By Harvey Thorleifson

At first glance, The Forks seems a simple feature – the confluence of two rivers etched into a dry lake bed. But to explain how it came to be requires a review of more than three billion years of Earth history, a story of colliding continents, a tropical sea, caves and sinkholes, a time of brine, a thick layer of shale shed by the Rocky Mountains, deep erosion, a glacier that covered Canada, one of the largest lakes in Earth's history, a 4,000-year drought, a missing

## GEOLOGICAL TIME GUIDE

| TIME (In millions of years) | EON | ERA | PERIOD | EPOCH |
|---|---|---|---|---|
| .01 | | | | **Holocene** (Large mammal extinctions; Humans come to North America) |
| .02 | | | *Last extensive glacial cycle* | |
| 2 | | | **Quaternary** | **Pleistocene** |
| | | | | **Pliocene** (First hominids evolve in Africa) |
| | | | | **Miocene** |
| | | | | **Oligocene** |
| | | | | **Eocene** (Great erosion; first grasses, horses, tapirs) |
| 65 – 2 | | **Cenozoic** (Modern life) | **Tertiary** | **Paleocene** (Mammals begin to evolve rapidly) |
| 65 | | *Extinction event* | *Dinosaurs die – About 65% of life on Earth disappears* | |
| | Phanerozoic (visible life) | | **Cretaceous** (First flowering plants) | |
| | | | **Jurassic** (Central Atlantic Ocean opens) | |
| 248 – 65 | | **Mesozoic** (Middle life) | **Triassic** (First dinosaurs, early mammals) | |
| 248 | | *Mass extinction event in the oceans* | *More than 90% of species disappear* | |
| | | | **Permian** | |
| | | | **Carboniferous** | |
| | | | **Devonian** (First insects) | |
| | | | **Silurian** (Land plants, jawed fish) | |
| | | | **Ordovician** (Tyndall stone) | |
| 544 – 250 | | **Paleozoic** (Ancient life) | **Cambrian** (First vertebrates) | |
| 2500 – 544 | **Precambrian** | **Proterozic** (Early life) | | |
| Before 2500 | **Early Precambrian** | **Archean** | | |

river that suddenly appeared from the west, and a populated region that regularly turns into a temporary lake. Despite all this, people have chosen to live here for thousands of years and in that time, The Forks has become a focal point of the region and a significant meeting place.

This is the Red River Valley, but if you climb the tower at The Forks, you will see the surprising result of all that spectacular geological history – a flat landscape. Indeed, this is a remarkably flat landscape, compared to the rocky hills of the Canadian Shield of northern Ontario, or the rolling hills and lakes of the Prairie to the west – and far more serene than the majestic mountains of Canada's west and east. And even from the tower, it's impossible to see the valley walls (see page 18). The eastern wall, which consists of ancient granite hills, is more than a hundred kilometres away. An equal distance to the west, everywhere except along the gently rising Trans-Canada Highway, is the western valley wall, the abrupt rise of the Manitoba Escarpment, made of vastly younger shale. Between these distant valley walls, the Red River slowly winds along the middle of the flat valley floor, obeying a course dictated by the underlying layer of limestone, which slopes gently to the west beneath the sediments of glacial Lake Agassiz. This rock – the eastern granite, the western shale and the underlying limestone – gave us the foundation for the landscape and the rivers as we know them. But how did these rocks form?

THE PRECAMBRIAN EON: *Before 544 million years ago (mya)* The granites and other Precambrian rocks deep below Winnipeg constitute the fundamental factor that governs the character of The Forks today. These rocks are part of the North American craton, the core of the continent, which extends from Montreal to Calgary and from the central United States to the Arctic. This craton was assembled between two and four billion years ago as a jigsaw puzzle of rocks such as granite, gneiss and greenstone. As early continents drifted and collided, and as oceans opened and closed, new rocks were added onto the growing North American continent, and the core of stable, relatively immobile, mature rocks gradually expanded with time. Construction of the craton took place very early in Earth's history, during the Precambrian Eon, more than 544 million years ago.

The craton is therefore the sub-foundation of the region, both where it is exposed and also where layers of sedimentary rocks have buried it. Where the craton is exposed, it is known as the Canadian or Precambrian Shield. A traveller can observe the rocky hills and lakes of the shield along the Trans-Canada

Highway across Northwestern Ontario, but in the Prairie region, as well as in southern Ontario and the St. Lawrence valley, relatively thin layers of sedimentary rocks such as limestone, sandstone and shale cover this craton.

At The Forks, the granites and other rocks of the craton can be accessed by drilling to a depth of about 200 metres. Farther west, one would have to drill even deeper as the sedimentary rocks thicken. But even though they are buried deep below the modern landscape, these stable, mature, ancient rocks of the craton support Winnipeg and provide the gentle, earthquake-free substrate that rises up to form the eastern wall of the Red River Valley.

The Precambrian rocks of central North America consist of belts that lie in an east-west direction. This trend is characteristic of what is known to geologists as the Superior Province – the area of Precambrian rocks extending from the city of Thompson in northern Manitoba all the way to Lake Huron. The Superior Province was largely assembled during early Precambrian time, between 3.5 and 2.5 billion years ago, during the creation of the North American continent. Geologists call this process continental accretion and it culminated with a dramatic mountain-building episode known as the Kenoran Orogeny.

During this time, long, narrow ribbons of rock called greenstone belts were progressively built, defining the east-west grain of the rocks of the Superior Province. These belts are generally tens of kilometres across and hundreds of kilometres long, and typically consist of dark-coloured volcanic and sedimentary rocks. They lie between broader areas of typically pinkish granites and gneisses. In the dark-coloured greenstone belts, such as the rocks that can be seen from the highway along the north shore of Falcon Lake east of Winnipeg, are most of the mines in the shield. The volcanic rocks of the belts are the remnants of volcanic island arcs comparable to Japan of today, as well as sedimentary rocks that formed in ocean basins that opened and closed as the primeval continents drifted.

The greenstone belts include a full spectrum of volcanic and sedimentary rock types. The volcanic rocks include basalt in abundance, formed where molten magma erupted as lava flowed onto the sea floor. A dark-colored rock, basalt is quartz-poor but rich in iron and magnesium. Near West Hawk Lake, on the Trans-Canada Highway near the Manitoba-Ontario border, basalts that erupted on the seafloor in pillow shapes can be seen.

As the volcanic rock was exposed to air and the action of water, wind and gravity, it was worn down, forming sediments that later turned into sandstones and shales. The debris that washed from basalts became quartz-poor, dark-coloured sandstone known as greywacke. But other processes concentrated silica to form lighter-coloured volcanic rocks richer in quartz, such as andesite and rhyolite. Millions of years later, rhyolite would be used by Native North Americans to create projectile points for their atlatl darts.

The greenstone belts and the surrounding regions also include igneous rocks that crystallized slowly from completely molten magma. As the continents slid under one

COURTESY OF THE MANITOBA GEOLOGICAL SURVEY

*The swirls of rock, above, are the remains of pillow lava – rolls of basalt that initially looked like neck pillows or rolled up sleeping bags. They form when molten lava cools quickly in water.*

*Most people think of the Red River Valley as consisting of the muddy banks of the river, but as the lower computer model shows, the valley is in fact hundreds of kilometres wide, stretching from the Canadian Shield on the far right to the Manitoba Escarpment on the far left.*

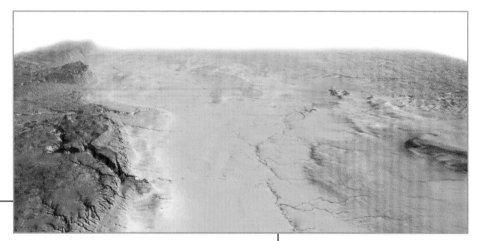

BOTH IMAGES: GAYWOOD MATILE / MANITOBA GEOLOGICAL SURVEY

*The deep cleft in the escarpment on the lower left is the Pembina Valley; the smaller Assiniboine River Valley can be seen above it. The vertical elevations in this model have been enhanced by thirty times to allow even relatively gentle increases in elevation to be easily seen. The upper model shows the elevations in the Red River Valley in a series of different colours, making it easy to see the outcroppings of limestone in the Interlake, for example.*

*Crossroads of the Continent*

another, rocks were deeply buried and, in the interior of the Earth, melted to produce magma in domes many kilometres across. These huge bubbles rose through surrounding rocks like droplets of oil in salad dressing, then cooled and crystallized to form igneous bodies of rock known as intrusions or plutons. The plutons range in composition from quartz-poor gabbro to quartz-rich granite.

Other things happened as the continents collided and mountains were built. Deeply buried rocks were "cooked", transformed by the heat and pressure of metamorphism, which turned shale into schist and sandstone into quartzite. These enormous pressures also deformed the rocks, pushing horizontal layers into vertical positions, folding layers in simple or chaotic patterns, and breaking the rocks along faults. Over large areas, these forces were sufficiently intense to partially melt and completely recrystallize the rocks, producing rock such as pink and black-banded gneisses.

Eventually, the volcanic and sedimentary rocks of the greenstone belts, the expanses of gneisses, and the intrusions of granite and other igneous rocks were welded together to form a stable foundation free of volcanic eruptions or large earthquakes. These processes, which took place over about two billion years of Precambrian time, assembled the North American craton. To this day, it forms a firm and stable footing for the Winnipeg region.

As a result, by late Precambrian time, the continent that would become North America had grown and matured so that its interior had become immune to the disturbances of collisions with other continents. Now erosion took over from volcanism, mountain building and sedimentation. Over the next billion years, the mid-continent mountains were exposed to air and water, causing chemical deposition and erosion by wind, ice and gravity. The surface of the Earth floats on the planet's mobile interior, so as rivers removed the newly-formed sediment from the eroding rock, the land rose to replenish the supply of rocks to be eroded, just as a boat rises as its cargo is removed. This is one of the factors that explains how metamorphic rocks that were cooked by temperatures and pressure at a depth of several kilometres can now be exposed at the surface.

Much later, the rocks that rivers and rain had been patiently

COURTESY OF ERIK NIELSEN

*Multicoloured gneiss (pronounced "nice"), above, found at Drumming Point on Lake Winnipeg's east shore, is testament to the fiery temperatures and tremendous pressures involved in the creation of North America.*

*Inset: A quartzite "Pelican Lake" point that was found at The Forks.*

removing were more deeply scoured by glaciers during the ice age, but there is evidence of the decomposed layer at sites that were protected from later glacial action. For example, in protected hollows under thick sediments in southeastern Manitoba, or where the ancient Precambrian rocks are covered by more recent sedimentary rocks, what was once sturdy pink granite occurs as a layer several metres thick of chemically altered rocks, in many cases consisting of soft whitish clay. It was this achievement of intracontinental stability, and the late Precambrian chemical decomposition of rocks and washing away of resulting sediment that was the first step in producing the gentle landscape that we see at The Forks today.

THE PALEOZOIC ERA: *544 to 250 mya*
The next major step in giving Winnipeg its geologically subtle landscape was the burial of the more rugged Precambrian rocks by the sedimentary rocks of the Paleozoic Era. These rocks were deposited early in the Paleozoic Era, which lasted from 544 to 250 million years ago (mya). The first sequence of deposits, consisting of sandstone and shale known as the Winnipeg Formation, is a layer about forty metres thick that lies about 160 metres below The Forks. The Paleozoic was the first or earliest era in the Phanerozoic Eon (see chart on page 16), which is defined as the 544 million years since the Precambrian Eon.

The sandstone in the Winnipeg Formation formed during a phase of high global sea levels about 460 million years ago. As continents drifted and what is now North America migrated to a tropical latitude, there came a time of bulging sea floors and sagging continents, when the continents were largely flooded by shallow sea water. As the seas flooded in, the gravel, sand, silt and clay that had formed from the decomposing rocks, were washed about by the water. These clastic sediments were separated by the flowing water and waves into deposits of varying size, and sand deposits blanketed what is now the Winnipeg region.

This sand became rich in quartz as it was acted on by the chemical and mechanical action that decomposed more chemically unstable minerals, and pulverized softer minerals. These processes decomposed nearly everything except quartz, which is chemically and physically very stable. As a result, the Precambrian rocks under The Forks were buried by sand rich in quartz, as well as layers of silt and clay. As other deposits buried these sediments, the temperature and pressure rose. When water-borne carbonate and silica percolated through these layers, the sediments turned into rocks. Sand layered with silt or clay became sandstone with layers of shale.

Deposition of the sandstone was another step in smoothing Winnipeg's landscape. Previously, during Precambrian time, the hills and valleys of the shield had been shaped by the processes of landscape erosion; tough rocks resistant to weathering stood high as hills, and soft rocks gave way to valleys. But when the sea inundated these hills and valleys,

*This map shows one of the seaways that bisected North America hundreds of millions of years ago. The outlines of the continent have dramatically changed since then, but the underlying modern map shows the areas covered at the time.*

COURTESY OF THE MANITOBA GEOLOGICAL SURVEY

*Crossroads of the Continent*

sand tended to accumulate in the valleys and the landscape levelled. Today, the sandstone lies well below Winnipeg and few people are aware of the important role it can play. The silica-rich Winnipeg Formation sandstone provides good well water in areas east of Winnipeg. And where it rises to the surface on Black Island in Lake Winnipeg, it has provided excellent quartz-rich silica sand for glassmaking. The sandstone is also a source of the sand that helps make Grand Beach such a famous attraction. But the sandstone is not the uppermost layer of rock beneath Winnipeg; it is simply the first layer that buried the Precambrian rocks.

**T**he uppermost layer of rock under The Forks, the layer that a driller would hit first, and the rock that has had the greatest direct influence on Winnipeg's character, is limestone. The limestone and related carbonate rocks together make up a sequence of layers about 130 metres thick that rests just thirty metres below The Forks. Limestones are exposed at Little Mountain Park near the Winnipeg airport, at Stony Mountain and Stonewall to the north, and at the Garson and Tyndall-area quarries northeast of Winnipeg. These limestones, which are rich in calcium, as well as zones and layers of dolomites rich in magnesium, together make up a complex series of layers that once blanketed the entire mid-continent. To the north and east, before they were removed by later erosion, they extended across what is now the shield all the way to Hudson Bay, where they can still be found. To the west, they extend from what is now the exposed Canadian Shield all the way to Calgary, where deep beneath the surface, today they contain large quantities of oil.

*The precision with which limestone is quarried today is evident, right, in this quarry in Garson.*

*Below: Now abandoned, the silica sand quarries on Black Island produced excellent material for making glass.*

COURTESY OF GEOLOGICAL SURVEY OF MANITOBA

PETER ST. JOHN

ROGER TURENNE

RUGGED LIMESTONE CLIFFS RISE ABOVE THE NORTH BASIN OF LAKE WINNIPEG.

*Crossroads of the Continent*

These carbonate rocks formed nearly a half-billion years ago, when the shallow tropical sea that covered the continent developed optimum conditions for an explosion of marine life. A good combination of a warm climate, shallow seawater depths, a ready supply of nutrients and an end to the early influx of sand and clay created a population explosion of marine organisms.

When they died, they littered the floor of the sea. Geologists call this material "calcareous biogenic debris". The word calcareous refers to calcite, which is a mineral made of calcium carbonate – the mix of calcium, carbon and oxygen that makes up the rocks. Biogenic means that the origin of the debris is living organisms – the body parts of shells, corals and other marine creatures.

Thus the organisms that abundantly stocked this half-billion-year-old central North American tropical sea are preserved in our midst as fossils. The rocks under Winnipeg are Ordovician in age. These seas would have been inhabited by creatures depicted on the opening pages of this chapter. To the west, younger carbonate rocks that were deposited during the Silurian and Devonian ages can be found near Portage la Prairie. These ages are readily confirmed by the quick eye of a palaeontologist, who is able to assign an age to the rocks on the basis of the fossils found in it. Though they may not realize it, many Winnipeggers can also do this with Ordovician limestone, for they easily recognize the dish-shaped fossils called *receptaculitids* or sunflower corals that are found in these rocks. Few would suspect that this organism was a plant, however, and not an animal. There are other recognizable fossils in the stone, such as giant snails, horn corals, chain corals, brachiopods, squid-like cephalopods and trilobites. Many of these fossils are the size of a person's hand or larger.

## RECEPTACULITES
### (*Fisherites receptaculitids*)

Though its fossilized remains would seem to be those of an animal, geologists now believe that *Receptaculites*, or sunflower coral, was in fact a plant – a type of alga that lived in large globular colonies about 350 million years ago. Each colony was made up of a series of plates of column-shaped algae, arranged layer upon layer in a series of clockwise and counterclockwise patterns. The colonies, which could be more than thirty centimetres across, may have looked rather like anchored balloons as they grew on the sea floor.

The fossils are seen in cross-section, however, for when the stone is quarried, the round colonies are bisected by diamond saws. The result is rather like an MRI scan of this ancient plant.

PETER ST. JOHN

Winnipeggers are familiar with these fossils because this excellent stone – known as Tyndall stone, one of Canada's best building materials – is quarried just thirty-seven kilometres northeast of The Forks near the towns of Garson and Tyndall. Most of us know it as Tyndall stone, but geologists have assigned this mottled limestone to the lower part of the Selkirk Member of the Red River Formation. Its tapestry-like branching pattern is created by zones of darker, more magnesium-rich dolomite, which make up about a third of the rock, in a lighter-coloured matrix of calcite-dominated limestone. Calcite is more soluble than dolomite, so in the case of old blocks of Tyndall stone, the dark, dolomitic mottles stand above the slightly receding lighter-coloured material.

The dark mottles are a result of burrowing by an organism whose behaviour was similar to that of shrimps. These creatures found the muddy debris to be a happy home – before it was turned to stone. Their branching trails are called trace fossils. The dolomite formed after the burrows were filled with sediment. As water with magnesium in it filtered through the sea floor sediments, the material filling the burrows incorporated the magnesium better than the surrounding floor of the sea. Then, much later during their history, these rocks were exposed to oxygen, which produced the beige colour so typical of this stone.

Quarrying of this remarkable stone began along the banks of the Red River north of Winnipeg during the fur trade era; the Hudson's Bay Company used it in the construction of Lower Fort Garry in the

*With its fascinating fossils, beautiful colour and workable texture, Tyndall stone is popular right across North America. It has been used for everything from busts and statues, above, to columns and exteriors of many public buildings, such as the Manitoba legislature, right.*

1830s. The Garson deposit has been quarried since the 1890s, but the town of Tyndall gave its name to the stone, as the closest railway point to the quarry.

Five quarries have operated in Manitoba; all worked the stone in much the same manner, though today's tools are far superior to those used by nineteenth-century stone masons. The stone is exposed by removing the overlying earth, and 2.5-metre diamond tipped saw blades are used to make metre-deep vertical cuts into the stone. The cut stone is raised with wedges and is then split into six or eight ton blocks using drills and wedges. Front-end loaders move the stone to the processing mill, where it is cut using diamond-toothed circular saws. The cut surfaces are smoothed using carborundum drums or diamond discs, or the stone is split to produce rough surfaces. Brownish stone is derived from the upper layers in the quarries; a more blue-gray stone is derived from the deeper layers that are harder and less desirable. In Winnipeg, thousands of buildings, including the Manitoba Legislative Building and the Art Gallery, are at least partly made of Tyndall stone. Elsewhere, structures such as the interior of the Parliament Buildings and the Museum of Civilization in Ottawa, as well as many other buildings across Canada and the U.S., are made of Tyndall stone.

But the cycles of global high sea levels that sustained the seas in which first the sandstone and then the

LOWER: PETER ST. JOHN / BUST: DENNIS FAST

*Crossroads of the Continent*

limestones of the Winnipeg region were deposited came to an end about 300 million years ago. The marine inundations that had lasted more than 200 million years gave way to a hundred-million-year phase of low global sea levels. The Forks region became land rather than sea, and the agents shaping the landscape again became wind and rain rather than waves and currents. What is now central Winnipeg was part of the terrestrial landscape over which early land animals lived and evolved, eventually culminating in the life forms we know as dinosaurs.

Their peaceful existence was devastated, however, by an explosion that rocked the region about 220 million years ago when a large meteorite or some similar extra-terrestrial body hit the area between what are now Lake Winnipeg and Lake Manitoba. The resulting crater, twenty-three kilometres wide, is now associated with Lake St. Martin near Gypsumville. Though not as large as the later event that killed the dinosaurs, it probably took decades for the life of the region to recover from this catastrophe, and it is possible that some species didn't recover.

During this long terrestrial period, the carbonate rocks of what is now the Red River Valley were slowly dissolved by rainwater, producing the characteristic features of karst terrain – caves and sinkholes. Like much of the Interlake to the north, the Winnipeg region is riddled with such karst features, though they are all buried by clay. We know a good deal about these caves and sinkholes as a result of drilling projects in Winnipeg, as well as detailed studies by caving enthusiasts in the exposed karst terrain in the Interlake region between Lake Winnipeg and Lakes Manitoba and Winnipegosis. We know, for example, that the caves are very old and in many cases were formed more than 250 million years ago, because they

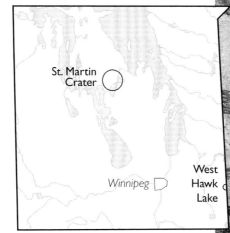

*Below: Meteorites left indelible marks on impact sites in the Interlake and the shield east of Winnipeg.*

St. Martin
Crater

West
Hawk
Lake

*Winnipeg*

are often filled with younger sedimentary rocks. And it is clear that the cave system is extensive, based on observations of rapid groundwater flow, springs, collapse features and the intersection of voids during drilling. A network of such voids was discovered during construction of the Grand Rapids dam.

THE MESOZOIC ERA: *250 to 65 mya*
About 200 million years ago, having been land for a hundred million years, the Winnipeg region was once again inundated by the sea. This was early in the Mesozoic Era, the time between 250 and sixty-five million years ago. There are few deposits to record the Triassic Period, which opened the Mesozoic Era, but rocks representing the Jurassic Era that followed have survived. As dinosaurs evolved to rule the Earth, southern Manitoba was inhabited by sea

BOTH IMAGES: COURTESY OF THE MANITOBA GEOLOGICAL SURVEY

*One of Manitoba's best-kept secrets is its remarkable caves. Those in the Interlake region north of Winnipeg, above, draw enthusiastic cavers every year. A similar cave system is located beneath Winnipeg, but these are mostly filled with clay and glacial sediments.*

**West Hawk Lake**

(~ 4km by 4km)

**A Fiery Birth**

West Hawk Lake is one of the few lakes which occurs in that part of the Shield, most of it is filled with approximately 111 m of water. About 5600 m in which is an astonishing 111 m deep. At the deepest point, the bottom of the lake is about 2000 m below the surface of the surrounding land. Most lakes in the region are shallow, typically only a few metres deep. West Hawk Lake is very different, its great depth due to a meteorite impact. During the late Jurassic or early Cretaceous period, a meteorite smashed into the region, creating a crater that eventually filled with water.

For more information about the origin and other scientific details of West Hawk Lake's origin, see the brochure produced by G. Clark & Associates on behalf of Manitoba and Ardberg Wood of the University of Manitoba.

BOTH IMAGES: COURTESY OF THE
MANITOBA GEOLOGICAL SURVEY

creatures. The rocks characteristic of this time are deposits of red and green shale, and more importantly for the regional economy, rocks called evaporites. These are deposits such as gypsum that form in a manner similar to the scaly deposits in the bottom of your kettle. Unlike the seas of the earlier era, the water was now a concentrated brine brought on by extreme evaporation; minerals from the seawater formed deposits that blanketed the region. Once again, any valleys that had formed when the land was above sea level were smoothed as they were filled with evaporite sediments. The resulting evaporite rocks, primarily gypsum and anhydrite – forms of calcium sulphate – have been quarried around Lake Manitoba and at Gypsumville. But these rocks are also present under southwestern Winnipeg, and have been mined underground south of the city. The drillers there are familiar with the red Jurassic rocks that they often encounter.

But these cycles of oceanic inundation and terrestrial exposure were about to be complicated by explosive events to the west. For millions of years, the North American continent had been on a collision course with islands of volcanic mountains that were riding north on the edge of the Pacific plate. About 170 million years ago, they slammed obliquely into the west coast of North America, initiating a violent era of volcanic activity and mountain building. Like a wedge, the edge of the continent peeled the lighter rock of the volcanic islands off the underlying ocean plate and an enormous sheet of territory cemented itself onto western North America.

The coastal collisions continued for millions of years and inland, the new territory served as a gargantuan bulldozer, rumpling the western part of the continent and forcing the land to buckle, creating a series of mountain ranges. About 140 million years ago, the Rocky Mountains were born, jackknifing skyward in a prolonged period of volcanic activity.

Even as they rose, the mountaintops were worn away by water and wind. Vast quantities of clay, silt, sand and gravel were borne by rivers into the sea east of the mountains. Initially, the sea was low, with the shore near Winnipeg and sandy river deposits were carried all the way to what is now the Red River Valley. Most of these deposits were later stripped off by glacial action, but patches of sandstone still exist here and there in the Interlake, as well as in buried caves under Winnipeg. To the west, however, the layer of sandstone survived; today it forms the base of the Manitoba Escarpment and extends even farther west beneath the surface.

Adding to the disruption brought on by this invasion of sand, an extraterrestrial body such as a large meteorite again smashed into the region, this time spectacularly excavating

*The graphics below have been vertically enhanced to show the rock layers that underlie Manitoba from border to border (bottom), as well as the nearly horizontal bedrock that gives Winnipeg its remarkably flat landscape.*

*At right: A few of the remarkable array of creatures that lived in and above Manitoba's Cretaceous seas.*

*Opposite: West Hawk Lake's almost perfectly round shape is a clue to its fiery origins.*

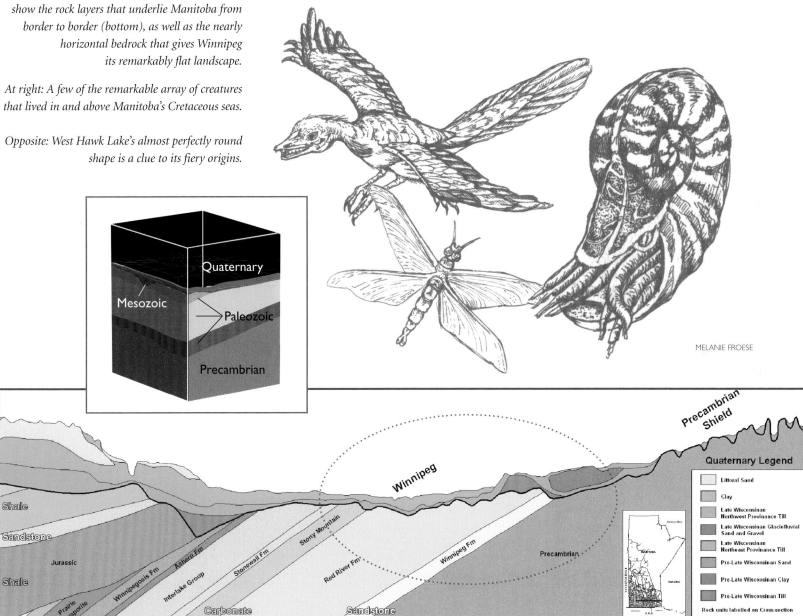

MELANIE FROESE

COURTESY OF THE MANITOBA GEOLOGICAL SURVEY

Quaternary

Mesozoic

Paleozoic

Precambrian

Precambrian Shield

Winnipeg

Shale

Sandstone

Shale

Jurassic

Prairie Evaporite

Winnipegosis Fm

Ashern Fm

Interlake Group

Stonewall Fm

Stony Mountain

Red River Fm

Winnipeg Fm

Precambrian

Carbonate

Sandstone

**Quaternary Legend**

Littoral Sand

Clay

Late Wisconsinan Northwest Provinance Till

Late Wisconsinan Glaciofluvial Sand and Gravel

Late Wisconsinan Northeast Provinance Till

Pre-Late Wisconsinan Sand

Pre-Late Wisconsinan Clay

Pre-Late Wisconsinan Till

Rock units labelled on Cross-section

*Mosaurs, above, were among the many large aquatic creatures that populated Manitoba's late Cretaceous seas. Their skeletons, below, have been found near Morden, Manitoba.*

one of the deepest lakes in Canada, West Hawk Lake. This well-preserved, almost perfectly round crater on the Ontario border east of Winnipeg has attracted the attention of meteorite-impact researchers from around the world.

But before long, the sea rose again, and an influx of clay and silt that lasted for tens of millions of years drowned the entire region with hundreds of metres of mud that gradually became shale. Through most of the Cretaceous Period, which ended the Mesozoic Era, the mud accumulated, supplemented by layers of volcanic ash, as dusty clouds of ash drifted in from volcanoes exploding farther west. Over time, these ash layers turned into bentonite, which has been mined for many uses, including kitty litter, near Morden, southwest of Winnipeg.

Increasingly sophisticated mosasaurs and plesiosaurs – giant marine reptiles – populated this muddy sea; their large skeletons have been found in quarries in the Morden area. At last the sea began its final retreat. The newly exposed landscape was near sea level, with a climate like Florida's and populated by a fantastic array of creatures that thrived in the verdant swamps. When the vegetation died, it fell onto the sand or into the swamps, creating the raw material for coal. A patch of this Cretaceous sandstone and coal has survived on Turtle Mountain in southwestern Manitoba.

The **Cretaceous Period** of the Mesozoic Era and much of life on Earth ended with an event of shocking devastation. About sixty-five million years ago, a comet or an asteroid slammed into what is now the edge of the Yucatan Peninsula. The impact created a crater 180 kilometres across and an explosion estimated to be 1,000 times greater than the detonation of the world's entire nuclear arsenal. Vast quantities of rock, dust and vapour were hurled into the atmosphere, blacking out the sun for months, or perhaps years. Heat from the impact created massive forest fires. Subterranean shock waves may even have triggered a chain of volcanoes on the other side of the globe.

A huge region, including southern Manitoba, was showered with debris that suffocated most plant life. Global cooling followed and the combination spelled the end for almost all the dinosaurs, along with every other species of land animal weighing more than twenty-five kilograms. Even the plankton in the world's oceans, the basis of the vast marine food chain, was affected. In total, perhaps sixty-five per cent of the world's species were culled.

Those that survived included birds – believed by many to be the dinosaurs' only living descendants – and some

BOTH IMAGES: LINDA FAIRFIELD

small mammals. Birds were more mobile and adaptable than the great land creatures, while even primitive mammals were capable of storing food. The survivors found themselves in a very different world, for before them lay a planet for the taking.

THE CENOZOIC ERA: *65 million years ago to the present*
As the Earth adjusted to the aftermath of the devastation and the loss of so many of its greatest life forms, the site that is now Winnipeg was also evolving. In the Tertiary Period that opened the Cenozoic Era, the land around The Forks was becoming a terrestrial landscape – after so many millions of years beneath the sea. Though sandstone and coal continued to be deposited for a short time, overall this was a time of deep erosion by rivers. And the depth to which the thick cover of shale and sandstone was stripped off is mind-boggling. By studying the Cretaceous and Tertiary coal to determine the extent to which it was cooked by the elevated temperature and pressure that result from burial, geologists estimate that as much as three kilometres of shale and sandstone were stripped off the region and carried by rivers to the sea. Between these powerful rivers was a landscape similar to southern Africa today, populated by ancestral horses and antelope, rhinoceros, camels, elephants, tapirs, turtles and alligators, as well as now-extinct mammals such as brontotheres and oreodons.

The final step in shaping the major features of the rocks in the region was the excavation of the Red River Valley. Today, the granites and other Precambrian rocks rise above the surface east of Winnipeg, where they form the eastern Red River Valley wall. But at the beginning of the Tertiary Period, these ancient rocks were nowhere in evidence; over the preceding 400 million years, they had been completely buried by sandstones and limestones. Now, in the early part of the Tertiary Period, these enormous layers of rock were almost completely stripped away in southeastern Manitoba. Today, only patches remain, such as the sandstone of apparently Cretaceous age at the bottom of West Hawk Lake. The early excavation work was done by rivers. Removing the sandstone, shale and limestone revealed the gross geometry of the eastern Red River Valley wall. But the shaping of its details would have to wait until the glaciations of the ensuing ice age.

The presence of the western Red River Valley wall, and therefore the presence of the Red River Valley itself, is, like many of our geological features, a fluke caused by one otherwise barely noticeable fact. Had the sequence of shales to the west accumulated slightly differently, there wouldn't be a Red River Valley at all. The key to creation of the valley and The Forks at its focal point is the Odanah Shale. Though there are hundreds of metres of shale in southwestern Manitoba, the Odanah Shale, which makes up the top layer of the Riding Mountain or Pierre Formation, is uniquely hard due to the high silica content, which acts as a kind of cement. The Tertiary rivers that stripped down the landscape, and the glaciers that later finished the task, encountered stiff resistance when they got down to the Odanah. Once the Odanah was out of the way, rivers and springs were able to clear away everything to the east, right down to hard limestone. But in western Manitoba, to this day, the Odanah forms a tough, resistant caprock that can be credited with forming the Manitoba Escarpment. Without the Odanah Shale, there would be no Manitoba Escarpment, and without the escarpment, there would be no Red River Valley. Instead there would be a landscape gently rising from the Canadian Shield to the Rocky Mountains, and no Red River, or Forks, as we know them.

# Laying Down

More than a hundred thousand years ago, during a break in the Ice Age, the land that is now *The Forks* might have looked something like the plains of Africa today. Central North America was home to Columbian mammoths (left), giant ground sloths and American lions (bottom right) and camels (centre) as well as the ancestors of today's pronghorn antelope, horses and bison.

# The Landscape

By Harvey Thorleifson

By about a million years ago, the rocks that form the foundation below The Forks were in place – granite to the east and deep below, limestone over-lying this ancient rock, and shale to the west. These rocks had been formed early in Earth's history, creating a solid basement, free of volcanoes and earthquakes.

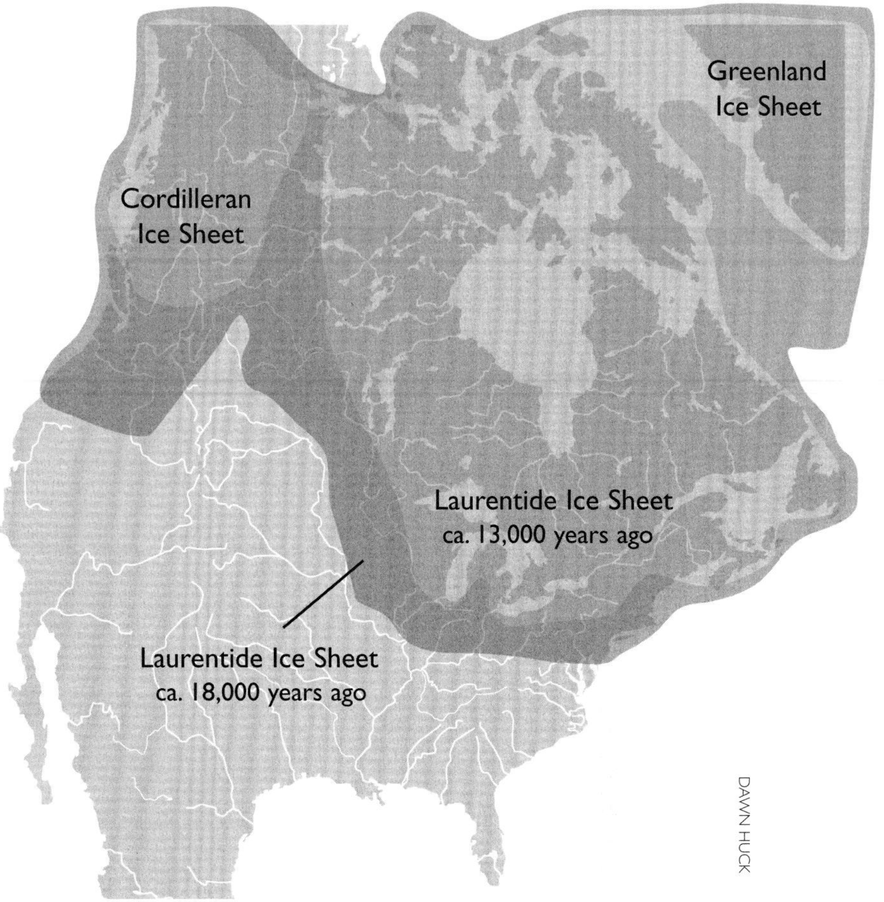

DAWN HUCK

The map labels read:

Greenland Ice Sheet

Cordilleran Ice Sheet

Laurentide Ice Sheet
ca. 13,000 years ago

Laurentide Ice Sheet
ca. 18,000 years ago

*The Quaternary Epoch, the label geologists have given the last two million years, has been a time of repeated glaciations. The last of these – the Late Wisconsinan – was among the largest. At its height, about 18,000 years ago, enormous sheets of ice covered almost all of Canada except parts of Yukon, as well as much of the northern U.S.*

In the millions of years since the demise of the dinosaurs, rivers and cycles of weather had stripped a thick layer of shale off the prairie region, revealing not only the beautiful limestone Winnipeggers would one day treasure, but also many of the caves that had been formed much earlier. To the west, however, the hard Odanah Shale had defied the eroding rivers, protecting the top of the steep Manitoba Escarpment and forming the western wall of the Red River Valley. In short, the foundation for The Forks was there, but the details of the understated prairie landscape that we all recognize today were sculpted only in the past million years or so – a time when Canada was repeatedly almost completely buried by ice.

The sixty-five million years since the dinosaurs roamed the Earth is known as the Cenozoic Era. And the Cenozoic is divided, in turn, into a long Tertiary Period, followed, two million years ago, by the Quaternary, the period in which we live (see the Geological Time chart on page 16). The Tertiary was the beginning of mammalian domination of the Earth; over many millennia the Manitoba landscape was populated by a remarkable assortment of mammals – including ancient ancestors of the hippopotamus and the camel, as well as, more recently, now-extinct creatures such as mammoths and mastodons.

During most of this relatively benign period, the eastern prairie landscape was slowly being stripped down to hard rock by rivers. But about two million years ago, things changed quite dramatically, as the Tertiary Period gave way to the Quaternary – a time of lengthy but intermittent glaciations. Geologists break the Quaternary down into the Pleistocene and the Holocene Epochs – the Ice Age and the time after the Ice Age. Those designations were created by early scientists who thought the Ice Age was a thing of the past. However, we now know better. The Ice Age is not over. We are in fact presently living in it, as any occupant of Greenland or Antarctica can testify, and sooner or later the great sheets of ice will once again cover Canada.

It just happens that our modern civilization has grown up during an interglacial period, one of the many respites, generally between 10,000 and 40,000 years long, that have occurred every hundred thousand years or so over the past two million years. During these interglacials, the normal ice-covered state of Canada and northern Europe is interrupted. The ice melts and recedes to the polar regions and global sea levels rise dramatically.

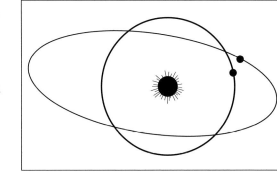

While it seems impossible to believe that an area the size of Canada could again become ice covered, essentially, it's simple. More snow falls during the winter than melts during the summer.

Why this happens has to do with several factors: the arrangement of the continents on the surface of the Earth; the tilt of the Earth's axis and the shape of its orbit as it rotates around the sun. Currently, as a glance at a globe shows, the major continents of the world are crowded around the northern half of the Earth's surface in a way that almost completely cuts the Arctic Ocean, which is centred on the North Pole, off from the Pacific and Atlantic. This continental configuration largely prevents warm ocean currents from reaching the most northerly regions of the planet. The result is summers at high latitudes that can be too cool to melt all the snow and ice that accumulate each winter.

But, one might ask, if the continents are arranged in much the same way as they were at the height of the last glaciation about 18,000 years ago, why has the ice receded from its vast expanse into what is now the midwestern United States? The answer depends on the other aspect of this complex equation – the astronomical part. Scientists observe that climate has a cycle of approximately 100,000 years. During a glacial age, glaciations lasting from between 60,000 and 90,000 years alternate with interglacials of between 40,000 and 10,000 years. This "Milankovitch cycle", so named for its discoverer, Serbian scientist Milutin Milankovitch, is determined by the Earth's orbit around the sun, which in turn is dependent on three other cycles.

The first is the 105,000-year variation in the shape of Earth's eliptical orbit; the second, the 41,000-year cycle in the tilt of the Earth's axis and the third, a 21,000-year cycle in the movement of the day at which Earth is closest to the sun as it moves along its eliptical orbit. This last cycle, called the precession of the equinoxes, shifts forward through the months from January, through February, on to March and so forth, around to January again at the end of 21,000 years. The cumulative effect of all these cycles for high-latitude countries like Canada is to determine the degree of variation between summer and winter temperatures. At one extreme, northern continents will have relatively warm summers and cold winters, as they've had for the past few thousand years. At the other extreme, the same areas will experience relatively cool summers and somewhat warmer winters. It is the summer temperatures that, more than anything except for the arrangement of the continents, accounts for the creation and disappearance of the great sheets of ice. Cool summers are not able to fully melt all the snow that falls during the previous winter and a lengthy period of cool summers will result in the slow, inexorable development of glaciers.

Research has shown that the beginning of a North American glacial cycle appears to occur in northern Québec and the Keewatin district of Nunavut, west of Hudson Bay. If a snowy winter is followed by a summer during which sunshine and temperatures are inadequate to melt all the snow,

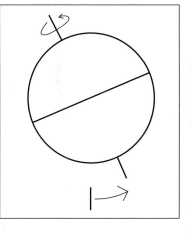

*The tilt of the Earth's axis, above, and the shape of its orbit are two of several factors that determine global climate.*

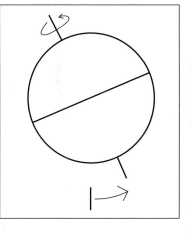

DAWN HUCK

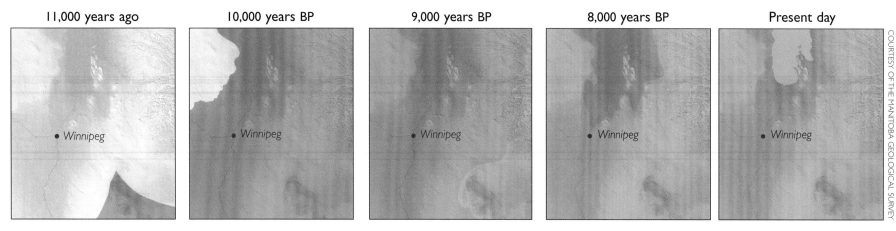

| 11,000 years ago | 10,000 years BP | 9,000 years BP | 8,000 years BP | Present day |
|---|---|---|---|---|
| • Winnipeg | • Winnipeg | • Winnipeg | • Winnipeg | • Winnipeg |

COURTESY OF THE MANITOBA GEOLOGICAL SURVEY

*This series of illustrations, created by Gaywood Matile of the Manitoba Geological Survey, shows the dramatic sequence of events that occurred on and over the land that is now Winnipeg between 11,000 and 8,000 years ago. Today's landscape is on the right.*

the following winter will start with snow left over from the previous winter. Just as a thrifty shopper's bank balance will grow if one spends less than one earns year after year, a landscape on which the summers are not melting all of the preceding winters' snow will gradually become inundated with snow. And as the pile of snow becomes thicker, the weight of it will compress the snow at the bottom of the pile until it becomes ice. When the ice is thick enough, it will begin to flow.

On a fairly flat continental landscape, glacial ice flows like pancake batter, and that pancake, or continental ice sheet, grows rather as government finances do. Snow surpluses lead to the steady growth of the ice sheet, while deficits lead to a reduction. The inputs are snowfall in the built-up interior of the ice sheet while the losses are the melting that goes on at the thinner margins, as well as the formation of icebergs in areas where the glaciers end in the oceans or lakes. In Canada, the result is a huge pancake of ice flowing out of Keewatin and Québec, until it covers most of Canada and the northern US.

Glacial ice flows by deformation, even when it is frozen to its bed, but it can also flow by sliding over the ground on a film of water. Sliding ice erodes the ground as it moves; loose material is bulldozed or dragged, and often incorporated into the bottom of the glacier. Rocks thus frozen into the ice are

DENNIS FAST

*Crossroads of the Continent*

scraped over the landscape, so the glacier becomes a giant sheet of sandpaper. This action strips off the softer exposed rocks and leaves hard rock with straight scratches known as glacial striations. Such striations are visible in the Whiteshell east of Winnipeg and on limestone outcroppings in the Interlake. As the glacier goes through cycles of eroding and depositing sediment, it leaves layers of debris called till beneath the bed of the glacier.

Scientists study these multiple layers of till, which are sometimes separated by soil and tree stumps, as well as the deep-sea record of sediment layers, to read the history of our Ice Age. What that record tells us is that our planet has experienced at least seventeen and as many as twenty of these glacial cycles over the past two million years. In southern Manitoba, the most recent of these unglaciated periods occurred between about 65,000 and 25,000 years ago.

During this time, and during the interglacial period between 130,000 and 120,000 years ago, the Red River Valley would have looked much as it does now, though populated by rather different animals. We know this from examining fossils and other aspects of deposits that date from these times. Southeast of Winnipeg, the St. Malo Formation tells us that the climate 120,000 years ago was similar to today's, with many large mammal species, such as mastodons and mammoths, roaming the landscape.

Soon after, what is known as the Wisconsinan glaciation began, reached a temporary maximum geologists call the Early Wisconsinan and then withdrew about 65,000 years ago, resulting in a warmer period that is recorded near Winnipeg by the sediments and fossils of the Vita Formation. Then about 25,000 years ago, the mighty Late Wisconsinan glaciation began. In a remarkably short time – about 5,000 years – the

## BLACK SPRUCE (*Picea mariana*)

As the margin of the continental ice sheet retreated, the exposed land surrounding Lake Agassiz was quickly colonized, largely by black spruce. In this cold, wet environment where many other plants could not survive, the black spruce – also called bog spruce – thrived. For a brief time, much of southern Manitoba looked like the province's northern forests do today, a dense woodland of hardy, rather spindly spruce, stretching above a forest floor covered with lichen and mosses.

Soon, however, southern Manitoba's forests gave way to grasslands, for the world was rapidly warming and even along the Red River the soil was too dry to sustain these moisture-loving spruce. Battered but not beaten, the forest migrated north and east with the shores of the retreating lake. Today black spruce are widespread throughout northern and eastern Manitoba, occupying bogs, moist lowlands and rocky outcroppings.

Both black and white spruce (the latter, *Picea glauca*, is much more at home in well-drained, sandy soil), were used by Manitobans in many ways for thousands of years. The Latin name means "pitch" and refers to the sap of the trees, which was used both for medicinal purposes and as a calking agent for birchbark canoes. The tough, pliable roots were also used to make baskets and to "sew" canoes by many northern cultures.

enormous Laurentide ice sheet expanded to blanket all of Canada east of the Rockies and much of the northeastern United States, all the way south to Iowa. In the west, it joined the Cordilleran ice sheet, which covered most of Alberta and British Columbia and a good part of Alaska.

Between 15,000 and 20,000 years ago, then, Canada was covered by one of the largest ice sheets in Earth's recent history.

*Glacial erratics can be found in many places in southern Manitoba. This one lies along Traverse Bay, at Lake Winnipeg's southeast corner; much larger erratics can be seen on the Ancient Beach Trail at Grand Beach Provincial Park.*

DENNIS FAST

In the past few decades, geologists have played detective on the workings of this glacier. Reading the character and composition of the multiple layers of sediment and measuring cross-cutting striations, they've been able to determine the changing behaviour of the ice. Like crime scene investigators, they've also traced pebbles, cobbles and boulders to their bedrock sources. These rocks, dropped or discarded by the ice as it advances or retreats, are called glacial erratics. They prove that the many phases of ice flow were able to carry debris from eastern and southern Hudson Bay all the way to Calgary or the American Midwest. In southeastern Manitoba, a trained eye can pick out distinctive Hudson Bay rocks in gravel pits.

About 15,000 years ago, however, Earth's climate switched from its glacial mode to its interglacial mode. Abruptly, the North American ice budget switched from surplus to deficit. Though the ice continued to be formed and to radiate, pancake-like, in all directions from Hudson Bay, the rate of melting and iceberg calving at the margins of the ice was greater than the replenishment at the sheet's interior. The result was a steady glacial retreat that ultimately led to the disappearance of the continental ice sheets. But this demise was slow – lasting thousands of years – and much happened during deglaciation.

Certainly, where the history of The Forks is concerned, the most important detail of the deglaciation was the creation of Lake Agassiz, an enormous lake that formed on the southern and western edges of the Laurentide ice sheet as it retreated. Lake Agassiz has been examined by many scientists, and this research has been led in recent years by Dr. Jim Teller of the University of Manitoba. About 14,000 years ago, the ice margin began to retreat from its southern maximum in Iowa and by 12,000 years ago, it had reached what is now Lake Traverse, on the South Dakota – Minnesota border. Up to this point, the landscape had sloped south, along the Mississippi River, so the melting water had flowed south. But now, the landscape began to slope toward the ice margin – a trend that would later became the slope toward Hudson Bay and determine the northward flow of the Red and Nelson Rivers. From this point on, the water pooled at the edge of the ice and what would later become the headwaters of the Red River became the southernmost shore of Lake Agassiz.

As the ice margin retreated, the ice-dammed or "proglacial" lake enlarged. Meltwater from the glacier and other nonglacial runoff from the prairie to the west ponded in Lake Agassiz, and initially some of that water overflowed through the southern outlet at Lake Traverse, draining to the Minnesota River and on to the Mississippi. Over time, as the lake grew and the shape of the great ice sheet changed, this drainage to the Gulf of Mexico switched back and forth with drainage to the Great Lakes, and even at times to the Arctic Ocean via the Mackenzie River. The initial drainage to the Gulf of Mexico, mainly through the southern Lake Traverse outlet to the Minnesota River, was interrupted whenever lower outlets to the Atlantic or the Arctic Ocean were uncovered by the receding ice margin. This switching of Lake Agassiz's outflow affected the workings of the world's oceans, so the global research community is now as interested in the history of Lake Agassiz as anyone in Manitoba is.

DENNIS FAST

WARREN UPHAM deserves recognition as the greatest Lake Agassiz scientist. After naming Lake Agassiz in his first Minnesota Geological Survey report, he made immense contributions to the advancement of science. Indeed, so great were his reputation and his influence that scientists who uncovered his errors were constrained, and the repercussions of those errors still affect today's research.

For example, Upham made the mistake of attributing the uppermost layer of clay in the Red River Valley to Red River floodwaters. Upham reasoned that buried logs and the location of deposits near the Red River reflected conditions that post-dated Lake Agassiz. He therefore concluded that Lake Agassiz formed and ebbed only once, while enlarging northward during a single, prolonged episode of retreating ice. He failed to recognize that the upper layer of clay was in fact deposited by the enormous lake as it emptied and refilled (see pages 38–39). This theory affected subsequent research for years.

Upham also entered into a debate with the great geologist Thomas C. Chamberlin, who was his supervisor after he joined the United States Geological Survey (USGS). So acrimonious was the debate that Chamberlin placed a dissenting chapter in Upham's greatest work, his monograph on Lake Agassiz published in 1895. Their debate focused on the Herman shoreline, which can be traced from Herman, Minnesota, to Brandon, Manitoba, and beyond. With his simple model of Lake Agassiz in mind, Upham claimed that the beach formed as the ice margin retreated from South Dakota to Manitoba's Riding Mountain. But Chamberlin reasoned that the beach would not have its weakly developed character if this were the case. He proposed instead that Lake Agassiz had somehow filled to the Herman shoreline.

This view invited dissent. In the late 1890s, Joseph B. Tyrrell of the Geological Survey of Canada (GSC) – the man for whom Alberta's Royal Tyrrell Museum is named – suggested that Lake Agassiz had filled when two glaciers collided in Hudson Bay. Upham vigorously resisted this idea, for it undermined his mission to promote the glacial theories of Louis Agassiz. His defence of the older theory can be compared to Charles Darwin expressing frustration with Steven Jay Gould. Attribution of the filling of Lake Agassiz to undetermined forces to the north hindered Upham's efforts.

# MAPPING LAKE AGASSIZ

The re-filling of Lake Agassiz was explained by William A. Johnston of the GSC in 1914, based on observations in Ontario's Rainy River district. But Johnston erred in suggesting that the same refilling could explain the char-acter of the Herman beach. A heated debate with Upham ensued and in 1918, Frank Leverett of the USGS tried to cool tempers by proposing a compromise – that the second high phase had only reached the shoreline at Campbell, Minnesota. The limit of the second high phase is still a topic of debate and it was only in the mid-1990s that an explanation for the Herman shoreline – the uplift of a northern Minnesota outlet – was proposed.

Despite these debates, progress continued. The advent of radiocarbon dating, as well as aerial photographs and topographic maps in the 1950s caused Lake Agassiz research to flourish under the leadership of John Elson of McGill University. But the early days of carbon dating were plagued by contaminated results, leading to almost as much confusion as clarity. This mess was finally tidied up in 1982, when North Dakota Geological Survey geologists Lee Clayton and Steve Moran separated the "good dates", free of contamination, from the contaminated "bad dates".

Benchmarks during this era occurred as conferences at the University of Manitoba in 1966 and 1982. Both resulted in important books on Lake Agassiz and drew attention to the increasing role played by university research as well as provincial and state geological surveys. This detective work, now led by Jim Teller of the University of Manitoba, has given us an understanding of how the Red River Valley landscape was formed.

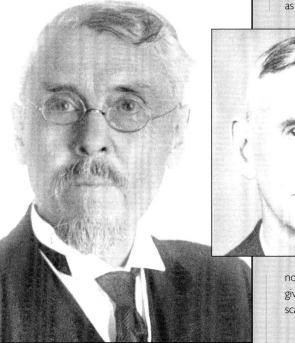
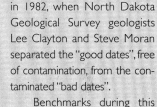

COURTESY OF THE GEOLOGICAL SURVEY OF CANADA

*Warren Upham, left, of the USGS, and William A. Johnston of the GSC, were pioneers in mapping Lake Agassiz.*

BOTH IMAGES: JERRY KAUTZ

*Spirit Sands, inset, in Spruce Woods Provincial Park, is part of a large underwater delta deposited by floods that reached Lake Agassiz when the shore was at Brandon. Following the retreat of Lake Agassiz, the Assiniboine River cut a wide valley into the delta.*

Another profound influence on Lake Agassiz was postglacial uplift. The continental ice sheet had a maximum thickness over the Hudson Bay region somewhere between three and five kilometres – approaching the height of some of the highest mountains in the Rockies. This enormous weight depressed the surface of the Earth by about a kilometre, rather like a bowling ball that creates a depression when it's placed on a trampoline. And just as the trampoline will rise when the bowling ball is removed, the portion of North America centered on Hudson Bay that was inundated by

ice has risen in response to removal of the ice, although the springing up of the Earth's surface may require something in the order of 20,000 years to be complete. But during the first centuries after the ice disappeared, the uplift was relatively rapid, and the Lake Agassiz basin began to tilt, even during the lifespan of the lake. Lake Agassiz's shorelines therefore now rise in elevation to the northeast, and the outlets that once drained the lake rose as the lake evolved.

Fluctuations in the level of Lake Agassiz caused by opening and closing of outlets or the uplift of outlets were recorded

*Crossroads of the Continent*

in layers of sediment deposited in offshore Lake Agassiz, in what is now the Red River Valley. In North Dakota, Minnesota and to some extent in Manitoba, a major fluctuation in water level is indicated by an upper layer of clay called the Sherack Formation, which is separated from clay in the underlying Brenna Formation by wood that has been radiocarbon dated at between 11,000 and 10,000 years. Sediments also record very large inflows of water from the west. Large sandy fans rapidly formed as underwater deltas; these occur where the glacial Sheyenne and Pembina Rivers entered Lake Agassiz in North Dakota, while the extensive Assiniboine Delta, with Spirit Sands near its apex, was deposited near Brandon, Manitoba. As the level of Lake Agassiz fluctuated, the rivers cut narrow valleys into these fans. These cycles of erosion and deposition in the river valleys give us a record of Lake Agassiz's fluctuations.

Beaches and other shoreline features also record the periods when Lake Agassiz stabilized for a time. In Minnesota, east of and connected to the southern outlet, four well-developed shorelines are present near the towns, in descending order, of Herman, Norcross, Tintah and Campbell. Shorelines above the Herman beach are poorly developed, indicating the short time span of events along the ice margin. But the Campbell shoreline is the most developed of all the shorelines. From Campbell, Minnesota, it can be traced up the western shore to Arden, Manitoba, and beyond; Highway 352 and Highway 10 at Ethelbert follow it for a considerable distance. On the eastern shore of Lake Agassiz, it can be traced all the way to Atikokan, Ontario.

Over nearly 200 years, the history of Lake Agassiz has been worked out by scientific explorers, government geological survey agencies and university researchers. The first documented recognition of the existence of the former lake

*This remarkable map shows the total area covered by the various phases of Lake Agassiz. The red dashed lines indicate the margins of the ice 9,900 and 9,300 years ago.*

COURTESY OF THE MANITOBA GEOLOGICAL SURVEY

was based on its gravelly beaches and offshore clay. A series of scientific explorers – William H. Keating, David D. Owen, Henry Youle Hind and Gouverneur K. Warren – crossed the eastern plains between 1823 and 1868, each adding something to solving the puzzle. In their footsteps came Robert Bell, George M. Dawson and Joseph B. Tyrrell, all early officers of the Geological Survey of Canada, which had been formed in 1842. And the first person to actually attribute Lake Agassiz to glacial blockage of northward drainage was Newton Horace Winchell, the first Director of the Minnesota Geological Survey.

But it took a young geologist from New Hampshire to begin truly intensive research on Lake Agassiz. His name was Warren Upham and he was hired by Winchell in 1879. Upham's first field season that year was directed at the geology of central and western Minnesota. But his very first report, in

*A small sandspit curves from the southern shore of Long Point, creating a quiet backwater on Lake Winnipeg. The point itself is enormous, nearly forty kilometres long and fifteen kilometres wide.*

1880, included a meticulous presentation of the glacial theory, a concept that was very contentious at the time. Upham also proposed the name Lake Agassiz, in recognition of the first prominent advocate of the glacial theory, the great nineteenth-century Swiss naturalist Louis Agassiz.

Supported by the Minnesota Geological Survey until 1885, and then by the United States Geological Survey for another two years, Upham continued mapping. In 1887, he extended his work as far north as Riding Mountain in Manitoba with the support of the Geological Survey of Canada.

But Canadians took the lead in the early twentieth century, when Canada's William A. Johnston of the Geological Survey of Canada made important contributions to understanding Lake Agassiz. Though he influenced thinking beginning right after his first field season in 1912, his work on Lake Agassiz wasn't fully published by the GSC until 1946.

The history of Lake Agassiz that has been worked out since the days of Warren Upham is now broken down into phases, beginning with the earliest or Lockhart phase. This began around 11,700 years ago as ice retreated from the Big Stone Moraine of South Dakota and Minnesota. Moraines are ridges of sediment deposited along the margins of the ice – Long Point, the peninsula that protrudes into the north basin of Lake Winnipeg is a good example.

During this early phase, the lake was alternately draining south through the Minnesota River and east through northern Minnesota to Lake Superior. The ice margin had moved north of what is now the U.S. border and torrents of meltwater from glaciers to the west were intermittently pouring into Lake Agassiz, cutting valleys along the Sheyenne, Pembina and Assiniboine spillways. These rivers carried sand and fine

IAN WARD

*Crossroads of the Continent*

particles of silt and clay; the latter, as Manitobans know well, settled in what is now the Red River Valley.

By about 11,000 years ago, the ice margin extended from a moraine near Darlingford, Manitoba, across the Red River Valley to the Rainy River area of Ontario, and on to eastern Lake Superior. East of Winnipeg, large sand and gravel deposits were laid down between glacial ice on the Canadian Shield and the faster-moving ice in the Red River Valley. These deposits now form the Sandilands.

When the ice margin reached what is now Winnipeg, a large, discontinuous moraine was built from Birds Hill to the Grand Beach area. Also about this time, glacial Lake Regina and other smaller lakes in Saskatchewan were filling and draining repeatedly, first causing the cutting of the Souris/Pembina spillway and later the Qu'Appelle and Assiniboine spillways, depositing the Pembina and Assiniboine Deltas.

But then, about 10,900 years ago, access to low outlets on the north shore of Lake Superior at Thunder Bay caused the huge lake to drain dramatically. This low phase of Lake Agassiz, which was lengthy enough to allow trees to grow on the clay of the southern Red River Valley, is known as the Moorhead phase – after the town of Moorhead, Minnesota.

It began when the ice margin in Northwestern Ontario retreated enough to allow drainage through several canyons similar to Ouimet Canyon near Thunder Bay; in fact, the Ouimet Canyon was created by an enormous outpouring of water, which literally cut through the rock. After an initial outpouring, Lake Agassiz reached a point of equilibrium for a time, with the water pouring into the great lake from the west being balanced by excess water draining through into Lake Superior. On the newly revealed clay shores around the edges of the lake, trees and grasses grew, attracting mammoths and bison and, who knows, perhaps early hunters. But it was not to last for long. Released from its great weight of ice, the land in the Thunder Bay area was slowly rising, gradually cutting off the outlet the same way a tap is slowly turned off.

Once again the water rose, creeping over the new forests, drowning them in the frigid water. But this was not to be a significant increase, for suddenly, water levels dropped again. Determining where the water had escaped this time was, until recently, one of many puzzles Lake Agassiz has posed. But this one appears to have been solved using data obtained by Gaywood Matile of the Manitoba Geological Survey. Aided by radiocarbon dating, Matile's work has shown that the dramatic draining must have occurred when melting glaciers opened a connection to the Clearwater Valley of western Saskatchewan, allowing Lake Agassiz to drain through the Clearwater and Athabasca Rivers in northern Alberta. Research continues, however; scientists clearly have many balls to juggle as they interpret Lake Agassiz history.

The second major period of high water, known as the Emerson Phase, began about 9,900 years ago; ice blocked access to both the eastern and northwestern outlets and Lake Agassiz began to flow once more to the south. This time Lake Agassiz grew large enough to merge with glacial Lake Kaministikwia, just northwest of Thunder Bay area, and red clay from Lake Superior was deposited in deep water across northwestern Ontario. Travellers can sometimes see this band of red clay as they travel the road between Kenora and Dryden, Ontario.

During this period, the second layer of Red River Valley clay, the Sherack Formation, was deposited offshore from Winnipeg to Fargo. Draining south, the water cut down to a bouldery bed of rocks.

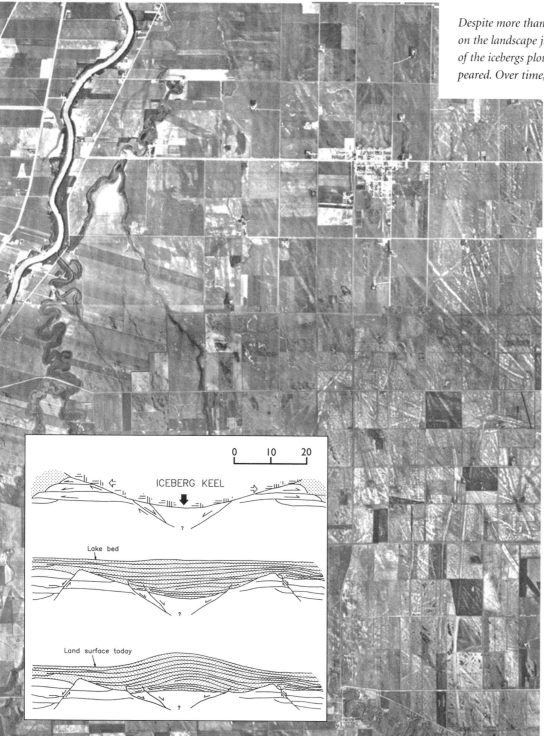

*Despite more than a century of cultivation, scour marks from Lake Agassiz's great icebergs can still be seen on the landscape just southeast of Winnipeg. These iceberg scours near Niverville were caused when the keels of the icebergs ploughed deep furrows in the clay bed of the lake, which filled with silt as the water disappeared. Over time, the clay shrank but the silt did not, leaving ridges that can still be seen today.*

**M**eanwhile, to the north, the ice was steadily melting and the edge of the ice sheet was retreating northeast. About 9,300 years ago, the sand and gravel from the edge of the ice built the enormous, C-shaped moraine that extends today from The Pas to Long Point and, crossing the north basin of Lake Winnipeg, forms Little Sandy, Big Sandy, Cannibal, George and Little George Islands, before finally disappearing on the east shore of the lake in the Canadian Shield.

This was Lake Agassiz at its mightiest extent. Stretching from central Saskatchewan in the west, south to South Dakota and east almost to Lake Nipigon, it was one of the greatest lakes in Earth's history. At The Forks, the water, which had once been 200 metres deep, was still well over 100 metres – about the height of the office buildings at Portage and Main.

Had you been standing at the top of one of those buildings, or sitting in a boat on the cold, windblown surface, you might have seen great icebergs, which regularly broke off of the margin of the ice and floated south. Sometimes, these mountains of ice were so large that they dragged on the bottom of the lake, forming features that geologists call "iceberg scours". Anyone flying in or out of Winnipeg airport in the spring or fall can still see these drag marks on the landscape. The chaotic pattern of scours, at left, is due to icebergs floating around the lake, driven by lake currents and wind.

Now Lake Agassiz was nearing the end of its life. As the ice margin retreated from the Sioux Lookout region in northwestern Ontario about 9,300 years ago, leaving behind another moraine, a succession of outlets draining into Lake Nipigon opened. Draining rapidly east, the final chapter of Lake Agassiz – the Morris Phase, as geologists know it – began. Research is still ongoing about the lake's next thousand years. Until about 8,200 years ago, the retreating ice continued to build moraines

*Crossroads of the Continent*

IMAGES COURTESY OF THE GEOLOGICAL SURVEY OF MANITOBA

IAN WARD

– including the one that separates Lake Winnipeg from Playgreen Lake to the northeast; then it was largely stagnant as the great lake continued to drain into Lake Superior.

About 7,800 years ago, Lake Agassiz briefly merged with the great proglacial lake of northern Ontario, Lake Ojibway, which drained at this time into the Ottawa River. Within a century, about 7,700 years ago, Lake Agassiz switched to a final episode of drainage, past the ice margin to James Bay.

The legacy of Lake Agassiz can be seen in Winnipeg's immaculately featureless landscape. As we've seen in the first chapter, achievement of this perfection required many steps –

the ancient assembly of the continents during the early Precambrian Era, the wearing down of the granites and other igneous and metamorphic rocks in the late Precambrian, the infilling of low spots with sandstone and carbonate in the Paleozoic, and the stripping of shales in the Tertiary. But the finishing touches were made by the continental ice sheet and by Lake Agassiz. Many areas of the world are flat, but few can match the near-perfect polish left by the ice, and the smooth plaster job done by Lake Agassiz clay, which filled the imperfections and leveled itself like soup in a bowl. Such a perfect landscape, and just the right substrate for two rivers to do their work – the creation of The Forks.

*Under the glowering clouds of an approaching storm, Lake Winnipeg still bears more than a passing resemblance to its distant ancestor, Lake Agassiz.*

# THE MAKING OF THE FORKS

ABOUT 8,000 YEARS AGO, as Lake Agassiz made its final retreat from what is now Winnipeg, a soupy layer of clay settled on the landscape from Portage la Prairie to Steinbach. This layer sagged slightly over streamlined glacial deposits, causing the subtle topography that forces all streams in the Red River Valley to favour a northwest-southeast course. Vegetation grew, soils developed and the selenite crystals so popular among Winnipeg rockhounds began to grow from the gypsum in the glacial Lake Agassiz clay.

But the climate wasn't glacial – 8,000 years ago Canada was warmer and drier than it is today; in fact, it was these warm conditions that had driven back the continental glacier. So not only did grassland quickly take over the Red River Valley, it also followed the retreating Lake Agassiz to areas that are now well well north of its current limit. This drought continued for thousands of years, ending abruptly 4,000 years ago.

As Lake Agassiz retreated, the Red River extended its course northward. The river mouth followed the lake's receding shoreline, carving a narrow, shallow inner valley on the flat landscape. Where it followed the northwest-southeast grain of the landscape, it formed a winding course, but this was interspersed by occasional straight sections – such as between Morris and St. Adolphe – producing the zigzagging river that is so familiar today. Meandering rivers like the Red tend to become more sinuous over time, for the meander loops shift slowly outwards – this is known as lateral migration. Eventually the meanders reach a point where only a narrow strip of land separates successive loops and a channel breaks through the neck of land, forming an oxbow lake.

Remarkably, over 8,000 years the Red River has barely begun this process, and few oxbow lakes have been formed. The initial development of the river was more rapid; half its progress was made in the first 2,500 years after Lake Agassiz disappeared, but its subsequent evolution has been docile. Greg Brooks of the Geological Survey of Canada (GSC) has found the rate of lateral migration is only about four centimetres per year in a winding stretch near St. Jean Baptiste. This slow pace is due to several factors: the tough clay through which the river flows, the gentle flow of the current and the effect of riverbanks that accumulate sediment and slowly collapse into the channel.

In addition to lateral migration, rivers also respond to the balance between sediments being brought in and sediments being carried downstream. In general, a surplus of sediments causes a build-up of the channel known as aggradation, while a deficit causes downcutting or incision. The deposits of the Red River tell us that it has been undergoing incision since Lake Agassiz drained, and the shallow river valley is getting deeper at a rate of about a half-meter every thousand years.

This slow pace is unlikely to change. In Manitoba, the Red River has lost half its gradient due to isostatic rebound, the gradual uplift of the land responding to the release of the weight of the Ice Age glacier. As a result, the river is gradually becoming more and more docile, and as it tries to deepen its valley, its progress is held up by obstacles such as the bouldery stretch at Ste. Agathe, and the bedrock at Lister Rapids near Selkirk, now drowned beneath the water of the Lockport Dam.

But even as the river slowly deepens its bed, it also leaves deposits of river sediments known as alluvium as it migrates laterally. These deposits occur within the meanders, and also here and there along both sides of the inner valley, which is about fifteen metres deep and two and a half kilo-metres wide. These deposits sometimes form benches that can be seen along the river; they are the most flood-prone sites due to their location one step down from the Lake Agassiz clay plain.

Geological and archaeological investigations tell us that the joining of two rivers at the Forks happened very soon after Lake Agassiz retreated 8,000 years ago. Excavations on Ruby Street in Winnipeg's Wolseley district in 1969 recovered wood and a bison skull at a depth of ten metres. Both were radiocarbon dated to about 7,500 years BP, indicating that the channel that the Assiniboine now occupies existed then. But if this was the ancestral Assiniboine, it didn't stay put for long.

Almost immediately, it seems, the Assiniboine became a river that couldn't seem to make up its mind. For nearly 4,000 years, it flowed north to Lake Manitoba, before flowing east to the Red River again between 3,000 and 4,000 years ago. Then, however, it joined the Red at St. Norbert, south of Winnipeg.

carving a channel used today by the La Salle River. The Assiniboine didn't return to its present course until perhaps 2,000 years ago.

There are several reasons for this complex history. At Portage la Prairie, the Assiniboine abruptly loses gradient, and also emerges from the V-shaped valley that it cut into the huge, sandy delta it created between Brandon and Portage la Prairie when it poured into Lake Agassiz about 11,000 years ago. The loss of gradient and loss of confinement combine to create a reduced ability to carry sediment, so downstream or east of Portage, the Assiniboine tends to drop its sediment and aggrade, causing it to build up its channels. We know this from the sandy soils at Portage la Prairie, and also because land rises slightly as you approach the river in this area – the rise is known as an alluvial ridge.

And as the accompanying map shows, small streams in the area, which carry water only occasionally, follow channels with a sweeping meander pattern similar to that of the Assiniboine. These meanders are determined by the amount of water a river carries, and the channels radiating from Portage la Prairie have a geometry that could only have been formed by the full flow of the Assiniboine. Indeed, it's surprising that these old channels have a geometry similar to today's Assiniboine, considering the drought-like conditions that existed when some of them were formed. Clearly, the occasional floods that dictate the shape of a river were similar to those of today, despite the long dry climate of the time. We therefore can see that the Assiniboine has repeatedly undergone what is known as avulsion – the abandonment of a river channel that has built itself up until it becomes unstable, rather like piling books in an ever-higher stack, until the whole stack is unstable. Having reached a point of potential instability, it would take only a small event like an ice jam to cause the river to abandon the channel.

Dating these diversions, can, to some extent, be worked out by crosscutting relationships – a channel that cuts across another channel must be the younger of the two. Studying alluvial deposits also helps. The channels extending north to Lake Manitoba have well-developed black topsoils known as the A-horizon. But the channels heading east to the Red are immature and lack black A horizons – clearly the northern channels are older. This is confirmed by radiocarbon dates obtained by Bill Rannie of University of Winnipeg, which show that the Assiniboine flowed north from before 7,000 years ago until after 4,200 years ago; that it flowed to St. Norbert before and after 3,000 years ago, and that it was flowing to The Forks before and after 1,300 years ago. Bill Last of the University of Manitoba, in his studies of Lake Manitoba, has also recognized the abrupt loss of the sediments that the Assiniboine River had been carrying into the lake. The switch to an easterly course may have been promoted by the accumulation of alluvium to the north, and also perhaps to some extent because the northerly course gradually became less steep as the land uplifted. It's possible that the Assiniboine could relocate again, although recently-built dykes and diversions have probably tamed the river.

Over the two centuries for which documented records are readily available, perhaps the most noteworthy characteristic of the Red River has been its tendency to flood – and not the sort of swift and brief flood that most rivers muster. The Red River prefers to occasionally convert itself into a temporary lake, as much as forty kilometres wide, that sticks around for weeks as the thaw progresses from south to north. This happened most severely in 1826, 1852, 1950, 1979 and 1997.

As a Red River flood develops in Manitoba, a lake forms upstream of Morris, where the river follows the grain of the landscape in a winding stretch that flows from southeast to northwest. The ponding in this area follows the lowland of the Morris River and the Red River upstream from Morris, in a trough that is in the same bedrock structure as Lake Manitoba. Downstream from Morris, the river is straighter as it cuts across the grain, and flooding is restricted. But at St. Adolphe, the river again heads northwest, and another lake forms. In the worst floods, these lakes merge.

This would have particularly been so in the great flood of 1826 that devastated settlements at The Forks. According to recent research, after a very wet 1825, as well as a cold, snowy and late 1826 spring, both rain and, possibly, south winds exacerbated flooding as it developed on both the Red and the Assiniboine. Ice at The Forks began to break up on May 5th, as

the waters abruptly rose, reaching a peak about May 20th. The resulting flow was about forty per cent larger than in 1997.

Our knowledge of water levels in this flood, as well as the 1852 event, was compiled by Sir Sanford Fleming in 1880 as part of investigations in preparation for railway construction, based on water level estimates provided by senior members of the settlement. These observations have recently been carefully reassessed for the development of flood protection strategies. Historical data is important because it provides a basis for anticipating what floods are likely to occur.

To obtain that historical data, experts have worked with

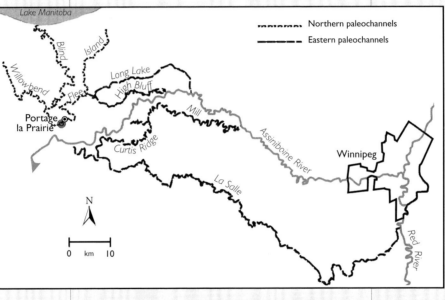

twentieth-century water level measurements that have been meticulously kept by experts such as Alf Warkentin of the Manitoba Water Branch. We can also rely on archival reports from fur trade and early settlement records, for information on nineteenth-century events. And scientists have now extended these records. A key source of information has come from the tendency of oak trees along the river to form an abnormal growth ring during severe flood years. Scientists Erik Nielsen of the Manitoba Geological Survey and Scott St. George of the GSC have pieced together a multi-century tree ring record by overlapping data from pencil-like cores taken from living trees, slices of logs from historic buildings, and slices from logs found

buried in riverbanks. By counting and measuring the tree rings, they have calibrated their observations to known floods of the past two centuries, and have found that major floods occurred in the preceding century, including major floods in 1747 and 1762. Additional floods, back to AD 1510, were recognized for the upper Red River and the Assiniboine. The character and frequency of occurrence of the 1826 flood-affected tree ring indicates that this flood was the largest since 1648, the beginning of the period for which data are available. And the tree rings do not support the old rumour of a flood in 1776.

Layers of sediments also can record floods, as we have learned from archaeological investigations such as those led by Sid Kroker at The Forks. Research by the GSC is underway on sediments from small lakes in the valley, and now additional investigations have turned up layers of silty sediments in Lake Winnipeg that correlate to Red River floods.

By collecting sediment cores 1.5 metres long from the Canadian Coast Guard Ship *Namao*, GSC scientists were able to recover this archive of sediment information, and results show one or two major floods in each of the past ten centuries. Clearly a flood along the lines of 1826 and 1997 is something that has happened regularly for many centuries, and is likely to happen again – assuming future conditions are comparable to those of the past.

But will conditions be comparable? We know that climate has changed, and floods have occurred in clusters, but the results also indicate that major floods have occurred even during dry periods in the past millennium. The landscape has since been altered, although archival compilations by Irene Hanuta of the University of Manitoba have shown that the flood-prone area was a mosaic of mostly grassland and wetland in the 1870s, not unlike today. And human engineering has resulted in both ditches that promote drainage, and roads that slow it down.

So the research shows that our Red River is the same Red River that has been slowly minding its business for 8,000 years – and boldly rising up to inundate the valley every few decades. Having been the case for millennia, this is likely to continue.

COURTESY OF THE MANITOBA GEOLOGICAL SURVEY

# A Continental

*Though the scene a thousand years ago was rather different than it is today, The Forks was recognizable in one fundamental way – it was a significant gathering place, where cultures mingled and goods and ideas were exchanged.*

# Crossroads

By Catherine Flynn and Barbara Huck

Across western North America, one long, hot summer followed another. Crops withered in the fields, streams dried up and disappeared and with them went the hopes of the people. Facing starvation and ruin, some left the land and moved elsewhere, seeking a new start in a new place. But the land they sought was already occupied and tensions grew between neighbouring groups. Soon, where peace had once reigned, conflict loomed like a dark cloud on the horizon.

**T**o twenty-first century readers, these might seem familiar circumstances. Was this the Dirty Thirties perhaps? Or the global warming that in recent years has devastated the western plains? In fact, it was neither of these relatively modern events. This was North America's heartland, more than 700 years ago. And both Native oral tradition and modern archaeology show that The Forks played a significant role in the attempt to find a solution to the trying times.

Between 1250 and 1325 A.D., it seems, there was a great gathering of nations at the place where the Red and Assiniboine Rivers meet. With their people, Native leaders came

COURTESY OF MANITOBA CULTURE HERITAGE AND TOURISM

from east and west, from north and south, travelling across the plains, down the rivers and through woodlands and forests to meet face to face with friends and enemies.

At The Forks, just north of the river junction, not far from where Festival Park often draws thousands together today, as many as eight or perhaps even nine different nations, from different cultures and speaking different languages, all camped together in a huge assembly. This remarkable Peace Meeting long predated the twentieth-century creation of the United Nations, or even the sixteenth-century Five Nations Confederacy, the visionary Iroquoian alliance that American historians now believe was a model for the creation of the United States more than 150 years later.

So important was the meeting at The Forks, that it is remembered even today by Aboriginal elders. Yet most of us know nothing about it. Why was such a crucial meeting held here? And what happened as a result?

Later in this chapter we'll investigate these questions, but the story of life at The Forks begins long before the great Peace Meeting, going back thousands of years to the first people who camped and hunted along the lower Red River.

From its earliest beginnings, very soon after the retreat of glacial Lake Agassiz left bare the fertile flats of the Red River Valley, the area's abundant resources drew people to it. Wood, water and wildlife; plants for food, baskets, mats, cordage and medicine; stone for tools, and a corridor to far-away places all made the banks of the river an appealing place.

Though any evidence of their passing has been lost in the periodic floods that have invaded the Red River Valley, it's possible that roving hunters came this way in the earliest post-glacial times. Certainly their prey – ancient bison, deer and moose – would have been here, though the majestic

*Crossroads of the Continent*

COURTESY MANITOBA CULTURE HERITAGE AND TOURISM

mammoths and mastodon were gone by the time Lake Agassiz drained from the valley. The remains of these great creatures have been found in more than fifteen sites in Manitoba, including several near Winnipeg, but these teeth and tusks were undoubtedly from an earlier interglacial period, for by the time Lake Agassiz drained from the Red River Valley 8,000 years ago, the last of them was gone.

**D**espite the importance of the Red River and its smaller, more recently arrived sister, the Assiniboine (see The Making of the Forks on page 44), surprisingly little archaeological information comes directly from the banks of the rivers. Though people have travelled along both rivers or followed their banks in both winter and summer for millennia, in some places erosion of the rivers has removed all traces of their passing, destroying campsites and breaking or moving tools and weapons, often redepositing them downstream in layers of sediment and silt.

Fortunately, however, in many other sites the rivers have also left heavy loads of sand, silt and clay behind, creating deeply buried and well-protected treasure troves of information on the distant past. In Manitoba a few of these, including The Forks and Lockport, fifteen kilometres downstream, have been studied. To the south, there are other well-preserved sites in Minnesota and North Dakota. Despite significant disturbances on these sites in the past two centuries, archaeologists have found grains of pollen and tiny shells, layers of fish bones and charred wood, as well as stone spearpoints, knives and tools deeply buried in chronological order beneath layers of silt and sand. In this way, a detailed picture of ancient life

along the Red River and around The Forks has been created.

Many pieces of the puzzle are missing, however, and for these, archaeologists have had to rely on information and artifacts gathered from elsewhere in the province. Evidence of people living in the lower Red River Valley during the Paleo Period, the "old" or "ancient" period immediately following the last

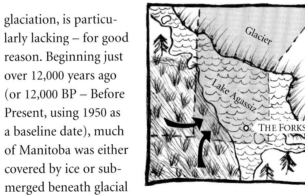

glaciation, is particularly lacking – for good reason. Beginning just over 12,000 years ago (or 12,000 BP – Before Present, using 1950 as a baseline date), much of Manitoba was either covered by ice or submerged beneath glacial Lake Agassiz. Because of these conditions, archaeological sites from this period are very rare. To date, the large spearpoints used by big-game hunters in search of mammoths, mastodons or ice age bison between 12,000 and 10,000 BP, have been found only in the southwestern corner of Manitoba or west of the Manitoba Escarpment near the province's western border. These areas were free of ice well before the rest of the province.

The discovery of even a handful of these beautifully-crafted points, sometimes called "Clovis" and "Folsom" points after sites in New Mexico where they were first identified, tell

*As this series of maps shows, the rapidly warming global climate not only created Lake Agassiz, the enormous lake that once covered much of Manitoba, but also precipitated a rapid series of environmental changes along its southwestern edge. In its early stages, spruce trees grew along the shores of the great lake. Later, as the climate warmed, grasses replaced the forests, which migrated north.*

COURTESY OF MANITOBA HISTORIC RESOURCES

AMANDA DOW

THE EARLIEST MANITOBANS WERE SUPERB BIG GAME HUNTERS WHOSE METHODS AND WEAPONS,
TOGETHER WITH GLOBAL CLIMATE CHANGE, TIPPED THE SCALE TOWARD EXTINCTION FOR MANY SPECIES.

us several things about the people who used them. We know, for example, that they were skilled artisans and knowledgeable hunters who travelled or traded over long distances. One perfect Clovis point was found near Riding Mountain. Made of Knife River flint, a translucent brown stone that produces fine sharp edges when knapped by an expert, it is a thing of beauty. The stone originated from glacial deposits found along the Knife River and elsewhere in western North Dakota, more than 400 kilometres from where the spearpoint was found.

The makers of these elegant points lived in an environment very different than our own. As the glaciers receded, tundra and spruce forest dominated the exposed uplands, while the central lowlands were drowned beneath the ever-changing shorelines of one of the world's largest lakes. Around the edges of the lake, nomadic hunter-gatherers and their families pursued their enormous prey. Archaeological evidence from Northwestern Ontario tells us that these people sometimes lived at the very edges of the glaciers, camping and hunting in a cold, windy environment much like the climate today at the toe of Alberta's Athabasca Glacier in Jasper National Park.

Yet global temperatures were rising and the great glaciers, and the lakes they spawned, receded remarkably quickly. Sometime around 8,000 years ago, the land around The Forks emerged from beneath the glacial waters and went through a rapid series

MANITOBA MUSEUM

## BIG BLUESTEM (*Andropogon gerardii*)

This most recognizable of native grasses is the one that gave North America's tall grass prairie its name. In fact, this tall, slender perennial can be found in all prairie regions from the Rockies to the Atlantic, but is most spectacular, reaching heights of between two and three metres, in the tall grass prairies of the eastern plains, including those in Manitoba.

It provides a constantly changing display of colour, ranging through the season from steely gray-blue to deep bronze and rusty brown. Big bluestem is leafy at the base, with roots up to a metre deep and branching flowers radiating from the stem in a "turkey foot" shape. It provides nesting and escape cover for many birds and small mammals as well as forage for deer and elk. Today, it is seeded by many ranchers and farmers, who have found it is preferred by livestock and unmatched for erosion control plantings.

of environmental changes. The latter Paleo Period, between 10,000 and 8,000 years ago, was the beginning of several millennia of global warming that climatologists call the Hypsithermal. Grasslands replaced the tundra and spruce forests as the western plains warmed and soon drought set in; now, instead of wooly mammoths, the hunters sought *Bison antiquus*, the ancestors of today's bison (*Bison bison*).

Though no direct evidence of the presence of these hunters has been found at The Forks, it is almost certain that as drought ravaged the central plains, the Red River

*The Clovis point that was found near Riding Mountain, left, is still sharp after nearly 11,000 years.*

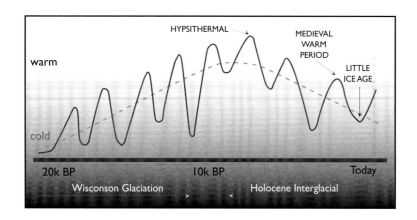

HYPSITHERMAL

warm

MEDIEVAL
WARM
PERIOD

LITTLE
ICE AGE

cold

20k BP                    10k BP                    Today

Wisconson Glaciation              Holocene Interglacial

DAWN HUCK

Valley and other sites in the eastern grasslands became a refuge for *Bison antiquus*.

The discovery of the Ruby Street bison, found on an old floodplain of the Assiniboine River about ten metres below the surface, makes it clear that these long-horned bison were here 7,500 years ago. And while in parts of western North America the ice age bison seem to have disappeared about 5,000 years ago, the discovery of the skull of one of them, along with copper spearpoints and other tools, along the Winnipeg River in Manitoba has led palaeontologists to believe that these remarkable animals found a refuge on the eastern grasslands until about 4,800 years ago. It seems then, that the great bison

must have inhabited the tall grass prairies of the Red River Valley for thousands of years, and it's almost certain that skilled hunters were not far behind.

Beginning about 8,000 years ago, these dramatic changes in climate and the natural environment led to significant and undoubtedly essential alterations in human lifestyles, weaponry and tools. This was a technologically and culturally vibrant period, a time of impressive growth and development all over North America, which archaeologists have recently begun to call the Intensive Diversification Period.

A greatly increased number of sites, as well as an increase in the number of people living in many of these sites are indications that the human population was growing dramatically. What they ate was also changing. To compensate for the demise of many of the large Pleistocene species – each animal essentially a well-stocked larder on the hoof – people were forced to broaden their diets, eating fish, birds, small mammals, as well as the remaining large

MELANIE FROESE

*Crossroads of the Continent*

mammals – bison, deer and elk among them. Not surprisingly, hunting and weaponry changed, as did methods of cooking, types of tools and styles of artwork. The same broadening of the economy and development of new types of weapons and tools was also taking place in Europe at about the same time, during a period known as the Mesolithic.

In North America, the spear-thrower or atlatl (as the Aztec called it), was being widely used on the eastern plains by at least 8,000 years ago. With its handle essentially an extension of the hunter's arm, the atlatl greatly magnified the power of his thrust. Just as important, it allowed hunting at a distance, both desirable and necessary given the smaller, speedier mammalian prey. The atlatl remained the weapon of choice for more than 5,000 years, until the introduction of the bow and arrow about 2,200 years ago.

But big game hunting was now only one of many ways of gathering food and a variety of new stone, bone and wooden tools was also conceived and developed during this period. Among them were net sinkers, fish weirs, harpoons and fish-hooks, as well as axes, gouges, wedges, mauls and hammerstones. The last of these might have been used for pounding nuts, seeds or berries, or for breaking bones for marrow.

Evidence of life during this period was found at The Forks during the initial construction activities. In 1989, two campfires containing charred fishbone were discovered at a depth of six metres, just west of today's Forks Market. Though they may not have thought of it as such, the people who fished and cooked here about 6,000 years ago were on the edge of a revolution, exploiting a source of food that had returned only relatively recently to The Forks. But soon this would be recognized as one of the best fishing places in North America.

During the Wisconsinan glacial period, the most recent of as many as twenty glaciations that have inundated North America during the past two million years, freshwater fish disappeared from Canada's frozen rivers and lakes. Those that survived were forced to find refuge either south of the great sheets of ice or in the unglaciated region of Beringia, which encompassed today's Alaska as well as the exposed Bering land bridge. When the ice melted, the fish repopulated the lakes and rivers, following the retreating ice sheets much as humans did. Because Winnipeg sits in the middle of the continental watershed, fish species from east and west, north and south all made their way to the Red and Assiniboine Rivers. In *After the Ice Age*, author E.C. Pielou writes, "It seems likely that the majority of fishes living anywhere in the interior of Canada and the northern United States today have ancestors that, at one time or another, lived in Lake Agassiz. The lake was the hub of migration routes leading from the unglaciated southern half of the continent into most of the drainage basins once covered by the Laurentide ice sheet [the ice sheet that covered much of North America]."

Zoologists have determined that 181 species of fish (including a few introduced in the past century) inhabit Canadian waters today. Of these, seventy-nine species are found in Manitoba and only two places in Canada have more

*Goldeye, left, a delicacy when smoked, can still be found at The Forks Market today.*

*The atlatl in action, opposite. The spear-throwing technology greatly magnified the power and distance of a hunter's thrust.*

COURTESY OF MANITOBA FISHERIES BRANCH

COURTESY OF MANITOBA CULTURE HERITAGE AND TOURISM

*This stemmed point discovered in a Winnipeg garden demonstrates how precisely hunting technologies were reproduced and how far they were traded. The Winnipeg point, shown below, is so similar in size and shape to a "Hanna" point found in southern Alberta, that it almost seems they were manufactured in the same factory.*

COURTESY OF BRENDA PANKIW

species of fish than the Red and the Assiniboine. Moreover, it seems that until fairly recently, the fishing was even better at The Forks than it is today. Lake sturgeon – enormous, primeval creatures that can reach 150 years of age and weigh more than seventy kilograms – were found in both rivers. Sturgeon Creek, a tributary of the Assiniboine in what is now Winnipeg's west end, was a favoured spawning site. Today, lake sturgeon in Manitoba are largely confined by locks and dams to the province's northern rivers, such as the Saskatchewan and the Nelson. And goldeye, deemed a delicacy when smoked, were also once much more numerous than they are today. Like the sturgeon, these silvery herring-like fish take years to reach sexual maturity and were vastly overexploited in the nineteenth and twentieth centuries. Stocks have only recently begun to recover.

Three thousand years ago, the situation was very different. The Forks teemed with fish, particularly in spring and fall when various species converged on the river junction en route to their spawning sites. Quite naturally, people were drawn to the place and excavations during the Public Archaeology Program in 1992 and '93 revealed that its reputation as a great place to fish appears to have made The Forks a significant gathering place and trading centre, much as it is today.

Working just southwest of Johnston Terminal, in an area that has since been designated an archaeological preserve, a team of archaeologists and volunteers led by Sid Kroker uncovered several hearths and literally tens of thousands of fish bones about three metres below the surface. Among the bones and charred wood from the fires were several artifacts, including nine projectile points. The points represented three distinct styles and four different materials, leading Kroker to believe that people had come together not simply to fish or process large quantities of fish, but also to trade.

The stone used to make the points included Swan River chert from western Manitoba, rhyolite from the Canadian Shield and Knife River flint from western North Dakota. Most of the points were triangular in shape with pronounced flared stems. Dart or atlatl points of this type are often called "Hanna" points, after the Alberta town where they were first identified, and have been dated to between 4,200 and 3,000 years ago. Examples have been found as far west as the Alberta-Montana border. One of the two found near Johnston Terminal was a "high-end" or deluxe version, crafted of Knife River flint, one of the most sought-after materials on the plains. Its appearance at The Forks is an indication of the extent of the trade networks at the time. The other points, which Kroker believed came from the east, included one made of chert from western Manitoba, another indication of how valuable stone was traded or carried over significant distances.

Also found among the refuse was a lovely bone harpoon head, possibly of wolf bone. It was neatly grooved at the base to allow a line to be attached. Used to spear large fish, the harpoon point would disengage from the wooden shaft when the target was speared, allowing both point and prey to be drawn in with the line.

It's likely that such a weapon would have been used for large fish, like sturgeon or catfish. Both were particularly prized for their oily flesh, a definite plus among populations whose protein intake came mainly from lean meat. Sturgeon were also valued for the roe, or caviar, that they produced during spawning season.

Fish can be caught in many ways, but one of the most expedient methods is with the use of a weir or barrier across a shallow river or in a backwater pond or slough. Forced into such confines, the fish can almost be scooped out by hand.

**S**uch a thing likely happened at The Forks, with weirs across the Assiniboine. Though Aboriginal fishermen were always careful to allow the majority of each spawning run to continue upstream to spawn, it's easy to see that catching as

IMAGES THIS PAGE:: THE FORKS NORTH PORTAGE PARTNERSHIP

*Winnipeggers took part in the public archaeology program at The Forks with great enthusiasm, from then-mayor Bill Norrie, seen at left (in gray trousers) with chief archaeologist Sid Kroker (in hat) and others, to budding anthropologists like the one shown above.*

*Among the artifacts uncovered was this lovely bone harpoon point, which, as shown on the adjacent page, was cleverly attached to both a shaft and a line to allow large fish to be caught and pulled in.*

THE FORKS NORTH PORTAGE
PARTNERSHIP

*Also discovered during the excavations were, from top, shell beads, and several points, including a stemmed or "Hanna" point of Swan River chert (light point with broken top).*

many fish as could be processed would have been a simple matter. In modern times, a team of two experimenting with a weir made of logs was able to catch nearly fifty kilograms of fish in just two hours. Working together for two or three weeks, even a small group of people could easily catch and preserve enough fish to provide a reliable alternative to the vagaries of hunting for months to come.

Excavating with great care, Kroker and his team of archaeologists were able to determine that three species – sucker, catfish and walleye or pickerel – made up the bulk of the catch. While some were undoubtedly eaten fresh, the evidence showed that most were preserved by hot smoking; scored filets were either laid or hung on racks over hot coals and rocks for between four and ten hours, depending on the size and type of fish. Fatty fish like sucker and catfish are prime candidates for hot smoking, for the smoke adheres better to oily flesh than it does to lean fish like pickerel.

It's possible that The Forks was used this way, as a fishing and processing place, again and again. For example, what was dubbed the "East Hill" excavation, beneath the terraced slope to today's Forks Historic Port on the Assiniboine, yielded a series of hearths and hundreds of bone fragments that were even more diverse than those at the Johnston Terminal dig. Here, everything from bison bones to tiny clamshells were

found, with catfish bones present throughout the site. When the bones were radiocarbon dated, the result yielded a date of about 2,800 BP.

Some of these people may have interacted with the "Old Copper" people, who made weapons, knives, fishhooks, harpoons and lovely crescents from raw copper mined along the north shore of Lake Superior. Though none of their tools or weapons have been found at The Forks, Old Copper artifacts have been found in a number of places right across southern Manitoba, from Bissett in the east to Melita in the southwest and Thompson to the north.

The Old Copper culture had its beginnings very early, perhaps 6,000 or 7,000 years ago, but its climax was between 5,000 and 3,000 years ago. The people seem to have had a culture based on a seasonal round of hunting, fishing and harvesting wild rice and nuts. Their tools and weapons were beautiful and highly valued, and its likely that both raw copper and fully-fashioned articles were widely traded. But it's possible too, particularly as the climate cooled about 4,500 years ago, that Old Copper peoples expanded into southeastern Manitoba to hunt bison, or perhaps to fish along the Red River.

There is also evidence at The Forks of early plains people who made pottery. In some parts of the world, especially in the Near East, pottery is associated with the beginnings of agriculture. In fact, for years many archaeologists assumed that the development of pottery automatically indicated a settled community focused on farming. But in North America, pottery is most often found among the encampments of people who were essentially hunter-gatherers. And in Manitoba, it makes its appearance about 2,200 years ago, predating any evidence of agricultural activities by hundreds of years.

*Crossroads of the Continent*

COURTESY OF THE MANITOBA MUSEUM

There are several likely reasons for this. When corn was domesticated in Central America nearly 6,000 years ago, it was a short-day, long-season crop. Moving it north to northern North America, where the growing season is short (about 100 days of reliably frost-free weather) and the days very long, required developing a strain – a short-season, long-day crop – that could grow fast and mature quickly. That not only corn, but also squash and beans (which were grown in the Missouri Valley just south of Manitoba) could be changed this way through selective breeding, is testament to the skills of early North American farmers. In fact, the cultivation of corn did come to the lower Red River Valley, but not until the creation and use of pottery was long established.

Archaeologists therefore believe that in Western Canada, the use of pottery arose not from agriculture, but from the need to extract more nutrients from all kinds of food. As every modern cook knows, stewing is an excellent way to

both extend a small quantity of meat and make poor cuts or hard grains palatable. Ceramic pots are better able to accomplish this task than the earlier skin or bark containers.

Both bark and skin containers were used with a technique known as "stone boiling", in which hot stones were placed in containers with water and food to bring them to a boil. By comparison, ceramic pots could be placed directly over a fire, creating hotter temperatures more quickly and allowing longer cooking times.

The earliest pots found at The Forks were the distinctive "Avonlea" pottery. Made by plains groups from southern Saskatchewan, they were created of thick coils of clay molded into a cone shape and decorated with a variety of surface finishes. Avonlea hunters were also noted for making some of the earliest arrow points that have been found. Delicately crafted and wafer thin, these lovely points were found among pottery sherds discovered at The Forks in 2002. Though the artifacts have yet to be carbon dated, they make it clear that Avonlea people were here between 1,700 and 1,300 years ago.

Some of the pots found at the site may also be what is called "Laurel" pottery, made by people from the Canadian Shield. Though similar in shape to Avonlea pots, they have a smooth surface finish and more ornate decoration around the upper part of the vessel. The coexistence of these plains and eastern woodland forms

*Created more than 2,000 years ago, ceramic pots initiated a revolution in the way food was prepared. Over time and among cultures, the shape, designs, ornamentation and methods of potting varied. As a result, pottery sherds are among the best tools archaeologists have to both date and locate cultures. The differences between cone-shaped Avonlea pots, at left, and the vessel below, distinctively marked with Thunderbird tail feathers, are evident even to amateurs. The latter, found at Lockport, was influenced by the Oneota people from the south.*

COURTESY OF MANITOBA HISTORIC RESOURCES

# FLOOD OF THE MILLENNIUM

IN ADDITION TO PROVIDING information on previous human occupations of The Forks, the archaeological excavations that have accompanied every development at the site have also illuminated other aspects of the distant past.

For example, excavations near the harbour unearthed evidence of a flood, an event to which Winnipeggers today can certainly relate. About a metre-and-a-half below the surface, the bones of both an adult bison and an unborn calf were found together near the bottom of a thick layer of sand.

Archaeologist Sid Kroker believes the presence of adult and fetal bison bone intermixed this way makes it clear that the body of the pregnant cow decomposed in situ. "It's likely," Kroker explained, "that the bison cow either died just prior to the flood and was washed downstream, or perhaps was caught in the floodwaters as it tried to cross the river. Either way, it was likely swept a short distance downstream, to the river junction, where the body was perhaps caught in the branches of a tree."

This would have been in the early stages of the flood, for a thin layer of sand underlies the bones, while the sand above them is much thicker. The depth of the sand layer, which in some parts of The Forks is a metre thick, is compelling proof that this was a massive flood of the Assiniboine River.

Having witnessed the flood of 1997, which many Winnipeggers have called the Flood of the Century, one can only imagine what an inundation many times that magnitude might have been like. Was this the Flood of the Millennium, perhaps?

LINDA FAIRFIELD

In 1997, most of the city was protected from the worst of the ravages of the water by the Winnipeg Floodway. Though water was backed up into the Assiniboine, the flood of 1997 was mainly on the Red River, which is wider and deeper.

In 1997, the flood was prefaced by classic conditions for a spring flood: a heavy April snow fall, followed by very warm temperatures. There was little city or provincial officials could do, expect pray that the floodway would do its job. Though it was touch and go for several days, the floodway gates held and the city was spared an inundation. To the south, Grand Forks, North Dakota, as well as many Manitoba communities along the river were not so for-tunate; they were devastated as the crest came through.

Scientists have compared the 1997 flood to the even larger one of 1826, which destroyed or seriously damaged most of the buildings at The Forks and elsewhere along the lower Red River Valley. Yet Sid Kroker says the deposits from the 1826 flood are in the order of twenty centimetres thick, just a fifth of those left by the flood 750 years ago.

The climate in 1250 A.D. was as warm or warmer than it is today, for this was the height of the Medieval Warm Period. In general, this was a time of drought, particularly on the western plains. But it's not hard to imagine a spring blizzard, with driving winds and heavy snow, a thick blanket of snow on partly melted ice and a herd of bison, seeking shelter perhaps, crossing the Assiniboine. The ice gives way and a pregnant cow slips through the gaping hole.

The rest, to paraphrase, is archaeology.

again suggests that groups from very different regions gathered at The Forks to trade.

In spite of many years of monitoring construction, as well as numerous digs at both The Forks and the The Forks National Historic Site, the latter led by archaeologist Peter Priess, the Avonlea campsite was found almost by accident.

Sid Kroker was monitoring the earth from the bore holes for the pilings of the new parkade when he found evidence of the campsite. Mitigative excavation of the parkade uncovered sherds from several cooking pots, and an arrowhead and other stone tools, as well as the remains of fish and bison.

Like atlatl points and later arrowheads, pottery is an indicator of where visitors to The Forks might have come from. Another such clue was found along Pioneer Boulevard, during excavations undertaken during the building of a road into The Forks. There, a hoe made from a bison shoulder blade was discovered, tantalizing evidence of visitors from the south and an indication that the same kind of agricultural activities that took place at Lockport about 600 years ago might also have occurred at The Forks. Certainly, with frequent flooding to nourish the soil and the rivers to water the crops, The Forks would seem a prime spot for growing corn.

At Lockport, several kinds of evidence – charred corn, bell-shaped storage pits, bison blade hoes and clay pots with distinctive chevron motifs – have led archaeologists to believe that people either related to or strongly influenced by horticultural groups to the south were living at Lockport in the early 1400s. Many cultures – the Mandan, Hidatsa and Crow of the upper Missouri River and the Oneota, from what is now Iowa on the upper Mississippi River – were accomplished

COURTESY OF MANITOBA HISTORIC RESOURCES

PETER ST. JOHN / HERITAGE CORN COURTESY OF MARY ANNE NYLEN

farmers during this period. And the Siouan-speaking Oneota were known to create pots decorated with the powerful Thunderbird motif, such as those found at Lockport. Provincial archaeologist Leigh Syms does not believe that chevron-decorated pots definitively proves that the Oneota were at Lockport, but clearly they either traded with or influenced the people who settled there 600 years ago. And to get to Lockport, people bent on farming would almost certainly have had to pass the junction of the Red and the Assiniboine. Thus it's easy to believe that farming began at The Forks not with

*Native horticulturalists, depicted here working their plots near Lockport, brought agriculture to Manitoba about 600 years ago. Their agrarian lifestyle may have been relatively short-lived, however, for even as they were planting their first crops of hardy corn, shown at left, the global climate was cooling. From about 1350 to 1850 AD, the Earth cooled dramatically during a period known as the Little Ice Age.*

*At The Forks, life continued much as it always had. As nations to the south and west experienced drought and hardship, the bison still wandered the northeastern plains and the fish filled the rivers in the spring and fall.*

the coming of Europeans, but hundreds of years before.

In the centuries prior to the establishment of the Lockport site, changes were occurring all over the Northern Hemisphere, in large part because of a relatively brief period of global warming that occurred between about 1150 and 650 years ago (or 850 and 1350 AD). Climatologists call this the Medieval Warm Period, or Little Climatic Optimum, and it was at least partly responsible for a number of well-known changes in European history, including the Viking invasions of Northern Europe and the Icelandic settlement of Greenland. Here in Canada, global warming made possible the brief but well-known Icelandic settlement in northern Newfoundland, but Canadians are less familiar with the even more momentous changes that were taking place in central North America.

Warmer winters, earlier springs and longer autumns seem to have accelerated both the hybridization of many plants, including corn, and to have greatly increased the number of areas in which they were grown. At the same time, populations across North America were exploding, a phenomenon that some archaeologists attribute, at least in part, to the addition of concentrated carbohydrates in their diets.

The cultivation of corn or maize (as well as squash and beans farther south) and the accompanying population increase led directly to other dramatic changes as hunter-gatherer societies began to adapt their yearly rounds to accommodate the need to tend their field plots. Soon, villages grew up around these plots of land, necessitating the establishment of more complex social and political organizations. In the Mississippi and lower Missouri Valleys, villages became towns, and the towns grew into small cities. During this period, life went on much as it always had at The Forks, but the people

AMANDA DOW

*Crossroads of the Continent*

who fished and hunted along the Red River would not have been unaware of these developments to the south.

As the warming continued, the mild climate began to give way to regular periods of drought. In Colorado and New Mexico, drought during the twelfth century was so severe that long-established towns were abandoned, many of them permanently. Farther north, drought between 1250 and 1400 created war between groups that had previously been at peace. Unfortified villages added fortifications and fortified towns moved into highly defensible locations, sometimes abandoning areas they had occupied for centuries. Often this movement seems to have been caused by the abandonment of upland settlements, which were too far from the major rivers for dependable irrigation; moving closer to the rivers often brought them into conflict with groups already resident there.

Archaeological excavations in many places show that this was a terrible time of hunger, malnutrition and warfare. By the fourteenth century, there is evidence of full-scale massacres, including the Crow Creek Massacre in South Dakota. Here, a huge mass grave contains hundreds of individuals with traumatic injuries to heads and limbs, as well as obvious signs of malnutrition.

It was about this time that the horticulturalists apparently moved up the Red River from the southeast. The Forks, meanwhile, had been occupied for centuries by Algonkian-speaking people from the east and north. Archaeologists have found broken sherds of ornate "Blackduck" pottery, widely associated with peoples from the forests to the east, as well as evidence of several occupations of groups from the Interlake. But there is no evidence that the arrival of the strangers from the south occasioned violence, either at The Forks or at Lockport.

To the contrary, along the lower Red River these corn-growing newcomers appear to have been accepted peacefully when they began to clear the land and plant their hillocks of very hardy corn – likely heritage varieties that are now called Northern Flint or Eastern 8 – at Lockport about 1400. As their neighbours did, these early farmers also hunted bison and fished and since there seems to have been enough for all, peace reigned.

In a world increasingly prone to scarcity and violence, it may have been these apparently simple realities – an abundance of food and an absence of war – that made The Forks the obvious choice for a great meeting of peoples in a time of scarcity and stress.

Aboriginal elders are aware of this meeting, for the information has been passed from one generation to the next for centuries. Literate cultures, with their dependence on written records, have often been quick to dismiss the veracity of oral history, frequently relegating traditional knowledge to the realm of myth and legend. Until, that is, such oral history is confirmed by a chance discovery.

Just such a confirmation occurred at The Forks. Very early in the development of the site, about 1990, Sid Kroker was approached by two elders. Because of the potential impact on the area, they had decided that it was necessary to share their knowledge with the archaeologist who would be spearheading the excavations there. The elders said that many years ago – perhaps 500 or more – eight or nine nations gathered at The Forks for a great Peace Meeting.

But for most of the decade that followed, archaeological excavations at The Forks recovered evidence of occupations much earlier than the Peace Meeting or, if in the same general time period, campsites that reflected a single culture. Then in

1997, during the archaeological work that accompanied the twinning of Pioneer Boulevard south of Water Avenue, the long-awaited confirmation of the elders' history was recovered.

The uppermost layer, the last in a sequence of occupations beginning about 1,000 years ago, contained stone and bone tools, ceramic fragments and extensive food remains – including

*As the centuries passed, the bounty of The Forks drew cultures from all directions. During the fur trade, easy access to large herds of bison, from which pemmican (right) was made, continued to make the junction of the rivers a place of importance.*

WILLIAM ARMSTRONG / NATIONAL ARCHIVES OF CANADA / C–10502

bison, elk, deer, beaver and rabbit bones, as well as the remains of catfish, drum, perch, sturgeon, sucker and walleye. Radiocarbon dating on the animal bones provided a date of 715 years ago. And among the bones was a fascinating diversity of pot sherds and broken vessels from North Dakota, Minnesota, Northwestern Ontario and Central Manitoba.

Pottery is still one of the best ways for archaeologists to establish the details of the past – the who, what, when and

CREE

THE FORKS

NAKOTA
(Assiniboin)

ANISHINABE
(Ojibwe)

LAKOTA

DAKOTA

DAWN HUCK

where – because for centuries pottery was distinctively linked to the people who created it. Now, spread over a large area at The Forks – essentially the section between today's baseball stadium and the large outdoor stage – were pieces of pottery that could be traced to as many as nine different nations. It was a unique collection, leading Kroker to believe that many cultures had gathered for a short period of time. Was this the Peace Meeting of which the elders had spoken?

It's an idea that begs to be developed. Did the people who gathered here recognize the passing of an old order? Many knew that instead of harvesting the bounty of the land, much of their time was spent growing their own food. They also knew that the land, or the weather, had betrayed them. The rain wouldn't come, the summers were hot and dry and the crops wouldn't grow. And now many people were hungry and sick. Others were on the move. What would the future hold? Had they displeased the gods?

From a distance of seven centuries, we can only speculate, but we do know that the Red River Valley has long been both a corridor and a meeting place, not only for humans, but geographically and environmentally. Lying west of the shield, at the eastern end of the Great Plains and the northern tip of the tall grass prairies, with great lakes in three directions, it was not the backwater that some have imagined. In fact, rather than a peripheral place of little importance, it seems that The Forks has instead been a significant crossroads, where people created relationships that extended in all directions, and were involved in exchanges of goods, technology and ideas.

It may be that the end result of the great meeting at The Forks was to encourage others to take advantage of the region's natural bounty. It does seem that over the next 300 years, the Anishinabe (or Ojibwe) from the east, the Cree from the north and the Nakota (or Assiniboin) from the south all regularly used The Forks as part of a seasonal round that covered much of central North America. The Siouan-speaking Nakota, for example, often travelled as far south as the Missouri River during the winter, to trade at the agricultural villages of the Mandan, then moved north during the summer months to the northern parts of Lake Winnipeg and Lake Manitoba. Quite regularly, they travelled as far north as Hudson Bay.

The Algonkian-speaking Anishinabe, meanwhile, moved seasonally from the boreal forests of the Canadian Shield to the parklands and prairies. Each of these nations would have travelled across Cree territory as they made these journeys, but though each must have defended its territorial and trading rights, and though young men undoubtedly went raiding from time to time, there seems to have been relative peace. Until Europeans came in significant numbers, there was a shared use of the land and its resources.

When the first, unnamed, French fur traders arrived at The Forks in the late 1720s or early 1730s, they found that all three nations regularly used The Forks to fish or trade or perhaps just to visit. In 1737, on the invitation of the Nakota, Pierre Gaultier de La Vérendrye journeyed from Lake of the Woods to The Forks on a trip that took eighteen days through "excessively cold" weather, according to his journal. Almost every day, he wrote, he came to lodges, whose inhabitants "wished me bon voyage and offered me provisions."

The same year, he noted that there were "two villages" of Nakota at The Forks, but the following year he found "ten cabins of Cree". Clearly, the junction of the two rivers was well used by different peoples for short periods.

At the time, and for decades to come, the banks of the Red River were thickly treed in many places with poplar and willow,

*In addition to all the other crucial tasks they performed and the furs they provided, for more than two centuries Native North Americans guided almost every European expedition. Here, in 1690, Nakota guides give young Henry Kelsey his first view of the vast herds of bison.*

REX WOODS / COURTESY OF ROGERS COMMUNICATIONS INC.

according to Alexander Henry the Younger, who passed that way in 1800. Appearing much as The Forks National Historic Site does today, these riverine forests would have provided homes for a variety of small mammals, adding variety to a diet of fish and large game such as bison and deer.

But life was changing for all the peoples that frequented The Forks. Beginning as soon as the first posts were established on Hudson Bay in the 1670s (see A Hub of the Fur Trade on page 66), the Cree, Nakota and Anishinabe had all become essential to the fur trade. Initially they served as trappers, but soon they also took over the role of middlemen, trading goods for furs to Aboriginal nations who lived farther inland. When the Hudson's Bay Company and its rival the Montreal-based North West Company began establishing posts inland in the 1770s and '80s, the Cree and Nakota assumed a new role as suppliers, hunting bison and processing meat and hides.

In 1810, when the NWC established Fort Gibraltar I at The Forks, the Native hunters and the Métis or Aboriginal-French population of the surrounding area were critical to its success. This was to be a "provisioning post", a place where pemmican – the fuel of the fur brigades – was dispensed in large quantities. Composed of dried and pounded bison meat, sometimes mixed with berries, with rendered lard poured over it, pemmican was high in calories, relatively light in weight and kept for months or even years.

Aboriginal employees also served as canoe men and York boatmen, as fishers and carpenters, as labourers and domestics. From the beginning of the fur trade, they had been crucial to its success, not only serving as hunters, trappers, traders and suppliers, but also actively assisting the newcomers in everything from basic survival techniques to actively providing protection from harm, as Chief Peguis did for the beleaguered Scottish settlers of the lower Red River in 1816.

In short, the business of the fur trade and even the very survival of Europeans in North America could not have been accomplished without them.

Yet as the years passed, Aboriginal hunters, trappers, traders and guides were gradually eased out of the trade, at The Forks as in many other places. By 1850, the buffalo hunters were mainly Métis and the company labourers were often Cree-Scots mixed bloods.

Even some of the most exemplary Aboriginal members of Red River society were pushed to its margins by sometimes subtle, and often overt racism. Aggathas Kennedy, for example, who grew up in the fur trade, raised ten remarkable children and almost singlehandedly ran the family farm, even before the untimely death of her Orcadian husband, was the victim of vicious racial slurs. Some of these came from newly arrived Englishwomen in St. Andrews on the Red, just north of The Forks. And prior to his death in 1864, Peguis, who had done so much for the settlers in the valley, had become disillusioned with the broken promises and disregard for his people and their rights.

By the time Manitoba became a province in 1870, not only the original inhabitants of The Forks, but their Métis and mixed-blood cousins – the latter forming the largest segment of the population around The Forks – were experiencing extreme bias and prejudice from expansionist newcomers.

For a century after Manitoba joined Canada, its Native inhabitants were treated as second-class citizens. Gathered onto reserves, educated in sometimes deplorable conditions at residential schools, they were little seen and less considered, their cultures and languages kept alive only by the efforts of individuals who were determined that they should not die.

In the past thirty years, however, a renaissance has begun to take place among Native Manitobans. Aided by

LARGE IMAGE: KEN GIGLIOTTI / THE WINNIPEG FREE PRESS; INSET: THE FORKS NORTH PORTAGE PARTNERSHIP

government programs to encourage education and develop skills, and spearheaded by elders who are determined that skill development must go hand in hand with a revival of cultural pride, Aboriginal citizens are at last regaining their long-lost place at the heart of Manitoba. Today, they serve as ministers in the government, practice law and medicine, and are involved in almost every aspect of society. But they are also taking great pains to revive their languages and cultures,

to ensure that their young learn their illustrious history.

At The Forks, there are many reminders of that history, from the Orientation Circle at The Forks National Historic Site, and the Wall Through Time, which wraps around the place where their distant ancestors once met in the spring to catch and process fish, to the North American Indigenous Games of 2002, and South Point, which awaits development by Winnipeg's Aboriginal community.

*In 1999, Douglas and Wilfred Keam paddled from York Factory to The Forks, a journey that took fifty-two days. Along the way, the pair was joined by many other paddlers.*

*Inset: The North American Indigenous Games at The Forks, 2002*

# A Hub of The

In 1815, the confluence of the rivers was a busy place during the winter, just as it is now. The second incarnation of the North West Company's Fort Gibraltar, which stood on the point about where Johnston Terminal sits today, drew trappers and traders, while the rivers provided fish for both the company and the Métis community that was growing on the east bank of the Red.

# Fur Trade

By Eleanor Stardom

The fur trade, the first European commercial venture at The Forks, had its roots in late sixteenth century fashion. While fancy furs, such as mink, ermine, martin and fox had long been prized by the aristocracy for their beauty and warmth, it was the rage for gentlemen's broad-brimmed felt hats that drove the North American fur trade and ultimately opened the continent to Europeans.

*The style of a "beaver" often announced its wearer's calling, political sympathies or station in life and many styles had names of their own. Here, from the top: the Wellington (1812); the hat worn by eighteenth-century clerics; the Regent (1825); a "Navy" cocked hat of 1800 and, right, the Continental (1776).*

HUDSON'S BAY COMPANY ARCHIVES / C–308

Beaver was considered the best fur for making felt. Its pelt consists of an outer layer of coarse guard hairs over an inner layer of soft fur. When this down was removed from the skin and mixed with adhesives and stiffeners, it produced a durable, water resistant felt fabric with a glossy finish favoured by felt-makers. The initial procedure of removing the guard hairs from parchment beaver pelts (*castor sec*) was a closely kept secret, known only to Russian processors. Anxious to avoid the extra shipping and processing costs involved in dealing with the Russians, in the late seventeenth century, felt-makers in London and Paris looked abroad for a solution.

Native North Americans had long used prime beaver for clothing, scraping the inner side to loosen the guard hairs and rubbing it with marrow to make the skin soft and pliable. The pelts were then cut into rectangles and sewn with sinew to make robes that were worn with the fur against the body. Over time, the guard hairs wore away and the natural oils of the skin polished the fur to a rich sheen. The result was *castor gras*, "greasy beaver" or coat beaver, which could be easily processed by western European felt-makers. Traders offered their highest price for them much to the amusement of the Natives, who gladly traded their second-hand garments for coveted manufactured goods such as hatchets, kettles, guns, awls and cloth as well as luxury items of Brazilian tobacco, brandy and beads. Both sides were satisfied that they had struck a good bargain.

Although other furs were collected, the prime winter beaver pelt became the standard (1 Made Beaver) by which the value of other furs and trade goods were measured. Since beaver are not migratory animals and are easily trapped, populations inevitably declined over time forcing traders to seek out new sources.

The strategic location of The Forks, at the junction of the Red and Assiniboine Rivers, offered ready access to fur-rich areas to the north and west. It was also a traditional assembly point for the Cree, their allies from the south, the Nakota, and the Anishinabe (or Ojibwe) from the east. Both made annual migrations through the parkland zone. As such, The Forks was destined to become the flashpoint for rivalry between two trade empires, the Hudson's Bay Company to the north and the Montreal traders to the east.

The Hudson's Bay Company had been established on May 2, 1670 by a Royal Charter granted by King Charles II of England to a group of speculators headed by his cousin, Prince Rupert. Under the terms of the Charter, the "Governor and Company of Adventurers of England Tradeing into Hudsons Bay", as it was formally known, was given sweeping powers. Among them was a trade monopoly over the entire Hudson Bay watershed, an area of 7,770,000 square kilometers that was henceforth, at least among the British, known as Rupert's Land.

The initial investors could have had little appreciation of the enormity of their acquisition; nor were the people who had occupied this land for thousands of years consulted. Europeans had never ventured into the vast majority of the territory, which today would include the provinces of Quebec and Ontario north of the Laurentians and west of Labrador, all of Manitoba and Saskatchewan, the southern half of Alberta and the southeast corner of Nunavut. In addition to its monopoly, but with no knowledge of the territory or its people, the company was granted the right to make

*Crossroads of the Continent*

and enforce laws and to establish a military force within the territory, all for the good of the company and the advancement of the trade.

A London-based Governor and Committee, elected by the shareholders, dictated policy and set annual fur rates while local officers and company "servants", as the rank and file employees were called, were responsible for the efficient operation of individual posts.

Initially the company built its posts at the mouths of major rivers flowing into James Bay, but soon expanded along the western shore of Hudson Bay. This was the territory of the Cree, who quickly established trade relations with the English. By the 1680s both the Nakota and Cree were making the long trip north to the Bay and it was estimated that in one year alone, three hundred canoes carrying more than seven hundred people had visited York Fort, later known as York Factory, the chief entrepôt or depot for the area's trade.

The Cree quickly recognized the advantage of acting as middlemen, departing from a life of game hunting to become traders, passing worn, well-used European goods to tribes to the south and west at a handsome profit. Since the English traders preferred to remain at their bayside posts, the Cree soon became indispensable as traders, agents and transporters. They held their own in the trade process, often dictating terms of the trade to both European and other Native North Americans alike. As their role as middlemen expanded, their association with the European traders and access to trade goods increased their personal status and reinforced their military power. They learned to exploit their strategic advantage and before long controlled the flow of furs and trade goods to and from Hudson Bay.

*While retaining its basic seventeenth-century elements, the Hudson's Bay Company crest has changed several times over the centuries. The version above is from the mid-twentieth century; according to experts from the HBC Archives.*

HUDSON'S BAY COMPANY ARCHIVES / P–237

For a time, a lack of direct competition ensured their allegiance to the Hudson's Bay Company, but it was not long before a threat emerged from the east. Independent French traders out of New France had made sporadic forays into the James Bay area as early as 1671, trying to intercept trade flotillas on their way north. They were a breed quite unlike their English counterparts. Montreal merchants, or sometimes individual voyageurs, would first obtain a trade licence (*congé*) from the French government in Québec, allowing them access to the interior or upper country, usually termed the *pays d'en haut*. Once financing was arranged, voyageurs were hired to transport trade goods inland by canoe, under the direction of a senior trader. Experienced voyageurs usually spent up to two years living and trading with the Natives, acquiring skills as canoemen and creating a culture of strength and endurance that was legendary. Unlike Hudson's Bay Company policy (though not practice) which restricted contact with the Natives, the French were permitted to take wives *à la façon du pays* (in the country fashion), which helped to cement trade alliances and promoted a certain stability. Despite the fact that their goods were often inferior

*With one sweeping stroke of a pen, Charles II granted his cousin Prince Rupert, below, a vast territory, not only unknown to and unvisited by the British, but peopled by more than a dozen North American nations.*

HUDSON'S BAY COMPANY ARCHIVES / P–129

HOWARD SIVERTSON / FROM THE ILLUSTRATED VOYAGER

TRADING *EN DÉROUINE*, IN THE WINTER CAMPS OF NORTH AMERICAN PEOPLES, RATHER THAN WAITING FOR FURS
TO BE BROUGHT IN TO THE FUR POSTS, MADE SENSE TO THE FRENCH FROM THE OUTSET. THE ENGLISH RESISTED THE IDEA FOR A TIME,
BUT EVENTUALLY REALIZED THE RESULTS JUSTIFIED THE INCREASED EFFORT.

*Crossroads of the Continent*

in quality and higher priced, the French traders provided a ready inducement to avoid the arduous trip to Hudson Bay.

It was adventurer and trader Pierre Gaultier de Varennes et de la Vérendrye who opened up the western interior to French trade. He was born at Trois Rivières in 1685, the youngest of thirteen children. After a career in the military he joined his brother as a partner in the fur trade in the area north of Lake Superior. He was intrigued with the idea of a western sea, commonly believed to exist in the middle of the North American continent. Opening onto the Pacific, this mythical body of water appeared to offer a short route to the riches of the Far East. At the beginning of the eighteenth century, the farthest point of western penetration was Rainy Lake, but information La Vérendrye obtained from local Natives suggested that the sought-after sea was within easy reach. To finance his explorations, he proposed a series of fur trading posts along the western route. In addition, he received financial support from French Canadian merchants and the Governor of New France, Charles Beauharnois, who was anxious to extend his economic and military power and to harass the English at every opportunity.

La Vérendrye received a three-year monopoly on the fur trade in the Lake Ouinipigon (Winnipeg) area and in June 1731 he set out from Montreal with a party that included his nephew, three sons and fifty *engagées* or employees. A new headquarters was established on Lake of the Woods. From this base, La Vérendrye directed trade and western penetration for the next two years, with help from local Natives, who played much the same role with the French as the Cree had with the Hudson Bay English.

To secure access to the trade and knowledge of lands

NATIONAL ARCHIVES OF CANADA / C14661I

to the west, he entered into economic and military alliances with the Cree and Nakota who, until then, had traded with the English. In June 1734, his son Jean-Baptiste reached Lake Winnipeg and, following the eastern shore southwards, came upon the huge delta of the Red River. Upriver from this confusing maze of channels, near the present site of Selkirk, he built Fort Maurepas. Progress was slow, for La Vérendrye was forced to make regular trips back to Montreal and Québec to shore up support and secure new financing. Still, he and his sons were convinced that the route to the Western Sea was still possible. It must lay, they felt, to the south through Mandan country, in today's North Dakota. In 1738, at the behest of the Nakota, who promised to meet and direct him,

*La Vérendrye and his sons, seen here at Lake of the Woods, have been rather heroically portrayed in several paintings from later eras. Surprisingly perhaps, no one is known to have painted any of the members of this adventuresome family while they lived.*

La Vérendrye pushed up the Red River from Fort Maurepas, reaching The Forks on September 24th.

He noted in his journal:

> I proceeded to the fork of the Assiniboine and reaching there on the 24th I found ten cabins (lodges) of Cree, including two war chiefs, awaiting me with a large quantity of meat, having been notified of my coming. They begged me to stay with them for a while, so that they might have the pleasure of seeing and entertaining us. I agreed to do so, being glad of a chance of talking to them.

La Vérendrye extracted a promise from them that as long as the French remained in their lands they would not trade with the English and would keep peace with their traditional enemy, whom La Vérendrye and his Cree and Nakota allies called the "Sioux". The uncomplimentary term – which literally meant "snakes" – referred to the eastern or woodland Dakota. La Vérendrye also urged the Cree to continue to hunt for food and supply the French forts, to which they agreed.

Two days later La Vérendrye headed west up the Assiniboine River, where he built Fort La Reine on or near the present site of Portage la Prairie. He left behind Sieur Louis Damours de Louvière and a small number of men to build a fort at The Forks, for the convenience of the people on the Red River. It was named, appropriately, Fort Rouge. Although probably not more than a storage depot, it was the first post built by Europeans on the site of the future city of Winnipeg. It lasted only a short time, however. Just over a decade later, in 1749, it was reported abandoned, likely due to the Red River flood of 1747.

Despite its brief existence, its presence was significant. As one of a chain of posts established by La Vérendrye, stretching west from Lake Superior to the mouth of the Saskatchewan River, it extended the French presence squarely across trade routes leading to the Bay, diverting furs and for a quarter-century boosting New France's economic wealth.

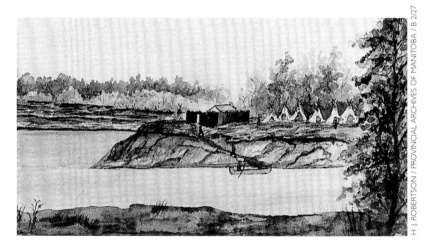

The struggle between Britain and France for control of the interior of North America ended in 1763 with the Treaty of Paris that concluded the Seven Years War. During the war, the French abandoned their western posts. The vacuum did not remain however. Soon Montreal traders, many of them Scots financed by capital from Britain and the American colonies, were once again plying western river routes. By 1765 they had reached the Saskatchewan River and by 1774 they were present in such numbers in the interior that one Hudson's Bay Company veteran complained that they were "... Interlopers of the trade who like the locusts of Egypt

*La Vérendrye's Fort Rouge, right, is believed to have been located on South Point, the tongue of land between the Red and Assiniboine Rivers.*

*Voyageurs, such as the colourful individual on the adjacent page, powered the French and later Canadian fur trades, often working eighteen-hour days and paddling at a pace that astounded even their Hudson's Bay Company rivals. East of Lake Superior, voyageurs lived mostly on dried peas and salt pork, but in the west, they were fuelled by pemmican during weeks of arduous travel.*

H. J. ROBERTSON / PROVINCIAL ARCHIVES OF MANITOBA / B 2/27

*Crossroads of the Continent*

bring Devastation & Ruin along with them." Competition for furs brought attendant abuses as each trader hoped to undercut his nearest rival. Posts proliferated, often within sight of one another, leapfrogging westward along major waterways. The Aboriginal people were quick to capitalize on the opportunities afforded by the competition. Even those who continued to frequent Hudson's Bay Company posts often traded their best furs inland, saving the remnants for their annual trip to the Bay.

The Hudson's Bay Company's monopoly appeared to be in tatters, but at first the HBC was slow to respond, preferring to remain in its "sleep by the frozen sea". Lacking both personnel and equipment to support inland travel, it continued to rely on the loyalty of Native middlemen. While it had been able to finance small exploratory expeditions into the interior between 1754 and 1771, they were not for the purposes of actual trade but rather to try and entice Native traders back to the Bay. One such expedition, led by William Tomison, reached The Forks in 1768. There, he found that English and French free traders were taking whatever furs were to be had.

Finally, in 1774, the HBC took action, sending Samuel Hearne inland to establish a post at Cumberland House near the Saskatchewan River. Unfortunately, as he noted in his journal, "Pedlars [as the free traders were often called] by this time has too much influence and that I ware too late in coming."

The HBC's new inland strategy slowly eliminated the middleman role enjoyed for so many years by the Cree and Nakota. This was at least partly offset, however, by an increased need for provisions and provisioners. Intense rivalry had resulted in a rapid depletion of woodland game with consequent food shortages at many posts. Lines of communication lengthened and traders were forced to establish food supply networks that drew heavily on the bison (or buffalo) resources of the parklands and grasslands for survival.

The food most in demand was pemmican. Bison meat was customarily cut into thin slabs, sun dried, tied into bales and consumed as dried meat (or jerky). To make pemmican, it was pounded into small pieces, sometimes mixed with saskatoon berries and packed into hide bags. Then lard, which had been heated in a kettle, was poured over the meat mixture. The resulting mixture weighed about ninety pounds or forty kilos and properly cured and stored, had a very long shelf life. One trader, who described it as unprepossessing in appearance with a good many bison hairs mixed with it, added philosophically, "After a time ... one becomes accustomed to those little peculiarities." It was estimated that a half-kilo of pemmican was the equivalent of two kilos of meat, an important factor given the long distances travelled by the fur brigades and the primitive state of the scattered posts.

In 1779, several Montreal partnerships amalgamated to form the North West Company, headed by Simon McTavish. They hoped that by combining their efforts they could reduce costs and present a united front to eliminate the Hudson's Bay Company, as well as other small independents. The gamble paid off. By 1800, the North West Company was shipping £144,000 worth of furs to London, compared to just £38,000 for the HBC. By 1805, having absorbed its major rival, the

BARBARA ENDRES

XY Company the previous year, and having neutralized many of its eastern competitors, the North West Company had captured fully eighty per cent of the trade, while the HBC accounted for just fifteen per cent. Now, much like compet-

WALTER J. PHILLIPS / NATIONAL ARCHIVES OF CANADA / C1108833

problems had been resolved with the development of the York boat. Rather like the Orkney yole, which had been used for centuries off the north coast of Scotland, the York boat was much heavier than a canoe, but had a shallow draught and required less skill to navigate. Even more important, it was durable and stable, particularly on large lakes such as Lake Winnipeg, and could carry more than 2700 kilograms of freight, twice the capacity of the typical Nor'Westers' *canot du nord*.

During these years, The Forks had continued to be a popular camping area for Aboriginal and European traders. While most were transitory, others remained longer. Two independent traders, Bruce and Boyer, overwintered at the Forks in 1781-82, building a small fort for protection. They were followed by Alexander Henry the Younger, a partner in the North West Company, in charge of trade

*When traversing large lakes, York boat crews, above, often rose before dawn to take advantage of a period of calm, working straight through until dusk.*

ing companies bent on supremacy today, the North West Company assumed an even more aggressive policy. It would even operate at a loss in order to maintain its dominance.

The stage was set for a showdown, but the Hudson's Bay Company refused to admit defeat. Its transportation

in the lower Red River Department. In September 1803, he established a small trading post at The Forks under the management of Louis Dorion, to serve as an outpost for the main trading post at Pembina, 110 kilometres south on the Red River. Like its predecessors, its tenure was short lived. Henry

74

*Crossroads of the Continent*

returned the following January to find Dorion and his men starving for lack of provisions. The post was closed the following year.

By the 1790s, the Hudson's Bay Company was actively competing on the Red and Assiniboine Rivers and The Forks became well-known as an important transhipment point for brigades travelling west and north. Here trade goods were resorted and assigned to various inland posts. As well, the confluence of the rivers had begun to be a vital provisioning centre for pemmican, fat and hides. These were often cached at The Forks and picked up by brigades moving west along the Assiniboine. Attracted by opportunities offered by this pemmican trade, in the early nineteenth century Métis began to settle at The Forks, intent on working as commercial bison hunters and contract freighters for the North West Company. As offspring of French traders and Native mothers, they had been raised within the culture of the fur trade and provided a ready labour pool that ultimately was indispensable to its operation.

With the demand for plains provisions growing, the North West Company built Fort Gibraltar at The Forks in 1810. Constructed on the north side of the Assiniboine and the west side of the Red, its primary purpose was to serve as a pemmican provisioning post to service brigades going to the Swan River, Saskatchewan, English River and Athabaska districts. It was described at the time as having ".. A wooden picketing, made of oak trees split in two, which formed its enclosure. Within the said enclosure were built the house of the partner, two houses for the men, a store, two hangards or stores, a blacksmith shop and a stable; there was also an ice-house with a watch tower over it; these houses were good

## KINNIKINIC (*Arctostaphylos*)

WHEN THE SNOW WAS STILL DEEP in the woods, this ever-green perennial, with its bright red or orange berries, provided a welcome meal for plains grizzlies as they emerged from winter hiberation. People, too, often used the rather tasteless berries as emergency food, cooking them to make them more palatable. Also called "bearberry", kinnikinic is a ground-trailing shrub with branches that are often a metre or more in length. Its shiny green leaves persist for more than one season, gradually browning as they age. In addition to bears and humans, the berries are eaten by grouse and wild turkeys, while deer and moose graze on the foliage. Steeped in boiling water, young leaves were used for centuries as an astringent tea, and dried and pulverized, the mature leaves served as an ingredient in a tobacco substitute. Fur traders learned this trick from Native North Americans, often using kinnikinic, shown here as a backdrop, to stretch their limited smoking supplies.

log houses, large and inhabited."

While the North West Company was expanding its operations the Hudson's Bay Company was experiencing financial trouble. In 1809, it had been unable to pay a dividend to its shareholders and the company was forced to operate on credit. To add to its financial woes, the Napoleonic wars had blockaded lucrative European markets, resulting in a glut of unsold furs in its London warehouse. At the same time the company was attempting to rein in soaring costs of competition in the western interior.

Thomas Douglas, the Fifth Earl of Selkirk, proposed a solution. A native of Scotland, he had long been interested in the plight of the Scottish and Irish crofters who had been dispossessed of their lands during the agricultural revolution. After touring the affected areas, he was convinced that assisted immigration was the key to improving their situation. He had proposed an Irish settlement in the Red River Valley as early as 1802, but had been rebuffed because its location would be within Hudson's Bay Company territory. Initial settlement projects in Prince Edward Island and Upper Canada had met with varying degrees of success, but Selkirk continued to pursue his dream of a settlement at Red River.

He began by buying up bargain stock in the HBC. That his brother-in-law, Andrew Wedderburn-Colvile, and his wife's cousin, John Halkett, had gained seats on the governing council helped to ensure a more sympathetic reception to his proposal. Colvile, an established London businessman, was committed to running the company in a more efficient manner. He undertook a program of retrenchment to stream-

line the company's operations and better enable it to challenge the North West Company's stronghold in the northern Athabaska area. The cornerstone of his "New System" was a requirement that inland posts rely more heavily on local provisions and reduce their dependence on costly British imports. Selkirk's plan of an agricultural settlement at The Forks would be a key component of the plan.

In 1810, Selkirk resubmitted his plan to the committee and on May 30, 1811 it was approved. For a nominal sum he was granted absolute proprietorship over a huge tract of land named Assiniboia, a 185,000-square-kilometre territory centred on the Red and Assiniboine Rivers. While the plan received support from the council, Hudson's Bay Company officers in the area were less enthusiastic; they feared the incoming settlers would interfere with the trade.

The North West Company stood to lose even more, for it had the most at stake. As it moved into the upper reaches of the Fraser and Peace Rivers, increasingly large amounts of pemmican were needed to support the canoe brigades and inland posts. Over the first decade of the century the NWC

had purchased, on average, more than 5,700 kilograms of pemmican and more than one metric tonne of grease from the Red River Department annually. This increased dramatically when the War of 1812 between Britain and the United States cut off the traditional supply route from Montreal, placing much of the burden of supplying all the posts west of Lake Superior on Pembina and Fort Gibraltar I. In 1813 alone, the company required 58,040 pounds (or 26,118 kilos) of pemmican to support its trade in Western Canada. In fact, the North West Company's very survival depended on the failure of Selkirk's settlement, for its location straddled two major rivers linking the fur country to the bison plains.

Selkirk's absolute proprietorship over Assiniboia and the territory's ties to the Hudson's Bay Company made the Nor'Westers justifiably suspicious of the earl's motives. Under the terms of the agreement, the settlement was to provide the HBC with 200 men annually, as well as land for retiring company servants, relieving posts of the costs of supporting them and their families. The Hudson's Bay Company was also entitled to establish trading posts within the territory of Assiniboia, but colonists were strictly forbidden to participate in the trade. In exchange, the company agreed to provide land and free transportation to the colonists, who were initially signed on as company servants to ensure some sort of discipline. In addition, the colony's first governor, Miles Macdonell, was given a commission by the HBC to add the weight of the charter to his rulings.

The North West Company responded in a variety of ways. Recruitment, for example, was initially slow, due in part to an effective newspaper campaign in Scotland, organized by the North West Company, to dissuade prospective settlers. After an arduous journey the first party of settlers reached The Forks on August 30, 1812. A site was chosen for the colony on a point of land about a kilometre and a half downriver from Fort Gibraltar on the west bank of the Red River. The settlers named the site Point Douglas, after the earl, began to clear the land and selected a site for Fort Douglas, the headquarters and official residence of Governor Macdonell, as well as a storage depot for company goods.

Despite the tensions, relations between the colony and the North West Company were cordial at first. Miles Macdonell's cousin and brother-in-law, Alexander Macdonell, was in command of Fort Gibraltar and they exchanged civilities upon Miles' arrival, the Nor'Westers even offering material assistance in the form of several horses. Miles reciprocated, inviting several Nor'Westers, local Métis and Aboriginal people to a ceremony on September 4th, where Selkirk's title to the land was proclaimed.

*The first incarnation of Fort Douglas, below, was built in 1812 on the Red River, not far downstream from The Forks.*

PROVINCIAL ARCHIVES OF MANITOBA / N10106

Given the lateness of the season, there was little time to do much before the arrival of winter so the party, augmented by a second group of settlers who had arrived in October, left to spend the winter to the south in Pembina. There, they would be dependent on the returns of the bison hunt for survival.

The winter at Pembina was dismal, however, for nothing had been prepared in advance for the settlers' arrival. Food was in short supply and North West Company officers, acting on instructions from their superiors, did their best to stir up trouble among the settlers, while urging local Nor'Westers to do everything in their power to oppose the colony. Miles Macdonell did little to ease the situation. Arrogant and vain, he was quick to flaunt his authority and Selkirk's claim to the territory. Finally, believing that even his cousin had turned against him, Macdonell ordered all association with the North West Company to cease.

*A Métis brigade of buffalo hunters, their Red River carts loaded with supplies, stops to rest.*

MANITOBA MUSEUM / MMMN7

Things were little better at Point Douglas the following year. Crops failed, forcing the colonists to again return to Pembina for the winter. On January 8, 1814, in an attempt to relieve ongoing food shortages, Macdonell issued the Pemmican Proclamation, forbidding the export of any provisions by either company or independent trader within the territory of Assiniboia without a special licence. Anyone caught would have all goods within their possession confiscated. As expected, the Nor'Westers were outraged, their worst fears realized. Métis bison hunters also resented the restrictions on their commerce with the North West Company and were quick to oppose any threat to their livelihood.

Copies of the proclamation were sent to all posts in Assiniboia and Macdonell ordered Sheriff John Spenser to confiscate almost thirty tonnes of pemmican, dried meat and fat, which had been intercepted as it came down the Red River. Finally in June, a compromise was reached. Macdonell agreed to return the goods seized in return for a promise of supplies for the following winter. The crisis was averted and hostilities ceased for the moment.

That summer Macdonell went north to meet a new group of incoming settlers. He returned to discover Spenser in the custody of the North West Company at Fort Gibraltar at The Forks. The terms of the June agreement were forgotten. Macdonell immediately ordered the Nor'Westers to quit their posts, but they wisely refused, knowing they would be destroyed as soon as they left.

Throughout the winter of 1814-1815, those who remained in the colony suffered continual harassment at the hands of the Nor'Westers and their Métis allies. One of the Métis leaders was Cuthbert Grant, son of a wintering partner and his Métis wife. In 1810, after he had completed

*Crossroads of the Continent*

W. DAY / HUDSON'S BAY COMPANY ARCHIVES / P-183

JUST AS WINNIPEGGERS DO TODAY, THE EARLY INHABITANTS OF THE FORKS USED THE FROZEN RIVERS FOR BOTH TRAVEL AND PLEASURE. HERE, IN A PRINT AFTER A SCENE PAINTED BY PETER RINDISBACHER IN THE EARLY 1820S, THE GOVERNOR OF FORT GARRY I ENJOYS A WINTER AFTERNOON OUTING WITH HIS FAMILY.

LORD SELKIRK / PROVINCIAL ARCHIVES OF MANITOBA / N10109

*Thomas Douglas, Earl of Selkirk, drew this sketch of Fort Douglas shortly after his arrival in 1817.*

his education in Montreal, Grant joined the company as a clerk in the Upper Red River Department. His natural leadership abilities were soon recognized and in 1814 the company appointed him one of four captains of the Métis.

The situation in the fledgling colony was now nearly unbearable. When Nor'Wester Duncan Cameron offered free transportation and assistance in obtaining land in Upper Canada, many of the settlers were convinced to leave. Soon after, a Canadian warrant was issued for Macdonell's arrest for the illegal confiscation of pemmican. He surrendered in return for a guarantee of the remaining settlers' safety and, in June was escorted to the North West Company's headquarters at Fort William on Lake Superior, en route to trial in Montreal. Within a week, in the face of continuing hostility, the remaining settlers fled to Jack River at the north end of Lake Winnipeg. Their homes were torched, their crops trampled and their livestock slaughtered. Only a few men were permitted to remain to salvage what they could.

At Jack River, the colonists were fortunate to meet Colin Robertson, a former Nor'Wester now with the Hudson's Bay Company, who was en route to the Athabaska country. Hearing their plight, he persuaded them to return with him to Red River and restore the colony. Additional colonists followed shortly thereafter, in the company of Robert Semple, the newly appointed governor of the Hudson's Bay Company's territories.

Relations between Semple and Robertson were strained. Like Macdonell before him, Semple regarded himself as the supreme authority in Assiniboia. He and Robertson were united in their belief that the key to the colony's survival lay in winning over the Métis, but they differed in their approaches. A vain and indecisive man, Semple alternated between attempting reconciliation and maintaining an aggressive stance.

Over the next winter, the Nor'Westers successfully continued to solicit the support of the Métis. Robertson, hearing of hostilities against the company in the Qu'Appelle Valley, seized Fort Gibraltar in retaliation in March of 1816. As tensions grew, Robertson persuaded Semple to destroy the fort and use the bastions and stockades to strengthen the fortifications at Fort Douglas.

On June 19, 1816 a party of Métis under the leadership of Cuthbert Grant, now bearing the title of Captain General of all the Half Breeds, was transporting a brigade of plundered pemmican down the Assiniboine en route to Lake Winnipeg. After sacking the Hudson's Bay post at Fort Brandon, they continued down river. Anxious to avoid The Forks, they attempted to go overland at Omand's Creek, but marshy conditions forced the heavy carts to detour within two and half kilometres of Fort Douglas. At Seven Oaks, approximately eight kilometres north of The Forks, they were met

*Crossroads of the Continent*

by a group of settlers headed by Robert Semple. Words were exchanged between Semple and one of the Métis; a shot was fired, then another. When it was over, Semple and some twenty of his men lay dead. One Métis was killed.

**E**mboldened by their success, Grant and the Métis seized Fort Douglas. Several settlers were imprisoned and the remainder escaped north to Jack River. Once again the North West Company controlled The Forks.

While all this was happening, Selkirk was en route to Red River from the east with a group of disbanded Des Meurons troops, arms and twelve boatloads of supplies. He was met at Sault St. Marie by Macdonell, who had learned of the colony's fate at Lake Winnipeg and had turned back to warn Selkirk. Outraged, Selkirk pushed on to Fort William, on the site of today's Thunder Bay, where he and his troops seized the fort and arrested nine North West Company partners. Selkirk's party occupied the fort over the winter and in January 1817 Macdonell pushed on to Red River with a small group of Des Meurons. On arrival, they retook Fort Douglas.

In the face of these ongoing hostilities, the British Government demanded that the two companies resolve their differences. The Prince Regent's Proclamation of 1817 called for a cessation of hostilities and restitution of all property and a commission of enquiry was established. Under the direction of William Coltman, representing the Crown, the

ALBERTYPE CO. COLLECTION / NATIONAL ARCHIVES OF CANADA / PA 31638

commission was authorized to determine what had happened and ensure the peace.

That summer an uneasy quiet ruled at Red River. The North West Company began construction of a second Fort Gibraltar at The Forks, just south of the original fort razed by Semple. Settlers returned to sow their crops and take up their lives again, bolstered by the presence of Selkirk and his troops. In an attempt to provide more security for the settlers, Selkirk entered into a treaty with resident Ojibwe, Cree and Nakota chiefs. Under the terms of this Selkirk Treaty of 1817, the chiefs transferred their rights of occupation to a two-mile or three-kilometre strip of land on either side of the Red River from Pembina to Lake Winnipeg and along the Assiniboine to a point just west of Portage la Prairie.

Coltman's enquiry, meanwhile, charged Selkirk for his actions at Fort William, but the Nor'Westers who had incited the Métis at Seven Oaks managed to slip away before charges of murder, theft and arson could be laid against them. The trials dragged on for years, draining Selkirk of his health and finances.

By 1820, both fur trade companies were in serious financial trouble. Preliminary discussions had begun regarding a union of the two companies, but Selkirk opposed such a move and it was not until his death that year that the final obstacle was removed.

The union of 1821 formally ended the strife between the two fur trade empires. Under the terms of the twenty-one year agreement the companies were reorganized under

*The Seven Oaks Monument was created to remember the Battle of Seven Oaks.*

*This lithograph shows the chief of the Red Lake Anishinabe speaking on behalf of his people at Fort Douglas in 1825.*

the name of the Hudson's Bay Company. Borrowing from the operating policy of the North West Company, profits of the trade would be shared by stockholders and officers in the field. But the traditional canoe route of the voyageurs through Fort William was abandoned in favour of the shorter and less costly route through Hudson Bay. Later that year, a royal licence was granted to the company, giving it exclusive rights to trade in British North America outside the bounds of Rupert's Land where it continued to enjoy the monopoly granted in the original charter, excluding Upper and Lower Canada. The result gave the company economic domination over territory stretching from Upper Canada, the predecessor of modern Ontario, to the Pacific.

Under the leadership of Governor George Simpson a rigorous program of retrenchment was undertaken. Simpson has been described as an uncompromising administrator, both thorough and tough, with boundless energy and physical endurance, often tested by his numerous reconnaissance trips throughout the territory. His strategy, which many modern administrators would easily recognize, was simple. In areas safe from competition, fairness and good management would ensure satisfactory profits. In areas of competition, the opposition would be crushed whatever the cost.

In the first years of his forty-year tenure, Simpson embarked on a major cost-cutting exercise. Officers were retired, surplus and unprofitable posts closed and salaries slashed. Many of the North West Company's labourers were Métis. It has been estimated that between one half and two thirds were laid off in the West. Many moved with their families to the area around The

W. DAY / HUDSON'S BAY COMPANY ARCHIVES / P–180

*Crossroads of the Continent*

Forks, settling on the east side of the Red River and along the Assinboine west to White Horse Plains, just west of today's Headingley. There, they continued to organize the Red River bison hunts, their principal source of income. When not engaged in the hunt, they formed a large labour pool for seasonal work on boat and cart brigades, as well as serving as clerks, carpenters and tradesmen.

By 1822, **Fort Douglas**, the Company's headquarters near The Forks had deteriorated to such an extent that Simpson opted to move to Fort Gibraltar. Subsequently renamed Fort Garry, in honor of Nicholas Garry, a member of the governing council, it was an unprepossessing structure. Alexander Ross described it this way in 1825:

*Instead of a place walled and fortified as I had expected, I saw nothing but a few wooden houses huddled together without palisades, or any regard to taste or even comfort. To this cluster of huts were, however, appended two long bastions in the same style as the other buildings. These buildings according to the custom of the country, were used as dwellings and warehouses for carrying on the trade of the place. Nor was the Governor's residence anything more in the outward appearance than the cottage of a humble farmer who might be able to spend fifty pounds a year.*

The fort was severely damaged in the flood of 1826 and fell into decline. In an attempt to escape the constant threat of floods, Simpson authorized the construction of Lower Fort Garry, otherwise known as The Stone Fort, at the head of deep water navigation on the Red River below St. Andrew's

Rapids. Though imposing, it was soon found to be ill suited for retail trade at Red River, and the decision was made to rebuild at The Forks.

Upper Fort Garry was completed in 1835 on the north bank of the Assiniboine River, on slightly higher ground than its predecessor. It consisted of principal dwelling houses, stores and offices surrounded by stout walls nearly five metres high. The walls boasted corner bastions that could be fitted with cannon, demonstrating the company's preeminence in the trade. The old Fort Garry I, slightly to the east, was used as part of an experimental farm operation, then leased to local settler Robert Logan. After further damage in the flood of 1852, it was demolished.

To consolidate its control over Rupert's Land the company had bought back the territory of Assiniboia from the Selkirk family in 1834. From then on, the governor and Council of Assiniboia were appointed by the company, restoring its administrative as well as judicial and economic control of the settlement.

By the 1830s, the Métis, both French- and English-speaking, formed the majority of population at Red River. After the 1821 union, many of the French-speaking men had signed on with their former rival, the Hudson's Bay Company. But as the settlement became more self-sufficient, demand for plains provisions decreased and Simpson's belt-tightening meant that there were fewer posts to supply. Most Métis were seasonal labourers; few reached the rank of officer.

There was therefore little opportunity in the fur trade for the educated or the ambitious. Often the only alternative to a life as an unskilled labourer was to become a free trader. And there was a burgeoning market in bison robes and hides to the south, where cheaper transportation routes to the west

C. W. JEFFREYS / NATIONAL ARCHIVES OF CANADA / C69353

*Following his appointment as governor, George Simpson, above, wasted no time putting his stamp on the HBC. With an eye always on the bottom line, he slashed staff and downsized operations in a way thqt would be very familiar today.*

Fort Rouge
1738-1747

ASSINIBOINE RIVER

200'

Fort Gibraltar 2, est. 1817,
was renamed Fort Garry 1
in 1821 (ruined by flood in 1826).

Upper Fort Garry
1835–1885

330'

RED RIVER

Fort Douglas
moved to this site
in November 1823?

1000'

Fort Gibraltar 1810

Stables

DAWN HUCK / AFTER GUNN

had also opened the door to a flood of American free traders. Norman Kittson, an American businessman who would soon dominate river transportation at The Forks (see By Water to Winnipeg on page 90), opened a post at Pembina. Here, close at hand, was an alternative market for the Métis.

Chief among the agitators for freer trade were retired Hudson's Bay Company servants Andrew McDermot, now a leading businessman and free trader, and Métis James Sinclair, another private trader. They were partners in a wide range of activities: freighting for the Hudson's Bay Company; private shipping; dealing in plains provisions and retail trading, to name a few. Most importantly, McDermot had been issued a special licence by the Hudson's Bay Company to engage in the fur trade, bringing in furs that would otherwise go to its American competition. After a brief sojourn in the Columbia River area, Sinclair returned to Red River where he established contacts with American fur traders. He imported American goods into the colony and helped to establish the Red River cart trail from Fort Garry to St. Paul, which was the head of steamboat navigation to the Mississippi and south until 1859.

By 1846 illegal trading was widespread, sorely testing the company's ability to maintain its monopoly. Suspecting McDermot and Sinclair of illegal trading and dealing with Kittson, the company abruptly terminated their freighting contract and their goods were refused passage on HBC ships.

The Governor of Assiniboia issued a proclamation against the illegal traffic in furs, but attempts by the company to stem the increasing flow of furs south only aggravated the resentment felt by many of the Métis.

Order was restored with the arrival of several companies of the 6th Royal Regiment of Foote sent to protect the company's charter, when war threatened between Britain and the United States over Oregon boundary negotiations. The reprieve, however, was temporary. Once the boundary was settled the troops left, to be replaced in 1848 by a small group of Chelsea pensioners, who would serve as a largely ineffective local force.

Alexander Isbister, a former company servant of mixed-blood parentage who had been educated in Britain, took up the Métis cause for freedom. Petitioning for their right to conduct their own fur trade in the land of their birth, he led a delegation to London in 1847 on behalf of nearly one thousand residents of Red River. There, he presented a petition against the company's "harsh conduct and mal-administration" to the British government. In commenting on Isbister's list of grievances the Earl of Elgin, Governor General of Canada, expressed the fears shared by others: "There is too much reason to fear that if the trade were thrown open, and the Indians left to the mercy of the adventurers who might chance to engage in it, their condition would be greatly deteriorated."

Though it might easily be argued that they were the cause of it, the British had seen first-hand the strife and bloodshed of open competition and had no wish to repeat it. The conflict between the company and the free traders came to a head in 1849. Guillaume Sayer and three other Métis traders were arrested for illicit traffic in furs with Aboriginal trappers. The case was tried on May 17th, Ascension Day. As the Métis congregated in front of St. Boniface Cathedral they were addressed by Louis Riel Sr., who urged a demonstration against Recorder (Magistrate) Adam Thom, a company appointee who was trying the case. An armed throng of several hundred Métis surrounded the courthouse, threatening to take matters into their own hands if the prisoners were not freed.

Sayer, represented by James Sinclair, pleaded guilty but evidence given in court stated that he had been given verbal permission by a junior company officer to trade in furs. The verdict was guilty with a recommendation for mercy. Sayer suffered no penalty and charges against the other three were dropped. When the news reached the crowd milling about outside they broke into cheers punctuated by gunshots. Cries of *"Le commerce est libre! Vive la liberté!"* spread quickly.

Though technically a victory for the company, the guilty verdict in fact opened the doors to free trade. From that point on, the company's monopoly was virtually indefensible; it would now have to rely on its competitive strength in the north west to survive. Despite the setback, the Hudson's Bay Company remained a major economic force at Red River, easily the largest employer in the region.

The Métis and free traders were the immediate

NATIONAL ARCHIVES OF CANADA / C750

PROVINCIAL ARCHIVES OF MANITOBA / N10448

*Through its trading posts, above, the HBC attempted to keep a tight rein on trade throughout its vast territory. But by the 1850s, free traders like Andrew McDermot, whose operation is shown at left, were challenging that authority.*

*Despite the protests of proponents of free trade and settlement, Upper Fort Garry continued to be the heart of commerce in Manitoba. And even in the closing weeks of the empire in 1869, there were those like Captain Armstrong, creator of the view below, who continued to view the HBC through romantic eyes.*

beneficiaries of freer trade. The Métis were quick to take advantage of wider opportunities and soon developed an economy independent of the company. Annual fur sales to St. Paul grew from $5,000 in 1845 to $45,000 ten years later and averaged more than $150,000 annually over the next seven years. But there was a darker side. With the influx of free traders into the area whiskey sales soared, resulting in a further deterioration of the lives of the original inhabitants of The Forks.

Within a decade the Hudson's Bay Company faced another challenge to its monopoly. The licence granting it exclusive trade outside Rupert's Land, which had already been extended once, was coming up for renewal in 1859. As a preliminary step, in 1857 the British Government undertook a parliamentary enquiry into the company's administration

of its vast territories. Until that time, relatively little was known of the climate and settlement possibilities of the north west. That was about to change.

Survey expeditions under Henry Youle Hind and John Palliser pushing west from Canada that year provided reliable information for the first time on the potential of the west for agricultural settlement. Palliser, in particular, spoke well of the company's role in the area, but his recommendations on how best to deal with the conflicting claims of the HBC, free traders and Natives were largely ignored. However, the expeditions' positive reports on the west's potential were eagerly seized upon by pro-settlement lobbyists in the east, many of them annexationists determined to extend Canada's control.

The result was that the Select Committee concluded that a change was needed in the north west; the company's licence was not renewed. It retained its territorial rights in Rupert's Land, but now it seemed only a matter of time before they too would be extinguished. And what would become of Red River and The Forks at the centre of it? There were several options. The territory could remain under British control as a Crown colony, but the British government was experiencing problems throughout its empire and was more interested in divesting itself of costly and troublesome dependencies than adding to its administrative responsibilities.

Secondly, there was the possibility of annexation by the United States. Red River had strong geographic and economic ties to the territory of

CAPTAIN ARMSTRONG / PROVINCIAL ARCHIVES OF MANITOBA / B10/8 N20893

Minnesota and local merchants and traders indicated they would welcome future railway links to the east and the elimination of custom duties. But the United States was about to become embroiled in the Civil War, placing any aspirations of territorial expansion on hold.

Finally, the territory could be annexed to Canada. This recommendation was endorsed by the Select Committee, since most of the arable land in Upper Canada had now been settled and many Canadians were eager to seek new opportunities in the west.

Events moved slowly toward this conclusion. In 1863, the Hudson's Bay Company was purchased by Sir Edward Watkin backed by the International Financial Society, a British investment group with interests in agricultural settlement and railway technology, rather than furs. Finally in 1869, with negotiations for the Canadian confederation successfully concluded, the company agreed to surrender Rupert's Land to the British Crown, which would in turn transfer the territory to the new Dominion of Canada on December 1st.

In return for its landed rights, the company received £300,000 from the Canadian government. It was also allowed to maintain all of its trading posts, the freedom to carry on its trade without hindrance and to select a parcel of land adjoining each in addition to land grants totalling one twentieth of the fertile belt. In Red River, the company claimed 1112 hectares surrounding Upper Fort Garry, commonly known as the Hudson's Bay Company Reserve. The area, bounded by Notre Dame Avenue and the Red and Assiniboine Rivers, stretched west to Colony Creek, just west of today's Osborne Street.

Throughout these negotiations neither party thought to consult the people of Red River, who were understandably anxious about their future. No assurances were given that their land titles would be guaranteed, there was no acknowledgment of Native claims to the land and no mention of self-government. Finally, determined to have their voices heard, many of the Métis rallied under the leadership of Louis Riel, Jr. and seized Upper Fort Garry, the colony's administrative centre. The resultant Riel Resistance succeeded in delaying the transfer until July 15, 1870, long enough to have their grievances addressed.

The sale of Rupert's Land ended two centuries of Hudson's Bay Company rule in North America. The settlement that was quickly growing around The Forks was now free to determine its own economic future, no longer subjugated to a larger fur trade policy administered by a distant council. Fort Garry lasted a little longer, ending in 1881 when it was demolished to facilitate the straightening of Main Street, in hopes of attracting more commercial establishments to the Hudson's Bay Company Reserve. The city was by then in the throes of a spectacular land boom, a time of steamboats, railways and immigrants from halfway across the world. The days of the canoe and the York boat were over. Railways and wheat, not furs, would now sustain its economic growth.

*Free traders, above, had been involved in commerce with the United States since the 1840s. Until 1859, that trade had mostly followed the Red River trails south to Minnesota by horse and cart. Now new avenues of transport beckoned.*

MANTON MARBLE / PROVINCIAL ARCHIVES OF MANITOBA

*We, the representatives of the people in council assembled in Upper Fort Garry, the 24th day of November, 1869 … mutually pledge ourselves on oath, our lives, our fortunes, and our sacred honour to each other.*

— The Declaration of Independence of the People of Rupert's Land and the North-West, adopted at Fort Garry, 8th December, 1869 —

# LOUIS RIEL AND FORT GARRY

WITH THESE LOFTY PHRASES, bearing echoes of the United States Declaration of Independence, a charismatic young man of just twenty-five began a tortured odyssey that nearly sundered Confederation's uneasy bi-national pact and transformed Canada itself by changing the course of western Canadian settlement. Powerful and misunderstood, this odyssey continues to reverberate through our national life today.

After more than a century, Riel's administration is finally receiving a balanced historical assessment. It is now obvious that his provisional government enjoyed support or acceptance from the majority of Red River's citizens of both languages with the notable exception of a small group of dissident Orange "Canadians", who never ceased their efforts to overthrow the "damned depraved half-breed", in Thomas Scott's words. But the Riel interregnum was marked by peace and order, in sharp contrast to the lawlessness and terror that followed the arrival of the troops and militia from Canada under the command of Colonel Garnet Wolseley.

History provides us with some memorable glimpses of Riel and his tenure at Upper Fort Garry from November 2, 1869 to August 24, 1870.

Louis David Riel was born October 22, 1844, the first child of Jean-Louis Riel and Julie Lagimodière, daughter of the first white woman to settle in the North West. All his ancestors were French Canadian save his paternal great-grandmother, who was a Franco-Ojibwe Métisse.

On the day of his birth, the baby was taken from his thatched-roof home near where the Seine River joins the Red River to the cathedral at St. Boniface, where he was baptized by Bishop Norbert Provencher. A bright, sensitive child, he was one of three Métis boys to be chosen by the bishop to be sent to Québec for a classical education. Riel excelled at his studies, but did not complete his training for the priesthood. He returned to Red River on July 26th, 1868, less than

a year before the people of Red River, half English-speaking and half French-speaking, learned they had been "sold", in Bishop Alexandre-Antonin Taché's words, to Canada without their knowledge or consent. This act, thus undertaken without consultation, sparked the so-called "Red River Rebellion" of 1869-70.

Most of the main events of this pivotal point in Manitoba's history occurred in or around Fort Garry's huge stone quadrangle. As the administrative hub of Rupert's Land, the fort, with its three-metre stone walls and ten bastions mounted with six-pounder cannon, was the obvious place to stage a response to the cavalier act of the Canadian government, itself just two years old.

No bloodshed was involved when Riel and 120 of his Métis guards took peaceful possession of the fort on November 2nd. They simply walked through the governor's private entrance (the North or Governor's Gate – the only part of the fort that still exists today). Nor was blood shed elsewhere the same day, when another group of Riel's men stopped William McDougall, Ottawa's choice as Manitoba's first lieutenant-governor, from crossing the border at Pembina.

Once established at Fort Garry, with patrols watching the roads and confiscating every weapon entering the colony, Riel resumed his efforts to win the support of the English-speaking community. On November 6th, he invited the English colonists to select two representatives from each of their eleven parishes and the town of Winnipeg to meet at the fort with the "President and Representatives of the French-speaking population of Rupert's Land in Council". The meeting would "consider the present political state of this Country, and … adopt such measures as may be deemed best for the future

welfare of same." The English parishes responded and Red River's first representative council met at the courthouse at Fort Garry on November 16th. The Métis celebrated with salvos of cannon fire and a *feu de joie*.

Meanwhile, the Canadian Party under its leader, John Christian Schultz, tried with some success to foment discord between French and English colonists while fortifying Schultz's compound on the south side of Winnipeg with arms and food. Hearing of the Canadians' efforts to raise a military force and of a plot by Thomas Scott and another man to assassinate him, Riel ordered his Métis guards to surround "Fort Schultz" on December 7th. Armed with two cannon, they gave the Canadians fifteen minutes to surrender, then marched the prisoners off to the fort.

The next day, the provisional government became a reality with the adoption of the declaration of independence and on December 10th, its flag was raised on the big flagpole in the centre of the square at Fort Garry. Despite bitter cold, two mass meetings drew more than a thousand to the fort on January 19th, and 20th, 1870. The atmosphere was one of goodwill all round. When the final meeting adjourned, as Riel's biographer George Stanley recounts, "men threw their caps into the air and shook each others' hands. They shouted and cheered. All of them believed the crisis was over. They had not wanted to fight Canada or each other. They merely wanted to be sure the Canadian government meant well toward them." Two days later, elections were held to choose a new convention and Riel sent most of his soldiers home, retaining only a small guard at Fort Garry.

The convention of forty met on January 26th and decided a new list of rights would be drawn up by a committee of three English and three French representatives. Formal approval of the provisional government occurred on February 10th and was announced with cannon fire from the fort. The convention members and the soldiers of Riel's garrison

**LE BATAILLON PROVISOIRE.**

poured into the cold, stormy night to celebrate with a grand display of fireworks. As the liquor flowed, Président Riel and A. G. B. Bannatyne, a prominent member of the English community, shared "a good horn of brandy".

During all this time, the fifty-six prisoners from "Fort Shultz" had been crowded into three rooms inside the fort. Riel visited, bringing newspapers, and on Christmas Eve, they were allowed to send out for a fiddle and hold a stag dance, which some of their Métis guards joined. On Christmas Day, they enjoyed roast beef, plum pudding and cakes. From time to time, they were taken to see Riel and asked to swear obedience to the provisional government or to leave the country. Nine accepted and were released. Those remaining made unceasing and sometimes successful efforts to escape. Schultz, for example, used a pocketknife his wife Anne had smuggled in to make a rope of buffalo hide, escaping over the wall on January 23rd.

On February 18th, guards at the fort spotted sleighs bearing armed men in the distance. The "Canadians", commanded by Major Charles Boulton, had regrouped and planned an invasion of the fort. Responding, a group of horsemen followed by fifty men on foot raced out the North Gate, but no shots were fired. Instead, the approaching armed men, including Thomas Scott, were peacefully arrested and returned to the cells.

Scott was hardly a naïve unfortunate, as he has so often been portrayed. A key lieutenant in Schultz's Canadian "army", he and another man had killed Norbert Parisien with an axe and, according to one account, dragged his body by the neck behind a horse. Encountering Riel on a Winnipeg street, Scott had screamed racial insults at him and threatened to kill him. Incarcerated a second time, he maintained a steady stream of threats against Riel, the Métis and the provisional government. Should he ever get out, he kept insisting, he would shoot the président. His conduct was so disruptive that even his fellow prisoners, including Major Boulton, implored him to stop. Riel tried to reason with Scott on

several occasions and personally intervened to save him from a savage beating by his warders after he and another prisoner overpowered two guards and attempted to foment rebellion.

Nevertheless, Scott's court-martial for insubordination has been called a travesty. He was not allowed to speak in his own defence or call witnesses. Moreover, the proceedings were held in French, with Riel translating for the unilingual Orangeman. On March 3rd, Scott was condemned to death by a split vote. Despite having pardoned Boulton, and in spite of pleas from prominent members of the English community, Riel was determined that Scott be executed. Fearing that he would never cease his agitation, Riel said, "I take a life to save many," adding, "We must make Canada respect us."

At noon on March 4th, Scott was taken to the Fort Garry courtyard where he said a short prayer with Reverend George Young. With a white cloth over his eyes, he was led before the firing squad. "This is horrible. This is cold-blooded murder," he sobbed as he was pushed to his knees. André Nault gave the signal and all six executioners fired, but only two or three bullets struck Scott. With a ghastly groan, he sank into the snow in a pool of blood. François Guillemette stepped forward and with his revolver put Scott out of his misery with a bullet to the brain.

In Canada, little note was taken of the execution for several months. Riel's emissaries were received in Ottawa and negotiated the terms of the Manitoba Act directly with Prime Minister Sir John A. Macdonald and his deputy, Sir Georges-Etienne Cartier. Riel's vision of provincehood, full parliamentary representation, the equality of the French and English languages and even his choice of name – Manitoba, "the God who speaks" – were all constitutionalized by an act of Parliament. The negotiators returned home and Manitoba became a province on July 15, 1870.

On June 17th, Abbé N. J. Ritchot, Riel's chief negotiator, arrived back in Red River on board the steamship *International*. As the ship proceeded north along the Red

River, families rushed to the water's edge to welcome him. When it docked at Fort Garry, a large crowd led by Riel was waiting while the fort's twenty-one guns boomed a noisy salute.

In Ontario, however, the remnants of the Canadian Party, in concert with the Canada First movement and the Loyal Orange Lodge had been holding "indignation meetings", fomenting a rising tide of anti-French fury. Fearing the loss of his political base, Macdonald allowed his expeditionary force to Fort Garry to become an "army of occupation".

Meanwhile, from the day of Scott's execution, the colony had enjoyed an unusual period of peace and tranquility. But just as he was preparing a celebration to receive Manitoba's new lieutenant-governor, Adams Archibald, Riel's world collapsed. In a few short hours, he was turned from statesman to fugitive. The storied gates of Upper Fort Garry closed on him forever the night of August 24, 1870.

That evening, an English settler, James G. Stewart, arrived at the fort on horseback and rushed in to Riel shouting: "For the love of God clear out, the soldiers are only two miles from the city and you are going to be lynched." Leaving his meal on the table, Riel crossed the Red River to Taché's house. When the bishop asked why he had left the fort, Riel replied that it appeared he had been deceived. "Rather than run the risk of being killed or murdered we prefer to leave the fort …"

As Taché gazed across the river at Wolseley's soldiers, Riel said: "No matter what happens now, the rights of the Métis are assured by the Manitoba Act; that is what I wanted … My mission is finished."

More than a century would pass before the truth of those words would be confirmed. Rather than being honoured as Manitoba's first premier and a Father of Confederation, Riel spent the rest of his life as a fugitive. He died on a gibbet at Regina's Central Police Barracks on November 16, 1885.

By Frances Russell

By Water

This view of the confluence of the rivers shows the tremendous activity that centred on The Forks during the early 1870s, as large steamships shared the busy waterways with a bevy of flatboats, York boats, rafts and canoes.

# to Winnipeg

By Frances Russell

On a beautiful sunny day in 1859, a strange, boxy and very noisy craft appeared on the Red River. It was a steamboat, the *Anson Northup*, the first of its kind to venture down the Red. The Cree, the original people of the Lake Winnipeg basin, had two names for this strange, seemingly half-alive vessel.

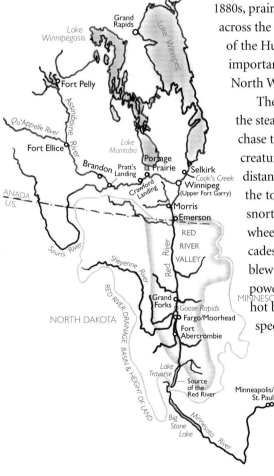

*Below: The Red River flows north from Lake Traverse in Minnesota to Lake Winnipeg.*

**T**he earliest of these, *Kuska pahtew oosi* or "fire canoe", painted a vivid word picture of the spectacle created by the *Anson Northup*, and all that were to follow in the path of her churning stern wheel.

During the early 1860s, most of the 1870s and the early 1880s, prairie steamboats – almost an oxymoron – held sway across the vast lands comprising the former fur trade empire of the Hudson's Bay Company. But nowhere were they more important than in Winnipeg, the hub of the new Canadian North West.

These majestic sternwheelers and sidewheelers, like the steam locomotives or "iron horses" that would soon chase them into oblivion, appeared as living, breathing creatures to all who saw them for the first time. From a distance, they made a sound like someone blowing across the top of an open bottle. Up close, they puffed and snorted like an overburdened horse. Their giant paddle-wheels thrashed even the most turbid water into cascades of sparkling crystal. When they vented steam or blew out their mud drums, they roared. Their whistles, powered by the steam produced in their shimmering hot boilers, shrieked deafeningly – often reducing their speed by up to two to three knots.

They were huge, reaching forty metres or more in length and eight to ten metres in width. Beautiful in the spectacularly ornate fashion of the time, they were also dangerous. Their lattice work and gingerbread accoutrements gleamed white in the sun. But their funnels not only spewed clouds of perfumed woodsmoke into the clear prairie air but also a steady shower of

live sparks sufficient to ignite shoreline haystacks or roofs and, all too terrifyingly often, the bouffant hair of the ladies on board.

They were indistinguishable from the floating palaces that had plied the Mississippi and Missouri Rivers in the 1830s, '40s and '50s, ferrying cargoes of river rats, gamblers and main-chancers of both sexes. And like them, they carried in their holds and on their decks all the raw necessities and material, animal and human, to allow the European settlement of a new land. They nosed to their berths at The Forks and disgorged their cargoes at the HBC wharf near the mouth of the Assiniboine River. There, just below the stone walls of Upper Fort Garry, was the "venerable company's" warehouse. An equal number of steamers would later berth at Winnipeg's Post Office Street (now Lombard Avenue) wharf, about a kilometre farther north on the Red.

Navigating the ever-migrating shallows and sandbars and ever-fluctuating river levels, these behemoths carried with them a significant part of the history of Western Canada. They ensured that the tiny settlement encompassing St. Boniface Cathedral on the east side of the Red River and Fort Garry at the historic confluence would blossom into a bustling metropolis. Ironically, it was in large part due to ships of another sort – ocean-going ones – that Winnipeg's glory days were prematurely cut short; the opening of the Panama Canal in 1914 spelled the beginning of the end of Winnipeg as the "Chicago of the North".

Since its founding in 1670, the Hudson's Bay Company had been shipping furs to and receiving supplies from York Factory on the Hayes River. But the Arctic shipping season was short. As the nineteenth century progressed, it became ever more difficult to find men prepared to undertake the

A. SHERRIFF SCOTT, RCA /
PROVINCIAL ARCHIVES OF MANITOBA

unbelievable travails of navigating and portaging the huge York boats the length of treacherous Lake Winnipeg and over the myriad portages of the Hayes River to the bay. In 1857, the company negotiated an agreement with the United States Treasury to have its goods shipped in bond through that country. This move gradually ended both the historic northern route and the isolation of the fledgling Red River Colony.

On behalf of the St. Paul, Minnesota, Chamber of Commerce, Captain Russell Blakely and John R. Irvine took a tour of the lower Red River in October 1858 and concluded that steamboat navigation was feasible for several months of the year. The chamber then offered $1,000 to anyone who would put a boat on the river the following year. A Mississippi steamboat captain by the name of Anson Northup offered to accomplish the feat for twice that sum – $2,000. Captain Northup brought his boat, the *North Star*, from the Mississippi above the Falls of St. Anthony to Crow Wing in the fall of 1858. There she was dismantled and during the bitter

winter that followed, her main parts, including a 5,000-kilogram boiler, were hauled overland 240 kilometres to Lafayette, a point on the Red River opposite the mouth of the Sheyenne River just south of today's Georgetown. Seventeen span of horses, thirteen yoke of oxen and thirty men were required for this amazing feat. They arrived on the evening of April 1st. The hull was built in about six weeks and the boat, re-christened the *Anson Northup* in honour of her owner, was launched in mid-May. On her first trip, she steamed upriver to Fort Abercrombie, above today's Fargo.

The *Anson Northup* had a capacity of between fifty and seventy-five tonnes and engines of 100 horsepower. She was twenty-eight metres long and seven metres wide and "drew fourteen inches [thirty-six centimetres] of water light," reported the Toronto *Globe* of July 9, 1859.

According to an article that appeared in the *Detroit Free Press* of July 16, 1859, the steamer left Breckenridge on June 6th and reached Fort Garry at The Forks on June 10th. The commander of the British force at the fort ordered the firing of the

*This mural, created for Winnipeg's main Hudson's Bay Company store, shows the* Anson Northup *being unloaded at the dock below Fort Garry. Also portrayed are a canoe and a York boat; the role of both, at least as vehicles of transport, would be greatly diminished in the years that followed the appearance of the doughty little steamboat.*

PROVINCIAL ARCHIVES OF MANITOBA / N1 3026

*This pastoral scene captures the brief, critical moment between the fur trade era and the sweeping changes that accompanied European settlement.*

cannon in honour of the event and the British flag was hoisted to greet the American stars and stripes waving at the head of the *Anson Northup*. The great bells of the Catholic Cathedral in St. Boniface chimed merrily and throngs of people pressed all around, "cheering and waving caps most energetically". The officers of the Hudson's Bay Company were also very cordial in welcoming this pioneer of progress and prosperity.

Following the momentous occasion, however, the doughty little ship quickly became the butt of many jokes. A correspondent for the *Nor'Wester* derided her as "a clumsy, labouring tub", writing: "The boat has such an extraordinary affection for the shore that at times no amount of rudder and wheel can cure her headstrong and landward fancies." He also quoted Captain C. P. V. Lull, one of her skippers, as characterizing her as "nothing better than a lumbering old pine-basket, Sir, which you have to handle as gingerly as a hamper of eggs."

*Crossroads of the Continent*

**S**he boasted three decks. The main one contained four staterooms to accommodate up to twelve "ladies" and a cabin with twenty-four curtained berths. The funnel ran from the lower deck's engine room straight up through the main cabin. As a result, the boat's interior was always super-heated. The hurricane deck and pilothouse provided the only respite.

Joseph J. Hargrave leaves us with a humorous account of her behavior as she attempted to negotiate rapids – possibly the St. Andrews Rapids between Winnipeg and Selkirk:

> *In consequence of the shortness [of the ship] it was found very difficult to manage her in turning the numerous and sharp points which we passed on our way … For more than an entire day the crew was engaged pulling the vessel over [rapids] by main force, by means of a rope attached to the capstan, and fixed to a spot ashore at some distance ahead. At intervals during this tedious series of operations [the ship] would partially ground, while the greater part of her keel would be floating in water flowing like the sluice of a mill. On such occasions she would whirl cork-like around, setting at defiance the utmost efforts of the rude stern wheel to regulate her motions.*

Samuel Taylor, a carpenter at Lower Fort Garry, noted in his diary that the ship with "plenty of people on board" took an excursion there on June 13th. Other accounts have her sailing into Lake Winnipeg before returning to The Forks. On June 17th, she departed for Fort Abercrombie with twenty-five passengers, including James Ross. Ross was quoted in both the Toronto *Globe* and the *Detroit Free Press* as saying that the

## THE MANITOBA MAPLE
### *(Acer negundo L.)*

**T**HOUGH NOT AS SHOWY in the fall as its sugar maple cousin, the Manitoba maple has recently earned a reputation for producing even sweeter maple syrup. This comes as no surprise to Native Manitobans, of course, who have long tapped the trees in early spring.

These medium-sized deciduous trees, also called box-elder, grow throughout southern Manitoba, particularly along rivers and streams. In Manitoba's steamboat era, they provided much of the fuel devoured by the ravenous engines.

The sap is not the only edible part of the maple. Mule and white-tailed deer, as well as elk and moose browse on the leaves and young twigs, and squirrels and chipmunks devour the seeds in autumn.

The Manitoba maple's compound leaves can be seen on this page.

return trip upstream took eight days. They sailed only during daylight and had to make frequent stops to cut wood on shore.

Having proven that steamboating was possible on the Red, Captain Northup collected his $2,000, but declined to shoulder the task of running the "lumbering old pinebasket" regularly. For a time, she was tied up at Fort Abercrombie and used to ferry passengers and Red River carts back and forth across the river. H. C. Burbank, Captain Blakely's associate, then purchased her and put Captain Edwin Bell in charge. She set sail again for Fort Garry, but had difficulty running Goose Rapids, north of Fargo, and was laid up at Cook's Creek, in East Selkirk, on August 18th. Her pumps were drained, her boiler blown and she was left to freeze over for the winter.

The spring thawed her out and in the summer of 1860, she made regular trips between Fort Garry and Georgetown just north of Fargo. The winter of 1860-61, again berthed at Cook's Creek, she sank but was refloated, repaired and re-christened the *Pioneer*. That same winter, the Hudson's Bay Company, which had quickly recognized the potential of steamboat transport for its own trade, formed a silent partnership with J.C. and H.C. Burbank and Company, stagecoach operators, to transport 500 tons of freight annually from St. Paul to Fort Garry on the little steamer.

The wily company knew it required a silent American partner. Under U.S. law, only American-owned ships could transport goods on U.S. waterways. The Burbanks' promises of regular ten-day or fortnightly service were never kept, because either navigation conditions or lack of freight continually delayed the boat. In the winter of 1861-62, the *Anson Northup-Pioneer* came to an untimely end as a result of a freak accident. Once again in her winter berth at Cook's Creek, a sudden fall in the water level so tightened her mooring ropes she turned turtle and sank in about three metres of water. Efforts to raise and refloat her proved futile and she ended her days rather ungracefully upended: her engines were removed and used to power a sawmill.

During this period, James Taylor, the U.S. consul in Winnipeg, was an enthusiastic promoter of steamboat traffic and particularly keen to encourage a water route to the gold fields of British Columbia via the Red and Saskatchewan rivers. His dogged advocacy earned him the name "Saskatchewan Taylor". He boasted that he had a friend in Archbishop Alexandre-Antonin Taché. Said Taylor: "When the whistle shall sound the advent of the first steamboat in Fort Garry, Archbishop Taché, who has prayed so earnestly and waited so long, will spring instantly to his feet and, raising his hands reverently above his head, exclaim, 'In the name of God, let the bells of St. Boniface ring, for civilization has come.'"

Taché's own account in his *Sketch of the North-west of America*, is quite different. He came to oppose the steamers because they injured the fish and consumed the scanty supplies of wood along the riverbanks. Perhaps most importantly, the archbishop objected to the fact that the profits from the steamboat trade went to Americans, not Canadians. The cleric wasn't alone. Flatboat operators and York boatmen agreed and attempted to push their vessels as alternatives, but to little avail.

Flatboats, especially, couldn't compete, particularly time-wise. George Winship crewed aboard a flatboat belonging to Dr. John Christian Schultz, a future lieutenant-governor of Manitoba. He recounts that it took the boat seventeen days to travel from Fort Abercrombie to Fort Garry in 1868. The fact that the boat had to put into shore so its passengers, including Dr. Schultz and his new bride, could cook and eat their meals was only part of the reason:

> The boat was equipped with two oars, fore and aft, with which it was easily kept in midstream during the day, and two-hour shifts of the men at the oars was the rule after the river had become free of ice; the stream got so wide that we had much difficulty in keeping the boat in midstream where the current bore it along more rapidly. At night, when the wind would blow the boat into an eddy, we frequently were obliged to lay-to until

*daylight. The old river was so wide that we did not know which way to steer the craft into the current. We had several experiences of this nature, and when we realized that we were lost in the vast expanse of water, we stayed where we were until morning. One night the wind from the north blew with such velocity that the boat was actually blown upstream for half a mile.*

The end of the *Anson Northup-Pioneer* was not to be the end of steam on the Red River. The Burbanks learned of the beaching of a Minnesota River steamer called the *Freighter.* In the spring of 1857, her captain had believed he could take advantage of the annual flood to run her from her anchorage ten kilometres below Big Stone Lake into the Red River, but the water receded before he could make it, stranding her. Sold at sheriff's sale, the Burbanks bought her.

The story goes that the company left her in the charge of a little Welshman who, away from his wife and children and living off the land, stood guard over her for nearly three years. When he was found, he was an absolute fright. His hair and whiskers were overgrown and he had been reduced to wearing coffee sacks and old window curtains for clothes. Burbank's men shared their garments and food with him and helped him take the boat to pieces. They brought it to Georgetown in the fall of 1860 to be rebuilt. Renamed the *International*, she was relaunched in 1862. A large and elegant boat, she weighed 135 tonnes, was forty-two metres long and had an eight-metre beam.

The *International's* first trip to Fort Garry in May 1862 took seven days, almost twice as long as the *Anson Northup*'s inaugural voyage, but she was carrying 200 passengers, including Archbishop Taché and the governor of Minnesota.

PROVINCIAL ARCHIVES OF MANITOBA / N10299

The *Nor'Wester* described the arrival in its May 28th edition this way: "It is really a grand affair. Its size and finish would make it respectable even amid the finest floating palaces of the Mississippi."

In August, the *International* attempted another trip to the mouth of the Assiniboine, but was forced back by the twin difficulties of descending Goose Rapids and the outbreak of hostilities with the Dakota.

The Aboriginal peoples' initial amazement at the fire canoes quickly turned to anger. The boats were denuding the riverbanks of timber, driving away their game and fish and disturbing the spirits of their dead. Initially, in exchange for

*The* Anson Northup *steams north into history.*

?F.G.SHEPPARD / WINNIPEG'S EARLY DAYS/ THE STOVEL COMPANY LIMITED

THE *CHEYENNE* SITS QUIETLY, DURING A RARE MOMENT OF INACTIVITY.

*Crossroads of the Continent*

four kegs of "yellow money" (gold) and an agreement only to blow the whistle on arrival and departure at Georgetown, Pembina and Fort Garry, they agreed to allow the boats to continue. But subsequently, navigation on the Red River suffered a hiatus of almost a decade because of the tensions created between First Nations and Europeans, in large part over the pressure of the the latter's ever-increasing encroachment into and settlement on the former's lands.

The so-called Sioux Uprising of 1862 kept the *International* anchored under the guns of Fort Abercrombie for an entire year. Meanwhile, the U.S. consul was fretting. In a letter to U.S. Major General Alexander Pope on November 10, 1862, Taylor underlined the benefits to American commerce of the Red River steamboat trade and the necessity to maintain it even through the agony of civil war:

*Sir: Under the revenue system of the United States, a very considerable diversion of trade and transportation to and from [the] Selkirk Settlement and other points of Central British North America, has taken place in favour of communications through Minnesota. The most prominent of these includes the navigation by steamers of the Red River of the North. The steamer* International, *a first-class vessel is now moored at Georgetown. The safety of the buildings and their occupants, as well as the steamer, seem to me of great importance to the continuance and extension of our international relations with Central British America. As special agent of the treasury department I beg leave to invite your attention to the fore-going consideration and to express a hope that you will direct the officer in command at Fort Abercrombie to assure himself of*

*the security of the settlement at Georgetown and the* International, *the steamer, from Indian depredations.*

Low water, scarcity of freight and nervousness about ongoing hostilities with First Nations dramatically curtailed Red River steam commerce for the rest of the 1860s.

The HBC bought the steamer from the Burbanks in 1864 but was unable to comply with U.S. regulations as a non-American entity. Some in Fort Garry thought the company had purchased the boat for exactly that reason, to halt the influx of settlers disrupting its lucrative fur trade. But in 1871, the company, which also now needed steamers to transport its goods and import its necessities, turned the *International* over to Norman Kittson, an American citizen who had been born in Canada and whose great-grandfather had fought under General Wolfe at the seige of Québec. Apparently the HBC had concluded that since it couldn't hold back the settlement tide, it might as well cash in on the profits to be made from ferrying passengers and other freight.

That same year, American captains Alexander Griggs and James J. Hill finished building the steamer *Selkirk* at Fort Abercrombie. The *Selkirk* weighed over 100 tonnes and boasted a flat bottom that required only a half-metre of water light but almost a metre and half fully loaded. On her first trip to Fort Garry in May 1871, she carried two passengers and a load of lumber for J.H. Ashdown's new store.

By the next winter, control over all the boats on the Red River passed to Kittson. In the spring of 1872, he organized and managed the Red River Transportation Company and joined forces with the Hill, Griggs Company of St. Paul to build the *Dakota* at Breckenridge. In the winter of 1873-74, the monopoly constructed the sidewheeler, *Cheyenne*, at

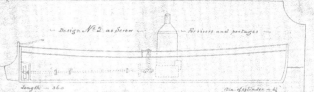

Grand Forks and bought the *Alpha*, which had been built at Breckenridge in 1873 by J.W. McLane.

After a decade of near-abandonment, steamer commerce on the Red River suddenly boomed. In the spring of 1873, the *Red River Gazette* reported that the HBC had about 350 tons of freight stored in its warehouse at Moorhead waiting for the spring breakup. The *Canadian Illustrated News* of November 27, 1874 stated that 1,100 Mennonites had already come to Manitoba and hundreds more were ready to follow in the spring. Next August, the *Manitoba Free Press* noted that 880 Mennonites had arrived on board the *International* and the *Cheyenne* in just two weeks.

*Above: Plans of small steamers, designed in England for the HBC in 1869.*

*Below: Just a year into service, the elegant SS Selkirk waits to be loaded.*

PROVINCIAL ARCHIVES OF MANITOBA / N16602

Kittson's monopoly was complete and his prices showed it. One angry Winnipegger complained bitterly after his jeweller charged him a dollar for a new second hand for his watch. The jeweller reportedly just shrugged and blamed it on outrageous steamer freight costs. A "Kitty Red River Transportation Line" notice dated St. Paul, Minnesota, on June 5, 1872 and addressed to B.R. Ross, a member of Winnipeg's first board of trade, states: "On account of extreme low water on the Red River we have this day advanced rates of passage and freight from Moorhead to Fort Garry". First class passage from St. Paul to Fort Garry was $23; second class was $18. First and second class freight charges were also $23 and $18 per 100 pounds respectively.

By the middle of the decade, anger at the steamboat monopoly was reaching the breaking point. The Winnipeg Board of Trade censured the federal government for its failure to provide adequate transportation facilities for Manitoba and indirectly blamed Canada for the province's $750,000 bill for eighteen million kilograms of freight, claiming it was more than double a fair price. Still, when the Dominion government hinted it might level the playing field for domestic steamship interests by banning American vessels on Canadian waters, it met with fierce opposition in Winnipeg. As is often the case in Canadian history, commercial interests trumped nationalist sentiment.

In 1874, the long-awaited competition arrived. Planned initially as a solely Winnipeg venture, it skirted the American law denying British "bottoms" navigation rights in U.S. waters by adding a few St. Paul merchants to its roster. The Merchants International Steamboat Line came into being in 1874. The next spring, the *Manitoba* and the *Minnesota* were on the Red. The *Manitoba* ran into customs problems on its first trip and was detained at Pembina for some time. A letter to

HUDSON'S BAY ARCHIVES / PROVINCIAL ARCHIVES OF MANITOBA / 363-P-80-K/3

the editor of the *Free Press* saw the fine hand of Kittson at work. Still, the steamboat war was on and prices plummetted.

The war took a decidedly ugly turn on June 5, 1875, described as "the most exciting event in the history of Red River transportation". The *Manitoba* was steaming towards Winnipeg having completed a fast trip of just forty-seven hours from Moorhead when it was rammed amidships by the *International* and sank in shallow water. There was no loss of life but the *Free Press* instantly blamed the *International* and her owner, Kittson. The rumour was that the ramming had been deliberate. All Winnipeg was agog and as late as June 29th, a little steamer named *Maggie* advertised special Dominion Day excursions to "Collision Villa" to view the half-submerged wreck. The *Manitoba* was raised, repaired and back in operation by July 22nd.

**B**ut her owner, the Merchants line, was steaming into financial difficulties. In September, the *Manitoba* was seized for a $1,700 debt. At about the same time, the *Minnesota* was taken into custody by the sheriff at Moorhead. The Merchants line ceased operations for the rest of the season and the gossip was that it had been bought by Kittson. A significant straw in the wind was that Kittson's Red River line immediately raised first-class freight rates from two dollars to $2.50 for the St. Paul-Winnipeg run. Then, on October 23rd, the *Free Press* reported that Kittson had indeed bought out the Merchants line. The next spring, he took possession of the *Manitoba* and the *Minnesota*, renaming the latter *The City of Winnipeg*.

PROVINCIAL ARCHIVES OF MANITOBA

Kittson was not the sole villain of the piece, however. It soon emerged that the American investors in the Merchants line, worried about the security of their stakes in the company, had made secret overtures to Kittson and ultimately received shares in the Red River line. Once again monopoly ruled, a monopoly that benefitted St. Paul over Winnipeg. In 1876, the Red River line was able to declare an eighty per cent dividend on its stock. The *Monetary Times* of Toronto wrote: "Being a St. Paul organization, the company arranged its tariff to discriminate in favour of that city, which drove Winnipeg merchants to purchase heavy goods in St. Paul."

From then on, putative rivals periodically popped up, but never managed to loosen Kittson's grip. By 1878, there were seventeen steamers on the river and an eighteenth was under construction. Flatboats could have posed a threat to Kittson's line, but in 1877 there were reports the U.S. Treasury Department was going to impose a tax on alien flatboats trading

*Inset: The indefatigable Norman Kittson, who by the early 1870s controlled almost all shipping on the Red River.*

*Above: the* International, *tied up at the Fort Garry warehouse during a period of low water.*

between American points. Steamboats already paid the tax, which was exacted only once in a boat's lifetime. This would put flatboat commerce at a serious disadvantage since a flatboat's life was a single trip downstream after which it was broken up for lumber. The *Free Press* suspected Kittson was behind that pressure, too.

Still, for all the travails imposed by the monopoly, the Red River's steamboat era was a colourful period in the history of the young City of Winnipeg.

Racing was a favorite sport of the steamboat men. A *Free Press* correspondent gives a blow-by-blow account of one exciting encounter in its June 13, 1876 edition: "The *Selkirk* and the *International* both wanted to get a leetle [sic] ahead of the other. They left here a week ago Monday evening, the *International* having three hours start, which she kept till arrival at Pembina, where a delay, caused by the breaking of one of her cam yokes allowed the *Selkirk* to catch up; both boats left that place, nose and nose together; the *Selkirk* took the lead, and kept it till she broke a wheel arm which occasioned a stoppage for repairs, during which the *International* passed her. At Grand Forks, the *International* stopped, but the rival boat hadn't time. Mitchell had just placed a 'rooster' on the safety valve and was standing over him with a monkey wrench to see that he kept in his place. Both boats tore up the river, stole wood from each other and kind of hustled things generally, the *International* reaching Fisher's Landing an hour and a half ahead, one says, and fifteen minutes

*Luxurious appointments, such as are evident in this lounge on the* SS City of Winnipeg, *were the norm, particularly in the last decade of the steamship era.*

ahead, according to the *Selkirk*'s version."

A night race between the *Manitoba* and the *Minnesota* is described in a letter by a passenger on the latter:

*The great lights of the two steamers gave a weird appearance to the scene. The pilots leaned over their pilot houses and cracked jokes with each other; and the roosters on deck crowed over each other, and the great chimneys puffed and threw out great clouds of sparks in unison, but we didn't spill any coal oil into the furnace nor break up*

PROVINCIAL ARCHIVES OF MANITOBA / N138

*the cabin furniture to make steam, but we forged quietly ahead, and soon left the* Manitoba *far in our wake.*

The *International* has the dubious distinction of having had a murder committed on board her somewhere between Grand Forks and Winnipeg in 1871. The story goes that an individual about forty-five years of age with a short brown beard disembarked from a stagecoach and climbed on board carrying two expensively-crafted leather suitcases. The purser

*Less romantic, but just as necessary, ferries across the Red and Assiniboine Rivers – such as this one leaving St. Boniface for The Forks in 1881 – played a crucial part in Winnipeg's development prior to the construction of the city's bridges.*

FREDERICK B. SCHELL / NATIONAL ARCHIVES OF CANADA / /C-120519

only got his name, G. Orton, which was later assumed to have been fictitious. When he failed to leave his cabin upon arrival in Winnipeg, the captain sent the smallest steward to break the porthole and crawl through. The badly-shaken boy reported that a chair was wedged against the door and the man was lying in a pool of blood on the bunk.

Police later established that he had been struck from behind and a knife used to sever a neck artery. His suitcases and identity were gone. The only item found on his body was a gold Masonic pin with square, compass and the letter "G" on his vest lapel.

Roy Brown, who wrote a book on the Assiniboine River steamers for Brandon's Centennial in 1982, may have solved

the mystery 110 years later. He writes that at the conclusion of a presentation he made on the boats to the Assiniboine Historical Society in 1980, "a man in the audience startled the crowd by saying that his grandfather had been murdered and robbed on a boat coming down the Red River. Apparently, his grandfather was coming out west to buy land and was carrying a considerable amount of money with him." The murderer escaped, "swallowed up by a veil of frontier anonymity".

On one occasion, the *International* literally steamed across the prairie to deliver a huge consignment of liquor for the Hudson's Bay Company on time. Her master, Captain Alexander Griggs, had to make the provincial Customs house by midnight, May 10, 1873, to avoid a new tariff that would cost the company thousands of dollars. The Red River was in full spring flood, submerging the prairies as far as the eye could see on either side. The daring feat was witnessed by a reporter for the *Manitoban:*

*The* Dakota *is shown here at The Forks a year before George Belhammer thrilled Manitobans with his selfless heroics.*

*"Capt. Griggs, on taking command, resolved to make a bold stroke to reach the goal in season, and very coolly turned the boat out of the bed of the river and made a short cut over the prairie thereby reducing the distance very materially and gaining the Customs House before the midnight tax hike on his liquid cargo."*

Yet another tale, this one of true heroism involved the

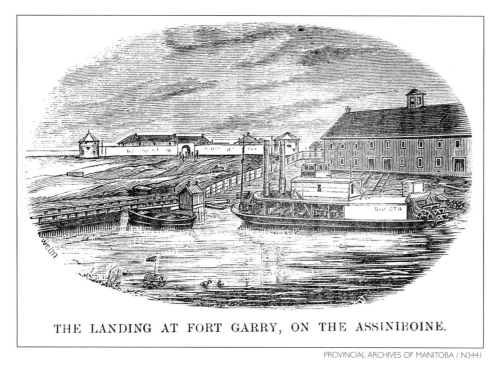

THE LANDING AT FORT GARRY, ON THE ASSINIBOINE.

PROVINCIAL ARCHIVES OF MANITOBA / N3441

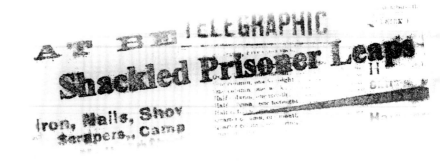

DAWN HUCK / HEADLINE
AFTER FARGO FORUM

*Dakota* and occurred sometime in May 1874. That trip, the ship's passenger manifest included the wife of British army officer Captain George U. White and their six children on their way to join him on their new farm at Teulon, as well as a consignment of fifteen shackled prisoners headed for trial at Pembina. The latter were guarded by a U.S. marshall with orders to shoot should any try to escape. Among the prisoners was George Belhammer. Thrown out of work when the North Pacific Railway had ceased to operate west of Fargo and with no money to buy food for his wife and child, Belhammer had broken into a commissary building at Fort Seward, Dakota Territory and been arrested.

Historian-pioneer George Keeney recounts that just as the call to breakfast was sounded one morning, little red-haired Emma White, just three years old, grabbed a low-hanging tree branch as it swept along the steamer's deck and, not letting go in time, was swept overboard and dropped into the swirling river. Belhammer, sprawling on the steamer's texas deck atop the sternwheel, saw her go. He yelled at the guard not to shoot and and took a seven-metre plunge over the rail into the river below, but the guard either didn't hear or didn't listen. A gunshot rang out, but the bullet missed Belhammer, splintering the ship's rail. By now, the captain had thrown the ship's giant wheel into reverse. Keeney's account continues:

*Crossroads of a Continent*

# from Steamboat to Save Child

*The child struggled in the water, buoyed up by the air caught in the folds of her garments. Belhammer was striking out sideways with his hands, held close together by the handcuffs. The child drifted towards him and just as she sank out of sight, Belhammer let himself under. When he came up, he had the child in his hands. With a backward fling, he threw her across his shoulder, holding on by taking grip of her dress band in his teeth. In her struggles, the child threw Belhammer off balance. Both went under … Raising his shackled hands above his head, he twisted and wrenched at them until the blood ran down his arms. He could not break the iron. As he sank he saw the instant appearance of the child's arm. With all his strength he pulled himself farther out into the centre of the river. We could plainly see his shackled limbs sticking out of the water. The irons glistened in the sunshine before they disappeared, as we all thought, for the last time. Belhammer again came up and once more he had the child, again, by the waist of her dress.*

**B**y this time, a boat from the *Dakota* had been launched and reached the child and her manacled rescuer. The passengers collected sixty dollars and presented the prisoner with the purse and a testimonial signed by eighty witnesses, including the captain. Belhammer received a reduced sentence and took his family north to the Teulon farm, where he was hired on by a grateful Captain White.

The Red's twists and turns meant the prows of her steamers pointed "as often towards the Antarctic as the Arctic pole", according to J.C. Hamilton in *The Prairie Province: Sketches of Travel from Lake Ontario to Lake Winnipeg.*

Perhaps the best and most detailed account of what it was really like to travel down the Red River on board a steamboat comes to us from no less a personage than Hariot Georgina Hamilton-Temple-Blackwood, Marchioness of Dufferin and Ava and the wife of Canada's second governor-general. She kept a diary, later published as *My Canadian Journal, 1872-1878.* In it, she recounts her visit to Manitoba in August 1877.

The vice-regal party, including Lord and Lady Dufferin and their twelve-year-old daughter Nellie, disembarked from their train at Fisher's Landing in Minnesota and climbed on board the steamer *Minnesota* for the trip to Winnipeg. The marchioness continues:

> *The steamer is a sternwheeler, such as we had on the Fraser River. She draws very little water, and certainly has an extraordinary passage to perform. The river, which to all intents and purposes is the Red River (the first few miles it is called Red Lake River), is very muddy, very narrow, and extremely sinuous. It twists and turns itself about. Think of a braiding-pattern, or of a zig-zag path up a steep hill. Or imagine sailing through hundreds of small ponds all joined together, the second concealed by the curve of the first and you may form some idea of it.*
>
> *I can only tell you that we go from one bank to the other, crushing and crashing against the trees, which grow down to the water-side. The branches sweep over*

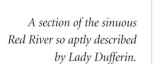

*the deck, and fly in our faces, and leave pieces behind them. I had just written this when I gave a shriek as I saw my ink-bottle on the point of being swept overboard by an intrusive tree; D's hat was knocked off his head by it.*

*The consequence of this curious navigation is that we never really go on for more than three minutes at a time. We run against one bank and our steam is shut off, and in some mysterious manner we swing round till our bow is into the other. Then we are bound, and go on a few yards, till the sharp curve brings us up against the side. Our stern wheel is often ashore, and our captain and pilot must require the patience of saints.*

Lady Dufferin also wrote about the hordes of mosquitoes that descended on the steamer towards evening.

*At dinner (a very good one) we were eaten while eating, and were glad to leave the lighted saloon, and sit on the bow of the steamer in the air. The night was dark, the river looked gloomy and mysterious, and we sat there and watched the black reflections in the water. Our steamer whistled, and in the distance we heard it answered. Slowly we turned a point and saw another boat [the Manitoba from Winnipeg] approaching. It looked beautiful*

*in the dark, with two great bull's-eyes, red and green lamps and other lights on deck, creeping towards us. We stopped and backed into the shore, that it might pass. It came close and fired off a cannon, and we saw on the deck a large transparency with the words "Welcome, Lord Dufferin" on it, and two girls dressed in white with flags in their hands. Then a voice sang "Canada, sweet Canada" ... They sang "God save the Queen" and "Rule Britannia" and cheered for the Governor-General as they began to move slowly away. He had only just time to call out a few words of thanks before they disappeared into the darkness .*

The vice-regal party reached Winnipeg on August 6th. The marchioness continues:

*We came in sight of Fort Garry about ten o'clock. The Red River appears to divide the town in two, but we left it and turned into the Assiniboine, round the corner of which we found a wharf. Some people came on board to see the Governor-General. He arranged for me to start half an hour before him, and go to the City Hall, where we ladies sat till the noise of bands and shouting announced his arrival.*

*The town of Winnipeg is rapidly increasing, and today, with its decorations of transplanted trees and flags, it looked gay.*

The vice-regal couple toured Manitoba for more than a month. They cruised around Lake Winnipeg on the Hudson's Bay Company steamer, *Colvile*, shot the Grand Rapids, where the Saskatchewan River descends nearly thirty-one metres in

*A section of the sinuous Red River so aptly described by Lady Dufferin.*

DAWN HUCK

*Crossroads of a Continent*

five kilometres, including a one-metre fall in the centre, visited the Icelandic settlement at Gimli and canoed the rapids of the Winnipeg River.

The conclusion of their Manitoba voyage was as ominous for the steamboat era on the Red River of the North as the marchioness' diary was vivid and immediate in its portrayal. On their last day in Winnipeg, September 29, 1877, Lord and Lady Dufferin "drove through Fort Garry and across the Red River to a place where D. and I each drove a spike in the Canada Pacific Railway, the first line in this part of the world".

Opened the following year, the railway linked St. Paul and Winnipeg and spelled the end of one steam epoch as another began. Further confirmation of the changing times greeted the governor general and his wife when they disembarked the *Minnesota* at Fisher's Landing on October 2nd. The marchioness picks up the story: "We went ashore, and saw the engine No. 21 of the Canada Pacific Railway; it is going to Winnipeg, with a train of railway-trucks, and it is to be called the 'Lady Dufferin' ."

The locomotive actually travelled to Winnipeg by barge, loaded with rail equipment and pushed by the steamer, *Selkirk*. She arrived on October 9, 1877. For the next year, she toiled up and down along the east side of the Red River, playing a significant role in building the CPR track from St. Boniface north to Selkirk and south to Pembina. In November 1878, she carried dignitaries and railway officials, including the Countess herself, to Roseau River for the first of six Western Canadian "last spike" ceremonies. It may have been this that prompted the renaming of the little engine the "Countess of Dufferin".

As outlined in our chapter on the railways, the story of the *Countess* over the next decades was filled with neglect and

PROVINCIAL ARCHIVES OF MANITOBA

St. Andrews Locks near Winnipeg,

near disaster, as well as valiant rescues. Today, Manitoba's first locomotive is home for good, and suitably esconced on Track 1 of the Winnipeg Railway Museum at the VIA Rail Station.

The steamboat era, however, didn't end suddenly. It simply faded away. One by one, its ships and their nervy and ingenious captains moved west or north, to service the rivers and lakes where the railway hadn't yet pushed its iron tentacles. At the time the steamship era went into eclipse on the Red River, it was just opening on Lake Winnipeg where it would last for more than another half-century. Because of the long delay in solving the problem of the St. Andrew's Rapids, all but impassable except during spring flood, the lake

*The* SS Winnitoba *at the opening of the St. Andrew's Locks. Prime Minister Sir Wilfred Laurier was aboard the ship as she slowly traversed the stretch of the Red that had bedevilled so many for so long.*

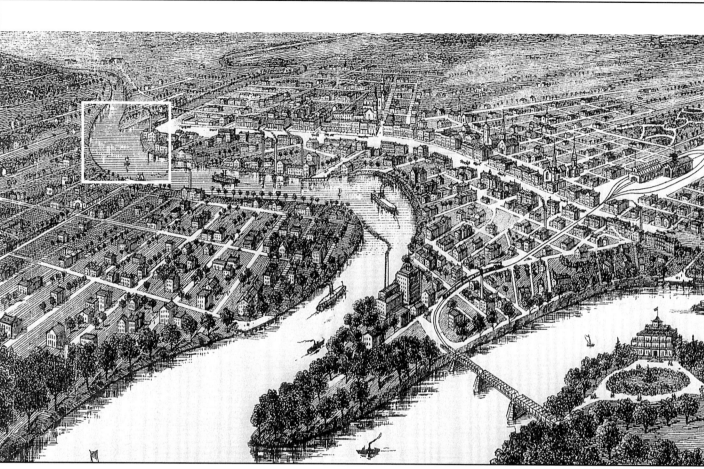

*This remarkable birds-eye view of Winnipeg, etched in 1881, shows the importance of river traffic to the burgeoning city.*

NATIONAL LIBRARY OF CANADA / C-11764

trade established its river port at Selkirk, not Winnipeg. In July 1910, Prime Minister Sir Wilfrid Laurier and a boatload of dignitaries steamed down the Red River from Winnipeg aboard the Hyland Navigation Company's *Winnitoba*. With another huge crowd watching on shore, the prime minister officiated at the opening of the Dominion government's St. Andrews Locks. But it was already too late for the Red River steamboat trade. The 100-ton *Grand Forks* was the last steamship to make the winding, 872-kilometre trip from St. Paul to Winnipeg, arriving on June 6, 1909. She brought

to an end exactly fifty years of steamboat commerce between Canada and the U.S.

The steamboat era on the 960-kilometre Assiniboine River was, in the words of one chronicler, "like a short burst of rockets in the passage of time. Even as the steamers strove westward, the steam locomotive crept along the bank behind them, inevitable winner of an uneven race."

In 1857, the intrepid Canadian surveyor, Henry Youle Hind, had measured the Assiniboine as being 15.4 metres wide and 1.8 metres deep at the mouth of the Souris. Many

*Crossroads of the Continent*

had long suspected the river was navigable beyond Portage la Prairie. And perhaps because of her shallowness and winding and twisting ways, she held a particular fascination for steamboat men. There were many of these characters and all were colourful. One was lumberman, boatbuilder and prairie shipping entrepreneur Peter McArthur, who had been held captive by Louis Riel at Upper Fort Garry in December 1869. A Presbyterian and strict teetotaller, he eventually lost his partnership in the Winnipeg & Western Transportation Company after it was taken over by the Hudson's Bay Company, because he objected to the company using his ships to freight its whiskey to Edmonton. He owned the largest steamboats ever to ply the Assiniboine, the sixty-two by ten-metre *North Star* and the forty by nine-metre *Marquette*. When he brought the *Marquette* from Minnesota to Winnipeg in the spring of 1879 for the Assiniboine trade, McArthur boasted that she would be "able to run on a light dew".

The *Marquette*'s first master was Captain Jerry Webber, a colourful Mississippi River boatman who had earned his papers by ferrying artillery for the Union Army on the flooding Mississippi and Minnesota Rivers in April and May of 1861, the opening months of the American Civil War. Captain Webber greeted every adversity with a string of ferocious oaths, at the conclusion of which he would throw his hat on the deck and jump up and down on it. He was always impeccably dressed, however, favouring a black frock coat, a semi-dress white shirt, and a string tie, along with the unfortunate and frequently-flattened broad-brimmed hat. His pet raven, nattily kitted out with a crimson ribbon strung around its wings, accompanied him on each and every trip he made on the Assiniboine.

**D**espite her size, Captain Webber was able to sail the *Marquette* all the way from Winnipeg to Fort Ellice, three kilometres downriver from today's St. Lazare, not far from where the Qu'Appelle River flows into the Assiniboine. In May 1879, her first season, she completed the round-trip distance of 1,440 kilometres in eight days. Her purser, A. D. Robinson, left a detailed account of the journey, including vivid depictions of the varied scenery:

> *As we left the flat marshy prairie behind we came to the bluffs where Pine trees covered high hills. It was a handsome scene. After travelling another hour, we arrived at Cyprus (Cypress) River where we put off a passenger and some freight The sand hills stretch for miles and great cracks and chasms show themselves. As we approached the hills, the prismatic colours were superb. The hills are covered with Spruce trees but the bald heads of yellow sand intermingled with red and yellow clay show above the tree line.*

There was a near-catastrophe on that trip when three members of the crew took to a lifeboat to "warp" the *Marquette* over the Assiniboine Rapids west of Crawford's Landing near the mouth of the Souris River. Their task completed, the men started rowing for the steamer, but the current was running fast. Sensing danger, the steamer's crew threw them a rope. They caught it, but the power of the current flipped the skiff over, plunging them into the river. Two managed to cling to the overturned craft but the third had been tossed too far out. Grabbed by the rapids' current, he hurtled towards the steamer. As he shot past, "a man reached out and grabbed him by the hair, thereby saving his life".

There were more than the usual adversities on the Assiniboine. Fast-flowing rapids could suddenly give way to a riverbed so shallow that ships literally walked "on stones", as one steamboatman put it. Sufficient water to keep a steamer afloat was as precious as gold. One story has it that an Assiniboine riverbank resident dipped his pail into the river one day only to hear the enraged skipper of a passing steamer roar: "Hey you! Put that water back!"

Still, steamboats eventually penetrated the entire length of the Assiniboine, a further 240 kilometres past Fort Ellice to the river's source near Fort Pelly in east-central Saskatchewan. McArthur's *Marquette* made the 480-kilometre Ellice-Pelly round trip in under one week in 1881.

Life aboard the Assiniboine's steamers was quite pleasant. The salon on the *North Star*, for example, boasted a $5,000 grand piano for singalongs and amusements. It was also amazingly cheap. The cost of a ticket from Winnipeg to Brandon was under ten dollars. "Several of the larger steamboats were well furnished with ornate tables and chairs, carpeted salons, costly chandeliers and first class staterooms arranged down each side of the second deck."

The captains resorted to a device called a "deadman" to "warp" their boats over rapids and across shallows. Roy Brown describes it in his book, *Steamboats on the Assiniboine*:

*...a sturdy log was buried in the bank to provide an anchor. A rod, having an eyelet at its upper end, was fastened to the deadman, the name given the buried log, and a rope was threaded through it and then attached to the steam-powered capstan on the prow of the boat. When steam was applied to the paddle wheel, the*

*mechanism also engaged the capstan and the boat was literally lifted over obstacles in the water.*

The first known trip up the Assiniboine was attempted on May 6, 1873 by the *Dakota*, the year before she was to witness the dramatic rescue of a little girl. The 118-tonne ship, twenty-eight metres long and just over a metre in the beam, couldn't get past the rapids at Sturgeon Creek due to rocks and low water. The next year, thanks to a flood on the river, she was successful and reached Portage la Prairie in two days.

The first steamboat to operate regularly on the Assiniboine was the *Alpha*, commencing service in 1878. "Of all the sternwheelers that traded on this river, she was probably the smallest, the homeliest and yet the most persistent," writes Loudon Wilson. She belonged to McArthur's Winnipeg and Western Transportation Company Ltd., formed in the spring of that year to carry freight and passengers on all the waters north and west of Winnipeg.

On her initial trip, the *Alpha* boasted a heavy cargo and two barges laden with flour, wheat, oats, potatoes, various goods and implements. She returned to Winnipeg with a consignment of valuable furs. In 1882, taking passengers from the CPR's Brandon railhead to Fort Ellice, she was overloaded and, barely three kilometres into her journey, began to sink. Recounts passenger H.A. Wilson: "We heard the captain shout: 'Blow the whistle like Hell for Heaven, we're going down.'" The river was less than four metres deep at this point so the captain ordered the crew to run her ashore. But the *Alpha* was too far gone to answer to her helm. All this time the whistle was blowing continuously.

The *Marquette* steamed to the rescue and the two ships were lashed together. Cattle, horses and people leaped for

PROVINCIAL ARCHIVES
OF MANITOBA / N.12234

their lives. Enough cargo was transferred that she refloated and returned to Brandon, but that wasn't the end of excitement aboard the *Alpha*. The next year, she experienced a near-mutiny after one of her boilers sprang a leak. The captain put the crew on giant sweeps bow and stern, using his rifle to make sure the stern contingent bent their backs to the task.

The Winnipeg and Western Transportation Company acquired the cream of the Kittson line, including, along with the *Alpha*, the *Minnesota*, the *Manitoba* and the *Cheyenne*, a sidewheeler that suffered a lot of damage when the water was low. Nevertheless, her owners had high hopes for her. They refurbished her fourteen staterooms, salon and ladies' cabins with white, green and gold-striped panelling, as well as inlaid flooring. Muralists painted a buffalo hunt scene above her paddlewheels. Thus outfitted, she catered to the dinner-dancing and excursion trade on both the Red and Assiniboine.

The brief heyday of steamships on the Assiniboine was the years 1880 and 1881. Then, on September 26, 1881, the CPR reached Brandon. By 1883, McArthur had taken his *Marquette* off the Assiniboine and put her into service on the lower Red in the Selkirk area. Five W&WTC ships were also moved to the Saskatchewan River, involving dangerous and daring voyages through Lake Winnipeg and up the plunging cataract at Grand Rapids. Only one was lost. Lady Dufferin's *Minnesota/City of Winnipeg*, the ship that had carried the vice-regal party between St. Paul and Winnipeg in 1877, sank in a fierce storm off Long Point on

Lake Winnipeg in 1881. But the *Alpha* stayed on the Assiniboine, making her last trip on April 27, 1885. She went aground outside the main channel of the river in the Spruce Woods north of Cypress River and, after a time, became known as "the mystery ship of the Spruce Woods". Her timbers can still be seen today, when the river is low. The last steamship on the Assiniboine was laid up in 1913.

For the last three decades of the nineteenth century, Winnipeg was the port of registry for all ships from Grand Portage at the western end of Lake Superior to the Rockies. But the Port of Winnipeg was actually split in two, reflecting the deep rivalry between the HBC and the growing city. The HBC's levee and warehouse were on the north bank of the Assiniboine just southeast of the Fort; Winnipeg's was at the foot of Lombard and McDermot Avenues. The waterfront

*Built for bigger waters, but perhaps safer on the river, the* Princess *lived up to her name in the first years after her launching. Two decades later, she was "shorn of her looks", stripped of her paddlewheel, lengthened and converted to a cargo freighter.*

CAPTAIN HAWES / COURTESY OF CAPTAIN CLIFFORD J. STEVENS

stretched between them. Immediately behind it was a triangular area known as the Flats, which, as we shall see in the following chapters, would go on to become Western Canada's "Ellis Island" – the immigration centre for the Canadian West – then Canadian National Railway's East Yards and much later, The Forks, Winnipeg's remarkably popular gathering place.

The *Steamboat Bill of Facts*, the journal of North American steamships, provides a final image for this storied era. It describes the gala day in 1881 when Captain William Robinson's new sidewheeler *Princess*, destined for the stormy waters of Lake Winnipeg and tragically claimed by them twenty-five years later, was launched at the foot of Post Office Street:

*A satisfied summertime crowd prepares to disembark as the gangplank is lowered on the Paddlewheel Queen.*

> *It was the greatest day of the year for the little city of Winnipeg. Along Main Street, crowds jostled for a better look at the procession passing on the wide thoroughfare. The procession, led by city dignitaries and the resplendent entourage of the Governor-General of Canada, Lord Lorne, who rode with Lady Lorne in the finest coach and pair the city could provide, had just passed by ... The (Winnipeg-St. Boniface) ferry is even now closing to her landing (at the foot of Water Street and Pioneer Avenue). Of the traditional type, Adelaide has a cabin housing the paddles on either side of the thoroughfare, with the boiler*

*and stack to starboard and the engine to port. She was built at Grand Forks in 1877–78 ... The passengers streaming off the ferry turn north on the levee, passing frame warehouses and a large mill. Here along the bank, flatboatmen used to tie their shanty stores and hawk "Yankee" goods from upriver till the city merchants had them ousted. On a continuous raft-like wharf, canoes and gears are strewn. Farther along ... is the sidewheeler,* Cheyenne *... Beyond her lies*

Marquette, *a sternwheeler with the main characteristics of the Missouri River "mountain boats" ... We skirt piles of lumber to pass the sternwheeler* North West *... Her hurricane deck is crowded with spectators. The riverbank is jammed. Every warehouse, tree, and pole has its quota of daredevils ... The crash reverberates across the river ... "I christen thee ..." A cheer rises ... There she goes!*

The *Princess* is sliding, racing for her element. There is a great splat of water, a deep furrow in the river, and a rending crash. The anchor-cable snaps out, whip-taut. The river current saves the *Princess* from the opposite bank. Now she lies just downstream, drifting gently, sans power, her relieved passengers waving and shouting.

PETER ST. JOHN

*Crossroads of a Continent*

THE FORKS NORTH PORTAGE PARTNERSHIP

Today's boaters can often hear the echoes of the past, for afternoon picnics, dinner dances and excursions are still popular on the Red River. Almost any sunny summer afternoon, riverboats can be seen carrying crowds of tourists downriver to Lower Fort Garry. And standing at The Forks after sunset, one might easily be carried back more than a century as dance music drifts across the water and the lights of a paddlewheeler appear around a bend. And one can only expect the traffic on the water to increase, as Winnipeggers rediscover their river heritage. A new system of water taxis and a growing network of docks have many city dwellers opting to travel to work between May and November by boat bus, rather than by the terrestrial equivalent. And where once they viewed the rivers as little more than aquatic back lanes, Winnipeggers, aided by municipal, provincial and federal dollars, have rediscovered the magic of the river valley. A system of groomed paths wind along the riverbanks, luring thousands down to the waterside. In winter, an ambitious system of walking, skating and skiing trails has created ice-level crowds of the kind not seen since the days of the fur trade. And as they always have, all roads lead to The Forks.

The docks and the picturesque harbour at The Forks (perhaps the most photographed scene in modern Winnipeg) are regularly crowded with pleasure craft, as their owners enjoy lunch or dinner in one of the site's many restaurants.

Dragon boat racers speed past the confluence of the rivers, paddlers and kayakers work out before the city wakes and lovers pause in the trees in The Forks National Historic Site on the banks of the Red, just northeast of The Forks.

"This," someone confided recently, pointing to the swollen Red, which has developed the disconcerting habit of rising during mid-summer, "is Canada's Rhine. It has the history, the mystery and a mind of its own."

*Topped by the Canadian flag, the glass viewing tower rises above The Forks, providing a wonderful overview of the plaza and the river junction.*

*Below: Dozens of dragon boaters gather for a weekend of racing.*

PETER ST. JOHN

# Western Canada's

For thousands, the confluence of the Red and Assiniboine Rivers was their first real view of Canada, their initial glimpse of a new life in a new land. And for many, it was a bittersweet experience. Between 1872 and 1884, conditions in the immigration sheds and the shanty town that grew up around them were often appalling, whether in the heat of summer or the bitter cold of winter. Yet most rose above the squalor. They laid the foundations for Winnipeg and Manitoba and opened the gates to Western Canada.

# "Ellis Island"

By Marjorie Gillies

People have been coming to the forks of the Red and Assiniboine Rivers for millennia. Beginning at least 6,000 years ago, Native North Americans established campsites here, along the shores of the Red. Later, they visited the site to observe important political, religious and cultural ceremonies at the confluence of the two rivers. In those early times, they came from east and west, north and south, some from remarkable distances given the means of travel at hand.

**M**ore recently however, Manitoba's immigration story is a chronicle of people from more distant places. In the past 130 years, tens of thousands have arrived here, rich and poor, privileged and persecuted, and for a brief period they all passed through The Forks en route to a new life in a new country. Indeed, between 1870 and 1885, The Forks was Western Canada's "Ellis Island", the immigration clearing house for all of the Canadian West, just as the infamous island in Upper New York Bay served immigrants to the eastern United States for a half-century after 1892.

Most newcomers to Manitoba made the journey for the opportunities that lay ahead, and some were rewarded with wealth and good fortune. But many faced hardship, loneliness, and a day-to-day effort to overcome the prejudice, racism and intolerance that prevailed in the early years of Western Canadian immigration.

Their letters home are filled with a collective complaint about mosquitoes in summer and cruel cold in winter. The

*In the early years newcomers often arrived by oxcart. Some came west over the all-but-impassable Dawson Trail, a patchwork of rough, wooden "corduroy" roads through bogs, and narrow trails over rocky outcroppings. Others, travelling the Great Lakes route via St. Paul, Minnesota, completed the trip by oxcart over routes along the upper Red River Valley.*

Mennonites from the dry steppes of the Russian Ukraine, where swamps were uncommon, had little familiarity with mosquitoes. One group sent an advance party to Manitoba. Appalled by the voracious insects, they decided on the United States instead. And the Icelanders, though they hailed from a northern country, knew winters moderated by the Gulf Stream. Especially in the first years, they found the cold of Manitoba's continental winters beyond imagining.

Despite the frigid temperatures and the biting insects, despite plagues of grasshoppers that stripped the landscape clean in the mid-1870s, hordes of immigrants arrived from eastern Canada, the United States, Britain and many parts of Europe after 1870. All were in search of new opportunities and a better life following Manitoba's entry into Canadian confederation that year and the City of Winnipeg's incorporation in 1873. Almost overnight, mosquitoes or not, Winnipeg was the gateway to North America's "Last Best West".

Many were responding to the federal government's national policy on immigration, developed in 1870. Anxious to promote rural settlement and stem the tide of people heading to the United States, the new program transformed Manitoba. Suddenly, the atmosphere was something akin to a gold rush, as thousands pursued free land rather than precious metal.

A million promotional posters distributed in Europe, Britain and the United States drew thousands of single men, as well as large family groups, all responding to the idea of living in the untamed West on free land that had never been cultivated. And thanks to its place at the confluence of the rivers, and later at the junction of the railways, Winnipeg became the hub of the movement west. Every person and every piece of equipment passed through the city en route to the great unknown.

THE FORKS NORTH PORTAGE PARTNERSHIP

*Crossroads of the Continent*

The first influx was mainly adventurers and opportunists from Ontario, Quebec and the Maritimes. Many were British remittance men, Irish Fenians or disbanded militiamen from the Wolseley Expedition, seeking employment opportunities and land grants offered by the Canadian government.

In the early years, many made their way overland on the Dawson Road between Fort William and Winnipeg. Before it closed in 1875, the unhappy travellers complained "this network of land and water was designed for commerce, not passenger travel". A trip of twenty-one days was not uncommon, involving accommodation at a variety of stations along the way that at least one traveller felt were "totally inadequate and filthy, unfit for women and children". Passengers had to heft their own luggage on and off wagons and boats and many of the men apparently lacked the "civility to restrain themselves from unseemly oaths". As well, a number of the boats carrying passengers and luggage were "leaky and unsafe ... belongings were damaged".

By early 1874, the population had grown from 200 residents of the tiny village of Fort Garry, not far from what were commonly known as the Portage Trail and the Main Road (today's Portage and Main) to a bustling city of 3,000, with hundreds more immigrants arriving each day. By 1880, the city had 66,000 inhabitants.

In 1879, government land agent William Hespeler had reported that "2,084 people were accommodated, a number only to be considered one-third of the actual immigration to this city." Moreover, he opined, the immigrants were "a class of people better provided with capital than those of early years."

What the Canadian government had largely overlooked in its early plans for attracting massive immigration to the prairies was the accommodation needed to cope with the flood of newcomers – especially those from Europe who had to be housed, fed and found employment at the same time as they were adapting to a new language and culture. Such services were almost non-existent in the 1870s.

As well, many of the unskilled poor from Europe had little money to bring to their new homeland. Often they neither spoke nor understood English or French and were therefore regularly victims of bias in land grant selection and acquiring jobs.

It was common policy for employment agents to post signs advising "No Irish", "No Scots", "No Jews" or "Aliens". By contrast, Ontarians or Americans who had sold family property to come west often had sufficient funds to establish banks, mills, stores, hotels and boarding houses, and also to build themselves mansions in Point Douglas or the Town of Broadway, just adjacent to The Forks.

During the land boom of 1881-82, when city lots sold privately for up to $20,000, land speculators and entrepreneurs became overnight millionaires. Some also became overnight paupers when the economy collapsed in 1883.

For the impoverished immigrants, life was very different. A first home in Winnipeg was often a rickety shack in squalid and unsanitary housing on the flood-prone "Flats", the property edging the west shore of the Red River just north of the confluence with the Assiniboine. This was the Hudson's Bay Company's Reserve Land, part of the property the company had kept when it transferred its vast holdings in Rupert's Land to the Canadian government in 1869.

Originally, this land had been slated to be Block 1 of the

PROVINCIAL ARCHIVES OF MANITOBA / N10095-95

*Posters such as this one painted a utopian life for Europe's land-hungry masses. The reality was often much harsher.*

Town of Selkirk, with lots laid out grid-style along the east side of Main Street. As early as the mid-1820s, the Hudson's Bay Company used the east and northeast part of the Flats as an experimental farm, including barns and fields, as well as houses for officers.

Later, the HBC sold or granted river lots, beginning on the north side of today's Pioneer and Notre Dame Avenues, to retiring company servants. The intent was to create a buffer zone between Fort Garry and the Red River settlers who had mainly settled north of what is now Point Douglas.

In 1870, the area dubbed the Flats extended to the southern boundary of Sinclair's Creek, between today's Bannatyne and Market Avenues, east of Main. From there it ran southward to

*"Looking North from Fort Garry, 1871", shows homes and businesses springing up north of the land the HBC had intended for settlement at The Forks.*

The Forks. Block 1 ran eastward on both sides of Broadway to the Red River. A similar strip of lots for private sale extended northward on the west side of Wesley Street to Water, excluding a large empty triangle of land south of Water, which had been a parking area for company-owned Red River carts. Block 2 of the reserve, which ran along Broadway westard from Main, became the Town of Broadway, a community of prosperous upper-class newcomers to the city.

Initially, the Hudson's Bay Company anticipated that it would have little difficulty attracting settlers to build on its vacant lots. But when Manitoba became a province in 1870, many pioneers were anxious to sever all ties with the HBC. They fought both the name Selkirk and the company's efforts to attract public buildings away from the fledgling city, which was centred north of Portage and Main.

Hostility between the two factions increased in 1873 when the city built a levee or landing place at the foot of Lombard and McDermot Avenues, diverting steamboat traffic away from the forks of the two rivers. And when the HBC won contracts from the federal government to locate a customs house, Dominion Lands Office, immigration sheds and the post office on south Main Street, the business rivalry was further intensified.

The first of the immigration sheds built by the federal Department of Public Works near the mouth of the Assiniboine River was completed in August 1872. Set on an empty triangle of HBC Reserve Land between Main Street, Broadway and the forks of the rivers,

F.G. SHEPPARD / WINNIPEG'S EARLY DAYS / THE STOVEL COMPANY LIMITED

*Crossroads of the Continent*

the one-storey wooden building was fifty-four by thirty-seven metres and divided into thirty compartments, each about the size of a small bedroom – "like pens in a pig stye", according to one observer. The building housed more than twenty-five families at a time.

The *Manitoba Gazette and Trade Review* described the 1872 shed this way: "A good substantial looking building. Rooms had separate entrances and were just comfortable enough for a temporary residence, without giving any inducement for a prolonged stay, as is the case in some instances.

"The cook houses are detached from the main building, so that there is no danger from fire. The interior of the shed is nicely whitewashed and the outside is painted a stone color ... A perfect arrangement."

A second shed, even larger and built a year later, allowed the accommodation of between four and five hundred people for short periods. Each immigrant was entitled to free shelter for a period not to exceed seven days. If space was available – a rare situation – newcomers were allowed to stay indefinitely at no cost. However, the sheds were generally filled to overflowing and additional space was often needed. In these circumstances, room was found at Fort Osborne Barracks on Broadway, in government buildings, vacant warehouses, hotels or – during the spring and summer – in large tents.

During the first year or two, a steady flow of early newcomers from eastern Canada and the U.S. were accommodated at the completed sheds, but crisis conditions developed in early October 1875 with the arrival of 285 impoverished Icelanders, who found that few preparations had been made for their journey north to Lake Winnipeg. Their homeland had been blighted by lava and volcanic ash following the

## PASTURE SAGE *(Artemesia)*

ITS DISTINCT "SAGELIKE" ODOR might fool some into confusing pasture sage with its southwestern cousin, sagebrush, or a western relative, prairie sage. But pasture sage is smaller, between fifteen and forty-five centimetres tall, and more delicate in appearance. Its leaves are gray-green, with tiny silver-haired leaflets on both sides. A perennial, it grows from a mat of grayish leaves that rise in a series of spindly stems when the plant is ready to flower. Despite this, the flowers – light yellow florets clustered in small dense heads. – are easy to miss. Like other species of *Artemisia*, pasture sage grows where the prairies have been overgrazed or disturbed. This is likely why it was increasingly noted around The Forks during the immigration period.

eruption of Mount Askja; for many it was the last straw after decades of Danish domination.

The newcomers were greeted at the Assiniboine River dock by a crowd of curious Winnipeggers, who expected to see "short .... stout, thick-set individuals with black hair like Eskimos". Their reaction, indicative of the racial sentiments of the time, was almost unanimous: "They're not Icelanders, they're white people."

One local newspaper described them as "smart-looking, intelligent, excellent people ... a valuable acquisition to the people in the province of Manitoba." It was also reported that the immigrants had "a particular manner of overcoming obstacles and an energy of character that will ensure them success here," a rather prescient comment, as it turned out, on the ordeals the newcomers would face.

A Voice from the Emigrant Sheds

To the Editor of the Free Press,

Can nothing be done with us poor emigrants, who have endured all the hardships of a Dawson Route to come here? We are willing to work, but there is no work to be had, and every week we are increasing in numbers. What then is to be done? Will the energetic Mayor of the city not devise something? Improvements, I understand, on a large scale, are contemplated. Why not proceed with them now, and give us poor fellows a chance to earn our livelihood; and by doing so keep up the reputation of what is destined to become a large city? If something is not done soon we will have to starve, or else look for redress from the Government to the extent of sending us back to where we came from, minus our hard-earned dollars, exchanged for privations, the record of which will retard immigration to this Province for some time to come. I consider it the duty therefore of every citizen of Winnipeg to guard against such a catastrophe, by urging on those they have placed in authority to look to the welfare of the city. Labor must be cheaper now, where there are hundreds in the sheds, than it will be for some time, should we be compelled to return. By inserting the above in your paper, you will oblige hundreds of impoverished men.

I am your, &c,
Emigrant Sheds, July 13, 1874

The reaction of the Icelanders was less enthusiastic. Touring the city of 3,000, with its muddy streets and ox-pulled carts, they described Winnipeg as, "a very

insignificant town with few noteworthy buildings".

Housed at the immigration sheds for a week, they embarked on October 20th for Gimli. Though the name means "paradise" in Icelandic, what faced them was anything but. The next months broke records for cold and the immigrants suffered incredible hardships. Their transportation to Winnipeg had been paid for by the Canadian government, but no plans had been made to assist them over the winter months. Having spent a year of hardship in Ontario, the Icelanders had arranged to take a small herd of cows north with them, hoping to ensure that they would at least have milk and cheese. On arrival, however, they discovered that the three men who were to have cut hay in Manitoba had found more lucrative employment elsewhere. As a result, there was nothing in the colony to sustain the cows for the coming winter. They would have to be left behind.

In fact, even food for the immigrants themselves would be hard to find and the Icelanders were encouraged to stay in Winnipeg if possible, where they might find jobs and housing. A cursory look around showed that both, however, were almost non-existent and the majority opted to continue north. For many, it was the wrong decision; by Christmas, food was in very short supply. Within months, half of those who survived had returned to Winnipeg. Some walked to the city, a distance of about eighty kilometres. Others journeyed on homemade sleds. Once back in Winnipeg, they found work digging sewers or laying out new streets. Others were employed in construction, the needle trades or as domestic servants. Determined to avoid a return to the sheds, they fashioned shanty dwellings on the Flats, using salvaged material found in the city, paying no regard to lot or street arrangement.

HUDSON BAY COMPANY ARCHIVES / F-131/32

*Crossroads of the Continent*

Even before their return, the immigration sheds had become cramped and squalid. Places of "considerable hardship, sickness and hunger", they were run like army barracks with "lights out" and doors locked at 10 o'clock each night.

At first the printed rules were written in English only, but soon they appeared in diverse languages, all stating that "any disorderly character who is not controllable by ordinary means is handed over to the police."

Sanitary conditions were soon totally unacceptable. Built without a foundation or weeping tiles, the floors frequently flooded and there was no provision for hot water. Unheated bathrooms were useless during cold weather. In summer, a corner latrine used by the men became a nuisance and a danger both to the establishment and the neighbourhood at large.

Meanwhile, the federal and civic governments were trying to shift responsibility for the shelter and care of the new arrivals

onto one another, while both spent money promoting immigration to Western Canada. Not surprisingly, increased immigration only worsened the demands on the system and its already inadequate services.

As one Winnipegger commented: "If City Council had concentrated on making the city healthy, beautiful and pleasant with an adequate water and sewage system, it would have had all the free publicity it could desire in the form of a contented citizenry."

Like the returning Icelanders, many immigrants' answer to such unacceptable conditions in the government-owned sheds was to build their own accommodation and the squatter town of jerry-built shacks near the HBC grist mill grew, and along with it, a cluster of bawdy houses adjacent to the sheds.

As early as the spring of 1874, complaints were being made to City Hall about how booze and brothels on the Flats were taxing the small police force under Chief John Ingram, who was himself a known patron of the houses.

Undisturbed by such reports, City Council felt "it was best to leave the problem of lack of accommodation to the Dominion government," opining that it was "not advisable to do anything that would diminish the energy or self-reliance of the new settlers which would inevitably happen if they were too comfortable."

If the first wave of Icelanders had faced cold and hardship, the second wave of 1,200, arriving in July 1876, encountered disease. At some point in their journey, the so-called Large Group had contracted smallpox, which unfortunately was not detected by the "duly qualified Quarantine officer". The immigrants moved on to Lake Winnipeg, where more than 100 died before the disease ran its course.

Back in Winnipeg, squalid conditions and inadequate medical inspection combined to make the Flats the site of

IMAGES THIS PAGE COURTESY OF NELSON GERRARD / FROM *ICELANDIC SETTLERS IN AMERICA*

*Opposite: This 1881 overview of the junction of the two rivers is one of very few that shows the long, low immigration sheds along the Red River and the nearby shanty town, as well as the relationship of both to Upper Fort Garry.*

*Above and left: At least initially determined to reach their intended destination before winter, the first group of Icelanders continued north along the Red River to Lake Winnipeg in a series of flatboats and barges.*

FRANK LYNN / PROVINCIAL ARCHIVES OF MANITOBA / N-1250I

*Crossing from St. Boniface in 1875, travellers used the ferry across the Red to South Point and a second ferry across the Assiniboine to Winnipeg. Six years later, a bridge replaced the ferries, linking Broadway with Provencher. This first bridge was short-lived, but was quickly replaced with a sturdier version that served both communities well for more than a quarter-century.*

periodic epidemics. Yet the problem was not tackled at all for almost a decade, when at last quarantine facilities were established. And it was not until 1898, when Clifford Sifton was head of the Interior Department, that the situation was finally resolved by improving living conditions for newcomers and providing relief and social assistance for those who were destitute.

In the meantime, in the absence of any effective government assistance, "respectable members of the community offered 'moral and spiritual encouragement' as well as economic assistance to the shanty population," according to city historian Gerry Berkowski.

The *Daily Sun* reported in January 1882 that the "respected Reverend Mr. Pitblado"... while investigating the condition of

the families in the sheds asked "how the folks were making out, how they liked the country" and whether the "good men had plenty of work". He always wound up his visit "by urging all to go to church", no matter to which denomination they belonged.

Despite the conditions, and the journeys most had to endure, some of the immigrants arrived remarkably well prepared. In July 1874, 327 Mennonite Anabaptists, members of sixty-five families, disembarked at The Forks from the paddlewheel steamer *International*. Their goal was to settle on almost 2500 hectares of free land bordering the Red River south and southwest of Winnipeg. Their exodus from the steppes of the Russian Ukraine had come with the termination of an edict by Czar Alexander II that had exempted them from military service. Refusing to serve because of their beliefs brought persecution, which in turn led to the desire to emigrate. From Canada's perspective, the Mennonites were ideal immigrants, for they had the lengthy agricultural experience sought by the Canadian government to open the west to farming communities.

So began their remarkable journey from the German language colonies in present-day Ukraine, by rail across Europe, by ship across the Atlantic and through the Great Lakes and finally by steamer up the Red River to Winnipeg.

They came bearing crates of grain seed from Europe and so anxious were they to take possession of their land that they stayed in Winnipeg only forty-eight hours. Leaving wives and children, the frail and the elderly aboard the steamer, they streamed through the city shopping for scythes, milling stones, hay forks, pots, pans, coffee mills, tinware, potatoes and groceries. By day's end they had spent $15,000 in gold on horses, oxen, carts and provisions, goods they complained were often "too expensive" and of "poor quality".

Despite this, Manitoba suited them well. Within five years, their numbers had grown to 7,000, mainly settled west of Emerson in today's municipalities of Stanley and Reinland and in an east reserve that is now the municipality of Hanover and the city of Steinbach.

A decade later, in 1882, at the encouragement of Sir Alexander Galt, Canada's High Commissioner to Great Britain, Winnipeg welcomed its first Russian Jewish immigrants. Galt was a vocal proponent of European emigration to and investment in Western Canada, according to provincial historian and researcher Henry Trachtenberg. Galt, he wrote, told Prime Minister Sir John A. Macdonald that "American

Jews were actively promoting emigration to the United States and I thought what was good for them could be good for us." In addition, Galt wrote to Macdonald, "A large percentage of Russian Jews will be found with sufficient means to establish themselves in Canada."

While the former may have been true, the latter was often decidedly not. The first group of 350 Russian Jews from Brody, a town on the Austrian-Galician border, had been the subjects of pogroms – government-sanctioned looting and murders – and were desperate to leave. Nor was Galt's interest in assisting these unfortunate people entirely altruistic. He was, in fact, cultivating the Rothschilds in Britain through his involvement as advisor to the board of the Mansion House Committee, a British organization of prominent Jewish and Christian political, business and intellectual leaders. He hoped "to establish an International Colonization Company with a capital stock of $1,000,000."

*The first colony of Mennonites arrives at the Hudson's Bay Company dock in 1874.*

F. HOBERER / HUDSON'S BAY COMPANY ARCHIVES / P-363

In part with the assistance of the Mansion House Committee, the Russian Jews arrived in Manitoba in May and June of 1882 and were ensconced in the immigration sheds. Most had been trades people and mechanics in Brody, but – at least initially – it seems that Galt expected them to become farmers. And rather than having "sufficient means", as Galt had once claimed, the group was destitute. The richest refugee was reported to have just $42 in his pocket.

F. G. SHEPPARD / WINNIPEG'S EARLY DAYS / THE STOVEL COMPANY LIMITED

*When the immigrant sheds were torn down in 1884, many of the Russian Jews moved to north Main Street, right, creating a vibrant community. The academic, business and artistic talent that developed here can be found in most of the major cities of North America today.*

**R**esponding to the initial emergency, the city organized a relief committee that soon raised more than $1,200 for the immediate survival of the newcomers. The Bishop of Rupert's Land personally subscribed $100. Ottawa donated 450 kilograms of flour, ninety kilos of oatmeal, almost five kilos of tea, two kegs of molasses, thirty tents and small per capita grants.

Though the immigrants were temporarily rescued, Galt's "new Jerusalem" idea quickly fell apart. Arrangements for fertile land for a colony were delayed for a number of bureaucratic reasons and many of the newcomers made it clear they were not cut out for an agrarian life. They sought work where they could, digging sewers, laying railroad track and loading gravel.

Made aware that most of the immigrants would never make farmers, Galt refuted his earlier enthusiasm, reporting

to the Mansion House Committee that the members of the would-be farm colony were "vagabonds who had turned to their natural avocation for peddling." He claimed to have been against the "experiment" from the outset. A cable dispatched on July 5, 1882 by John Lowe, secretary of the Dominion Department of Agriculture, was prophetic. It read abruptly, "Don't send more Jews."

Meanwhile the buoyant economy of 1881–82 had begun to slow and, despite their best efforts, by early January the Russian Jews still housed in the sheds and tents at the Flats were on the brink of starvation. In the face of disaster, the federal government responded with insensitivity. "It is not desired by the Department of Agriculture to encourage dependence by a general granting of assistance."

Fortunately, Winnipeggers were more charitable. They reacted quickly to appeals on behalf of the Russian Jews by City Council, the local churches, the YMCA and other agencies. Food, clothing, wood for fuel and financial donations poured in. City Council, which had spent less than $150 on charitable donations in 1881, appropriated $300 for the refugees in 1883 and Mansion House deposited $1,900 with Galt, to be dispensed at the rate of $5 per head.

However, as the months wore on, and the city experienced a severe real estate collapse, the Russian Jews faced growing antipathy, both from the community at large, which did not understand their religious practices, and from German Jews who had settled in Winnipeg earlier and feared the loss of their hard-won respectability from strangers who might be seen as pedlars.

Not only were the newcomers thus socially isolated, but as the city grew the Flats were physically isolated. Lumber and grist mills grew up along the Assiniboine and businesses sprang up along the north perimeter. The immigration sheds were demolished in 1884 in favour of new accommodation in Point Douglas and the squatters' shanties were removed in 1888, when the property became the terminus for the Red River Valley Railroad, the homesteader's main line to rural communities and their land grants.

With the demolition of the sheds in 1884, the Jewish refugees gathered in Winnipeg's North End, where they found and created employment and established synagogues. By this time, the city's Jewish population was the third-largest in Canada, after those in Toronto and Montreal, helping to create Winnipeg's multicultural mosaic.

The Jews also moved onto dairy farms in West Kildonan, agricultural colonies at Narcisse and small towns throughout the southern part of the province, where the Jewish-owned general store was soon as common as the Chinese restaurant. At one time there were 100 in Manitoba.

**S**oon all trace of the sheds was buried beneath a metre of fill along the banks of the Red and Assiniboine as the property became the passenger and freight yards for the Northern Pacific and Manitoba Railway. The fill protected the land from much of the flooding it had experienced in the past and by 1892, when all branch lines were amalgamated as the Manitoba Railway Company, the site was attracting attention elsewhere. The company was purchased almost immediately by the federally-owned Canadian Northern Railway and a year later a station, freight sheds, work shops and a round-house encompassed one-third of Block 1.

Its brief period as a transition point for tens of thousands of newcomers was over. And while some might call this one of the less glorious moments in the history of The Forks, it played a critical role as the first "Gateway to the West" in the creation of Manitoba and Western Canada and laid the foundation for the multicultural nation Canada has become.

The descendants of the Icelanders, Mennonites and Russian Jews who arrived between 1872 and 1884 have gone on to become leaders in Manitoba's – and Canada's – business and industrial communities. And though some departed for other provinces, or other countries, many have stayed to build a firm foundation for the legions of immigrants who followed in their wake.

Over the past 125 years, people of all races and religions have come from even more distant points – Chile, Vietnam, El Salvador and the Philippines, to name just a few – to create one of the most multicultural communities on the planet. When Manitoba earned the right to play host to the 1999 Pan American Games, visitors from the farthest reaches of the hemisphere were startled to find, in Winnipeg, cultural communities representing almost every nation of the Americas. And every summer Winnipeggers celebrate this diversity in a plethora of festivals and events.

THE FORKS NORTH PORTAGE PARTNERSHIP

*Forks Ambassadors Paul Dugue and Jane Huminuk are among nearly two dozen Winnipeggers who volunteer their time for a variety of events at The Forks.*

*Gateway*

By 1896, the rail business was firmly esconced at The Forks, and the Northern Pacific & Manitoba's elegant Manitoba Hotel (seen in the middle distance) had earned a national reputation. There was still room for fun, however, at the newly-created Fort Garry Park, located behind what is now Union Station.

# to the West

By Sarah Burton

The sun rose in a clear, blue sky on the morning of October 9, 1877, bathing the crowds that had gathered on both sides of the Red River in unexpected warmth. By 9 o'clock, many were shedding their coats as they gazed intently upstream. A half-hour later, the word came: the *Lady Dufferin* was just south of the junction of the Red and the Assiniboine. The crowds hushed in expectation.

L.FAIRFIELD '03

**T**hen the steamboat *Selkirk* rounded the point, drifting with the flow of the river, Union Jacks and Stars and Stripes flying from her upper decks. In front of her, on the first of three barges, was the object of the crowd's anticipation – the *Lady Dufferin* – the first locomotive in the Canadian Northwest. Smoke from her stack spiralled into the clear sky as her whistle repeatedly sounded its long sharp note.

The crowd burst into cheers, flags waving and caps flying in the air, as the whistle at the Hudson's Bay Company mill blew furiously in welcome. A new era had begun, and Winnipeg was about to embark on one of the most remarkable periods of growth of any urban centre in the British Empire.

This initial connection of the *Lady Dufferin* – later renamed the *Countess of Dufferin* – with The Forks was destined to be brief (see page 131), for she belonged to the CPR and her work lay across the river in St. Boniface. But the rousing reception at the junction of the two rivers was prescient, for the Flats were about to be transformed and rail transport was at the centre of the transformation.

In 1877, this was Block 1 of the Hudson's Bay Company reserve. When Manitoba was created as a province in 1870, the company rule in the area ended. But the HBC retained a certain amount of reserve land around each of its posts. At Upper Fort Garry, this reserve totalled about 500 acres (or 245 hectares).

As we have seen in the preceding chapter, though the company initially had great plans for the Flats as a residential area and had surveyed the land and drawn up lots, none of these lots was ever sold or occupied. Bounded by Water Street and the Red River on the north and east, and Main Street and the Assiniboine River on the west and south, the area had instead become a thriving shanty town. Following the creation of two immigration sheds near the junction of the two rivers, the surrounding area was soon attracting newcomers to the province who could not afford land of their own, as well as certain unfortunates of society.

Rather than a safe, stable, even upscale neighbourhood – as Block 2 of the HBC reserve, just to the west along Broadway, would soon be – the Flats had become the unsavory part of town, where poverty and destitution ruled, where prostitution and vice thrived.

But not for long. The arrival of the *Lady Dufferin* prefaced something that in a generation would transform the village on the Red into a metropolis and change the face of the river junction for the best part of a century.

*Its serpentine journey at an end, the Selkirk steams into sight, with the long-awaited engine, caboose and flat cars.*

COURTESY OF THE MIDWEST-ERN RAIL ASSOCIATION

*Crossroads of the Continent*

*This is an appeal to the citizens of Winnipeg! A momentous crisis is upon you. The fate of Winnipeg depends upon your instant and united action ... It **may** be made the Chicago of the North-West – it **can** be – let us say it **must** be and do it.*

**S**o wrote **H.G. McMicken**, alderman from 1876 to 1877, to the editor of the *Winnipeg Daily Times* in the spring of 1879. The momentous crisis to which he was referring was the decision of the Dominion government to pass the main line of the Canadian Pacific Railway through the town of Selkirk rather than the fledgling City of Winnipeg.

At the time, Winnipeg was not completely devoid of rail transport. A year before McMicken's letter, the first rail line in Western Canada had been laid from St. Boniface to the Minnesota border to join another travelling north from St. Paul to form the St. Paul and Manitoba Railway. But the advantages of having an east-west transcontinental line pass through the city far outweighed the benefits of this minor north-south line.

The Hudson's Bay Company and the city of Winnipeg both agreed that Canada's rail line, when built, should pass through Manitoba's most populous city, which had already established itself as an important distribution centre. City council also argued that being at the junction of the Red and Assiniboine Rivers gave Winnipeg a geographical advantage over Selkirk. Before the advent of the railroad, transporting large or heavy loads was generally done on the Red and Assiniboine Rivers via barges or steamboats. Beginning in 1859, the Red River colony had established important trade relations with the United States this way (see By Water to Winnipeg on page 90).

Since rail lines were still few and far between, the rivers would have to continue to be used in conjunction with the railways to ship goods to areas not served by rail. The City of Winnipeg and the Hudson's Bay Company both felt these reasons justified the passage of the transcontinental line through the city. But there the agreement ended.

The Hudson's Bay Company wanted the rail line to pass through its reserve. Since the creation of the Province of Manitoba, the company had been trying to establish its Forks

*Drawn in 1874, the year after the City of Winnipeg was incorporated, this plan clearly shows Upper Fort Garry, as well as both Block 1 (occupying the area just north of The Forks and east of Main Street) and Block 2, centred on Broadway, west of Main. Interestingly, the south end of Main is labelled "Garry or Main Street."*

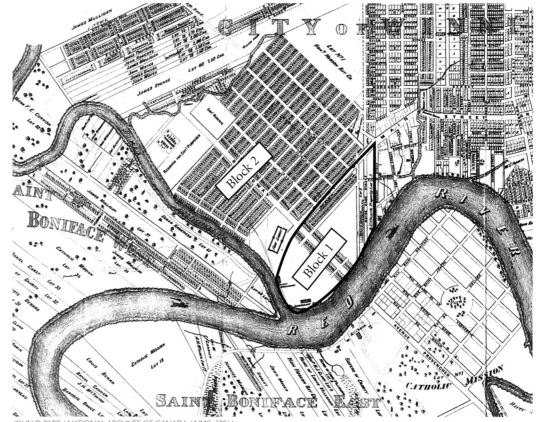

JOHN D. PARR / NATIONAL ARCHIVES OF CANADA / NMC–23816

G.A. STOVELL / WINNIPEG'S EARLY DAYS / AFTER PHOTOGRAPH BY STEELE & CO.

THE *COUNTESS OF DUFFERIN* DOCKS BRIEFLY AT THE FOOT OF LOMBARD STREET ...

# THE COUNTESS OF DUFFERIN

FOR ANY CHILD IN THE YEARS FOLLOWING World War II the *Countess of Dufferin* at Christmas was a magical sight. As it would until 1967, the locomotive stood in the forecourt of the Canadian Pacific Railway station on Higgins Avenue and in December become adorned with thousands of tiny white lights that traced its classic lines, from cowcatcher to smoke stack to cab. The marvel was the wheels. Lights sequenced around their perimeters made it seem as if the Countess was chugging off to a new destination.

It wasn't, of course. As David Harris writes in *Countess of Dufferin, A Brief History of the Lady In Black*, the engine hadn't moved under her own power since the early years of the twentieth century, when she was last seen ignominiously labouring at a lumber mill in Golden, B.C., under the unaristocratic name of *Betsy*.

Her beginnings were equally ordinary. She was one of about seventy wood-burning locomotives built by Baldwin Locomotive Works in Philadelphia in the 1870s and she spent the first five years of her life serving the Northern Pacific Railway in northern Minnesota. It wasn't until she got to Canada in 1877 that she became the stuff of legend.

Purchased by the CPR for the construction of its Pembina Branch to the American border at Emerson, the locomotive, then known as engine #21, was scheduled for shipment by barge from Fisher's Landing, Minnesota, down the Red River to St. Boniface in early October 1877. As it happened, the Earl of Dufferin, governor general of Canada, having completed a vice-regal visit to Manitoba with his wife, had stopped at Fisher's Landing en route to Ottawa via St. Paul and Chicago. To mark the occasion, locomotive #21 was renamed the *Lady Dufferin*. When she arrived at the Forks on October 9, 1877 on a flotilla decorated with flags and bunting, she was greeted with whistles and bells, and gave as good as she got with her own steam whistle. For the

tiny, remote Red River community, the arrival of the first locomotive was electrifying.

She was not, it should be noted, the first engine in the Canadian West. Two small engines. built in England and shipped around South America, had previously been used in

PROVINCIAL ARCHIVES OF MANITOBA

the coal mines on Vancouver Island. But the *Lady Dufferin* – renamed the *Countess of Dufferin* – was the first on the prairies.

For the next twenty years, she worked in earnest, first constructing the Pembina line, then working on the CPR main line. But by the end of the nineteenth century, coal-burning locomotives were replacing wood-burning models, and the CPR sold the engine to the Columbia River Lumber Company of Golden, B.C. With too little power to climb the Rockies under her own steam, she was taken west on the flatbed of a more powerful train. In Golden, she was put to work in the lumberyards, then eventually dismantled. By 1909, her boiler was being used to supply steam for a planing mill and her gearing was operating the lumber mill. She was about to be sold for scrap.

The story might have ended there if Winnipeg Board of Control member Richard Deans Waugh hadn't come across her in 1909. Aroused by this disappearing piece of Manitoba history, he spear headed a campaign to return the *Countess* to Winnipeg. Restored at the CPR's Weston shops, she was put on display in 1910 at Whyte Park, and then, in 1943, moved to the CPR station where she became one of Winnipeg's most beloved sights.

Since then, the *Countess* has had her ups and downs. The weather and an excess of affection combined to undermine her proud bearing. She was removed and furbished in the late 1960s, then went into warehouse seclusion in the late 1970s and '80s. It wasn't until the 1990s that local railway enthusiasts brought her back to glory.

Fittingly, her association with The Forks, which began with so much joy and ceremony in the nineteenth century, has been renewed in the twenty-first. Today, spruced up and shining, the *Countess of Dufferin* is open for public viewing at the Winnipeg Railway Museum (Tracks 1 and 2 at the Via Rail Union Station on Main Street). Long may she remain.

THE

# Manitoba

## AND
## NORTH-WESTERN RAILWAY
### LAND DEPARTMENT,

OFFICES        622 MAIN STREET, WINNIPEG,

OFFER FOR SALE, WITHOUT CULTIVATION OR SETTLEMENT RESTRICTIONS,

## 2,750,000 ACRES OF LAND
IN THE WELL KNOWN
## Park Lands of the Fertile Belt.
GOOD SOIL.    GOOD TIMBER.    GOOD WATER.

**TERMS OF PAYMENT.**—If paid for in full at time of purchase a discount will be allowed; but the purchaser may pay one-sixth in cash and the balance in five annual instalments, with interest at six per cent. per annum.

**IMPROVED FARMS** along the line to rent or for sale; a list of which can be seen at the Offices of the Company.

**TOWN LOTS FOR SALE** along the Manitoba & North-Western Railway in the following places: Arlen, Neepawa, Minnedosa, Newdale, Strathclair, Shoal Lake, Solsgirth, Birtle, Fox Warren, Binscarth, Harrowby, Langenburg.

Maps showing settlement and lists of free Government Land open for entry. Folders (in English and foreign languages). Maps, &c., and any further information can be obtained at the Offices of the Company, or by letter addressed

**A. F. EDEN, Land Commissioner M. & N. W. R.,**
*622 MAIN STREET, WINNIPEG.*

Representatives from Minnedosa, Birtle and other districts along the line can be interviewed at the above address.

PROVINCIAL ARCHIVES OF MANITOBA / N12268

*The railways and the opening of the West to settlement and agriculture went hand-in-hand. And for a time, Winnipeg was the gate through which all prospective settlers passed.*

(or Flats) site as the commercial centre of Winnipeg. To this end, in the early 1870s, it had granted land to the provincial government to construct immigrant sheds, while the company itself built a warehouse and grist mill. These buildings were all located east of Upper Fort Garry, on the north side of the Assiniboine River at its junction with the Red. The warehouse and mill were on land that is now the terraced harbour on the Assiniboine, while the immigration sheds were farther east, on what is now The Forks National Historic Site.

**W**innipeg's business community, however, had no desire to support an HBC monopoly and chose instead an area north of Upper Fort Garry, near present-day Portage and Main, to develop its centre of industry and commerce. The Flats remained undeveloped, a periphery populated by immigrants and prostitutes, largely ignored by both the HBC and the city. In the late 1870s, Winnipeg's politicians were less concerned about precisely where in the city the transcontinental rail would pass than that Winnipeg would have the railway at all.

Alexander Mackenzie, the Liberal successor to Sir John A. Macdonald as Canadian prime minister in 1873, favoured Selkirk and was immune to blandishments made by Winnipeg delegations to Ottawa. At first, Winnipeg asked only for a branch line to connect the city to Selkirk. Then it offered to build a station and a bridge across the Red if the line came through Winnipeg; finally it upped the ante by offering to pay a $200,000 subsidy to any company willing to build a rail line from Winnipeg to the province's western boundary. Mackenzie was unmoved.

There was, therefore, no joy in Winnipeg until Macdonald returned to office in 1878. During his campaign, seeking votes from the west, he had hinted at his willingness to put the main line through Winnipeg. Mass meetings were held in the city, petitions were drawn up, and subsidies offered. Leading merchant J.H. Ashdown suggested the city offer $300,000 toward building a bridge across the Red River from St. Boniface and in 1880, the city began construction of the Louise Bridge, a rail and traffic bridge across the Red about two kilometres north of The Forks. Now city council offered to pay the entire cost of building the bridge if the Dominion government would build the CPR line from Winnipeg westward.

WESTERN CANADIAN PICTORIAL INDEX / WCPI 11

S till, little progress was made until 1881, when Macdonald's government finally awarded the contract to build the Canadian Pacific Railway to a consortium of business interests led by Donald A. Smith, later Lord Strathcona. Unlike the federal government, the syndicate was more willing to consider Winnipeg's argument for a main line. In the summer of 1881, the CPR made a formal offer to locate shops in the city and build a line from Winnipeg to the southwest of the province in return for a $200,000 grant, permanent tax exemption, and land for a station. City council accepted and work began. Much to the HBC's disappointment, the new CPR station and yards were to be constructed on Point Douglas, where Main Street and Higgins Avenue meet today. Winnipeg got its rail line, but The Forks, for the interim, languished.

Winnipeg had fought hard to get its railroad and it transformed the city, bringing in immigrants, opening new markets for shippers and investors, and sparking a real estate boom that turned the city in name into a city in fact. But as the only major railway in the province, with a monopoly clause forbidding competition, the CPR had enormous power. High tariffs and rates charged by the railway angered many. Farmers in particular were up in arms over the company's monopoly. Not only did the CPR charge high rates to ship grain, it also controlled elevators and grain handling, under the direction of William Ogilvie. Ogilvie refused to ship grain that had not come from the company's own elevators. These elevators were often accused of cheating farmers by lying about the amount of dockage, or waste material, present in a sample of grain. Farmers with good grain were often paid at "damaged-grain" prices. Irate and desperate, they demanded a change.

Responding to these concerns, Manitoba Premier John

Norquay began a seesaw battle with Prime Minister Macdonald over provincial railway charters. The Manitoba legislature would pass charters allowing local companies to build lines from Winnipeg to the American border, and Ottawa would disallow them because they opposed the CPR's monopoly clause. Norquay tried chartering the Red River Valley Railway as a public works project (and therefore beyond the federal government's jurisdiction), but Macdonald used his influence to prevent London banks from loaning Norquay money. The financial scandal collapsed the Norquay government, and Norquay himself died soon after.

Thomas Greenway, Manitoba's first Liberal premier, then took up the cudgel, threatening to bring in American companies to get the lines built and offering police protection if the federal government interfered. Finally Ottawa backed down, ending the CPR monopoly and the federal disallowance of Manitoba railway legislation. In 1888, an American company, the Northern Pacific, took over the Red River Valley Railway and four other Manitoba lines to become the Northern Pacific and Manitoba Railway. The NP&M Railway

*A true Manitoban of Orcadian and Cree fur trade stock, Premier John Norquay did not hesitate to go to bat for the province's farmers. Though he didn't live to see the final outcome, his efforts initiated the struggle that led to the end of the CPR monopoly.*

PROVINCIAL ARCHIVES OF MANITOBA / N10299

# UNION STATION

CONSTRUCTED BETWEEN 1908 AND 1911, at the peak of the railway boom in Canada and amid the feverish growth of the city, Union Station was designed by Warren and Wetmore, architects of New York's Grand Central Station. Its plan and classical details were based on the Beaux Arts style, architecture that typified the City Beautiful movement so popular in North America at the time.

An imposing structure built entirely of stone, the station runs 100 metres along Main Street with its main entrance at street level in the centre of the building. In the Beaux Arts tradition, it has a three-part facade composed of a centre block and two rectangular wings.

Four storeys high with an elaborate rotunda lit by great arched windows on all four sides, it is topped with a copper dome that sits directly over where Broadway once ran through The Forks.

Using the latest in early twentieth-century design, the station incorporated innovative traffic patterns that quickly moved passengers from ticket booth to baggage area, along an undertrack subway and up to the train tracks. Passengers waiting for trains exited through the north side of the lobby to an adjoining 836-square-metre waiting room.

In its early years, immigrant passengers had an entirely different view of the station, however, for this was an era when discrimination based on race, religion and language was prevalent. To serve the needs of immigrants and yet maintain class distinctions, much of the basement area was devoted to huge waiting rooms, with a lunch counter, laundry and separate men's and women's washrooms and lounge areas.

A 1912 issue of *Railway and Marine World* carried an article that assessed the segregation of travellers this way: "It will therefore be seen that immigrants will be well provided for and will be handled to and from both trains and station without coming into contact with other passengers."

Today's basement facilities are quite different. The lower level houses a physical training center for VIA Rail, as well as tenant storage rooms. The upper floors of the station are occupied by government and corporate tenants, while on the main floor are federal and provincial government offices.

Today's ticket office is near the passenger waiting room, but the balconies, set between ribs that arch upward to the dome, still over look the gray terrazzo floor and the metre-high brown-and-tan veined marble wainscotting. Lighting for the rotunda was once provided by ornate bronze sconces; today it comes from contemporary cylindrical tube fixtures.

Despite these modernizations, Union Station at ninety is still classically beautiful. A stroll through the soaring rotunda and out onto Broadway can still elicit the same sense of wonder expressed by Parisienne artist Paul Maze, the man who taught Winston Churchill to paint. He called Union Station "one of the most beautiful sights in Canada". Little wonder that since 1990 Union Station has had Heritage Railway Station designation from the Historic Sites and Monuments Board of Canada.

Once, Union Station routinely handled as many as 8,000 passengers a day. The rumble of iron wheels on steel tracks and the lonely whistle of the engine could be heard day and night.

Today, it's a much quieter place. Twelve passenger trains a week travel the rails through Winnipeg — three from the east, three from the west and six heading north and south to and from Churchill. In an average year, slightly more than 40,000 passengers travel through the station, an average of about 110 a day.

The grand old station is still linked to The Forks, though in a rather different way than it once was. Where its twentieth-century connection was all business, with repairs, warehousing, deliveries, even heating all provided at The Forks, today the association is tourism. On arrival in Winnipeg, Via Rail's transcontinental passengers are offered tours of the market, the harbour and, if there's time, the national historic site. Many say it's the highlight of their visit to Winnipeg.

By Marjorie Gillies

DENNIS FAST

PROVINCIAL ARCHIVES OF MANITOBA / PAM 45

*Rotunda, Union Station, Winnipeg, Man.*

VALENTINE & SONS / NATIONAL ARCHIVES OF CANADA / C-14827

FROM THE DAY IT OPENED, UNION STATION WAS A CENTRE OF ACTIVITY, AS THIS 1912 RENDERING SHOWS.

*The heart of CN's success was the skill of its labour force, shown below outside and inside the B&B Building.*

bought land at the Flats and – finally – a dream of the HBC was fulfilled and the Flats were transformed.

In 1889 construction began on workshops, a roundhouse, station, train shed and freight shed. One structure survives from this era – the engine house built by the firm of Rourla and Cuns for almost $16,000, a significant sum at the time. It is the oldest surviving train repair facility in Manitoba and likely the oldest in Western Canada. It is also the oldest structure at The Forks today. Fittingly, perhaps, it now houses a facility for some of the site's youngest visitors, the Manitoba Children's Museum.

Originally, the building housed a machine and blacksmith shop, an engine house and a ten-stall roundhouse. Locomotives entered the roundhouse on tracks that ran the length of the building, then were pivoted on a turntable, enabling them to enter the appropriate repair stall. In both the engine shop and the roundhouse, large pits in the ground enabled repairmen to work from beneath the locomotives, while cranes were used to lift the chassis off the wheel assemblies. The roundhouse was demolished in the mid-1920s; the other major change to the complex was the roof. Once peaked, after a fire in 1938, the present-day flat roof was built. The pits were filled before the building, often called the B & B Building (initially for the Boiler and Brake Building, and latterly for the Bridge and Building Department) was transformed.

The immigration sheds were torn down in the early 1880s; by the 1890s, the shanties on the Flats had all disappeared. The prostitutes moved on to Point Douglas, the poor and the destitute dispersed and in their place stood the NP&M rail yard and, nearby on Water Street, the luxurious Manitoba Hotel. Built in 1891 and foreshadowing the grand CP and CN hotels that would rise in the decades to follow, it was considered the finest hotel in Canada.

Two years later, a group of Winnipeg citizens announced plans for an athletic park to be built on the Flats, complete with race track, grandstand and concessions. Land was leased from the HBC and the company, which supported the idea, started building. Though uncompleted, a three-square-block facility opened that summer, bordered by Christie and Main Streets to the east and west, and Broadway to the north. The park had a frontage of 200 metres on Main Street, with a two-storey grandstand – which burned down in 1906 – not far from where Union Station sits today. But most of the Flats still

LACOME COLLECTION / LA7

LACOME COLLECTION / L10

DR. F. MATHEWSON / WESTERN CANADIAN
PICTORIAL INDEX /504-16116

lay empty and unused, and before long, the athletic park would be cleared for bigger and more profitable schemes.

In February 1899, the Manitoba Hotel was destroyed by fire. Burdened with debt, the NP&M was unable to rebuild. But the year before, in 1898, William Mackenzie and Donald Mann, former contractors for the CPR, had created the Canadian Northern Railway, from an amalgamation of rail and shipping companies. In 1901, the CNoR took over NP&M's yard, operations and equipment, and enlarged its Winnipeg repair shops.

In 1903, the CNoR bought twenty-four additional acres of land from the HBC and made an agreement with its rival, the Grand Trunk Pacific Railway, to share the facilities in Winnipeg. In return for the land purchase, the HBC required that the CNoR build a passenger station and an office building within three years. When the *Manitoba Free Press* published a map of the CNoR's plans for improving the Flats in November that year, it was clear that those plans would not include an athletic park. The site was to be solely a rail yard.

After thousands of years as a largely accessible public meeting place, the junction of the Red and Assiniboine very quickly became what they would be for most of the twentieth century — private property.

Until the late 1980s, this area would be inaccessible to and largely unseen by anyone but railway employees and the few train passengers who cared to cast their eyes over an industrial landscape. A 1.5-metre embankment, extending along the western edge of the riverbank from Main to Lombard Avenue, had been created in the late 1880s when the NP&M Railway had raised and levelled the Flats in preparation for building its railyard. For a decade, the embankment had kept the freight yards from a river view. Now Broadway east of Main Street was closed, severing the historic connection to St. Boniface, once made possible by ferries and since 1882 by the Broadway Bridge. Even from Main Street, the view of this historic area was eliminated by the four-metre railway embankment that stretched along the east side of Main from the Assiniboine River to Lombard Avenue. When the Hudson's Bay Company built a warehouse on part of the Fort Garry Park site in 1911, access to the East Yards, as the property was now called, was effectively sealed.

Here in the heart of Winnipeg, but removed from public view, the Canadian Northern and the Grand Trunk Pacific built an up-to-the-minute transportation facility. Operations were conducted in enclosed sheds and platforms, including the two buildings, constructed in 1909 and 1910, that contain today's

*Elegant and sophisticated, the Manitoba Hotel, left, was also very convenient. NP&M trains passed right under a covered platform at the rear of the hotel, allowing guests to debark in comfort at their destination. The same concept would be used in Ottawa when the Chateau Laurier was built.*

*This 1892 plan, below, shows Fort Garry Park, with its double track and grandstand.*

NATIONAL ARCHIVES OF CANADA
NATIONAL MAP COLLECTION /
GUINN P-353

Chapter 7 | Gateway to the West                                                                                                137

*This watercolour, right, of Water Street, at the north edge of the East Yards, gives a sense of the industrial power the railways brought to Manitoba.*

*Troops leaving Union Station in 1915, below, apparently had little inkling of the horrors that awaited them overseas. War was still believed to be an adventure.*

PROVINCIAL ARCHIVES OF MANITOBA / PAM 36

PROVINCIAL ARCHIVES OF MANITOBA / 31

*Crossroads of the Continent*

Forks Market. Originally designed as stables by Warren and Wetmore, the architects of both Union Station (see page 134) and New York's Grand Central Station, the larger, more northerly building was built for the Canadian National Cartage Company, an affiliate of the CNoR. Two storeys high and thirty by twenty-nine metres, it could house 120 horses. In 1938, the stables were converted into a garage to accommodate the replacement of horses and carts with cars and trucks.

The second building, for the Grand Trunk Pacific Railway, was an almost exact replica of the first, but 14.4 metres shorter, with a peaked rather than flat roof. It could accommodate 100 horses. This building was converted into a garage at about the same time as the National Cartage stable next door.

By 1911, the year Union Station opened, twenty-four rail lines radiated out from Winnipeg. The following year, Winnipeg's Joint Terminal project was completed, with three new freight sheds. In the eyes of some, in the space of just over a quarter century, the Flats had been transformed from "a disreputable flood plain" into a thriving industrial centre.

The fortunes of the East Yards ebbed and flowed over the course of the next seventy-five years. The Canadian Northern and Grand Trunk Pacific, financed by heavy borrowing, became increasingly financially troubled when the 1914 outbreak of the Great War – World War I – diverted the credit of English banks. While the war turned Winnipeg into Western Canada's military centre, the departure or stopover place for thousands of soldiers and transfer point for myriad war goods, Winnipeg's remarkable – and unsustainable – period of exuberant growth came slowly to a halt. Mackenzie and Mann declared bankruptcy in 1917. The Canadian government, itself cash-strapped by war, refused a loan and instead took over the CNoR. Between 1917 and 1923, the CNoR, the Grand Trunk,

# NARROW LEAF SUNFLOWER (*Helianthus*)

THE EASILY RECOGNIZABLE SUNFLOWER is thought to have originated in South America, perhaps in Peru. Today as many as sixty wild species are found and many more have been cultivated. True to their name, they resemble a child's drawing of a sun, and turn their showy heads to follow the sun from morning till night.

The narrow-leaf sunflower, a smaller-flowered member of the family, can be found in tall grass prairies from Manitoba to Texas. Like its cousins, it is tall and slender, with long narrow leaves.

The yellow ray flowers or petals give the plant its name, but it is the disk flower, the dark seed-filled centre, that has always been prized for food. Humans have been using the hard-shelled seeds for centuries, perhaps millennia, eating the seeds raw or roasted, pounding them into a meal or crushing and boiling them for oil. But animals, from songbirds and game birds to moose, deer and antelope also crave them.

Sunflowers quickly became one of the most ubiquitous cultivated plants as the railways brought settlers to Western Canada. Tall and showy, they could be seen growing in almost every farmyard. Interestingly, when farms were abandoned during the 1930s, cultivated sunflowers, with their huge disk flowers, would quickly revert to the native type of the area.

Today, huge fields of sunflowers are grown across North America and provide one of our most widely-used cooking oils.

and three other financially troubled railways were amalgamated; Canadian National Railways, the CNR, a rival, government-operated national carrier to the CPR, emerged.

In 1917, workers in the East Yards were affected by the influenza epidemic that killed more people worldwide than did the Great War itself and two years later, in 1919, the

PROVINCIAL ARCHIVES OF MANITOBA / PAM 39

*Crossroads of the Continent*

Winnipeg General Strike significantly affected activities at the yards, auguring a postwar economic depression that dragged on for several years before giving way to the Roaring Twenties.

PROVINCIAL ARCHIVES OF MANITOBA / PAM 50

By the mid-1920s, a spirit of emancipation was sweeping North America; hemlines rose, music – and musicians – changed and for the first time, large numbers of people were travelling simply for recreation. Confident and innovative, a man of the times, CNR president Sir Henry Thornton recognized the potential of combining these enthusiasms. With jazz taking hold of the music world, and radio creating new audiences, Thornton established the first coast-to-coast network in North America by installing radio receivers on CN passenger trains. To ensure a steady diet of programming, he built radio stations in the company's major hotels across Canada, including the Fort Garry, and hired professional bands and

PROVINCIAL ARCHIVES OF MANITOBA / 40

orchestras. The performers often played for two audiences at once, one dining *in situ* and the other thundering across the country. The network, which also aired political speeches, foreshadowed the establishment of the Canadian Broadcasting Corporation by a full decade. Music also infused the company's rank and file. CN employees put together bands of their own, some of which – the Railroad Porters Band, for example – drew national attention as it toured the country in the 1920s.

At Union Station, the stirring music of bagpipes could be heard from time to time, as pipers welcomed visiting royalty or Canadian prime ministers. And music filled the huge space every New Year's Eve during the 1920s and '30s, as public celebrations were held, at no charge, for as many as 1,500 Winnipeggers.

This lightened mood was not to last for long, however.

*The Railroad Porters Minstrels Band, opposite page, is seen on tour here in May 1922.*

*Another Winnipeg band, lower left, the Transcona Shops CNR Band.*

*All this musical talent was beamed across the country to radio cars such as this one, above, pictured receiving a transcontinental broadcast in 1930.*

*Grand Trunk Pacfic Railway workers are pictured about 1913, perched atop the railway turntable.*

Six years after the CNR was formed, the stock market crashed and the Depression of the 1930s forced lay-offs and cutbacks. CN did what it could to lessen the impact on its employees, reducing work weeks to keep more of them on the job. The effort was generally appreciated, for working fewer hours was

better than not working at all.

There was also growth and change at The Forks during this period. In 1928, a four-storey cold-storage warehouse was constructed just east of the two stables and immediately leased

by the National Cartage Company, which was experiencing an increase in traffic. Despite the Depression, two years later the building was greatly expanded. In 1962, a new tenant, Johnston National Cartage Company (later Johnston Terminal) occupied it. This name has remained with the building to this day.

Today's visitors to Johnston Terminal's shops and restaurants may notice the building's unusual shape; its southeast corner looks as though it has been cut off. In a way, it was; the warehouse was constructed to conform to a track that once curved against its east side.

Over the decades, the East Yards were used not only as a freight and terminal centre, trans-shipment point and repair location, but also as a junkyard. For nearly a century, beginning in the 1880s, chipped ceramics and broken glass were routinely dumped in designated areas. And even before that, it seems that the burgeoning City of Winnipeg had used at least one riverbank location as a refuse dump. The entire site was, in short, a historical repository – an archive of sorts.

Years later, when the junction of the two rivers was transformed, yet again, and rejuvenated as a meeting place for the people, hundreds of pieces of china and glassware helped to tell the story of the last century. Archaeologists had a field day, identifying hundreds of pieces of china and glassware. Initially classified by colour, the dinnerware was then examined more closely to determine whether manufacturers' marks (and therefore dates) could be found. By cross-referencing  several pieces of white dinnerware decorated with blue lines, it was found that they had been decorated with the railroad logo "CNR", but whether that denoted the Canadian Northern or Canadian National Railway was not clear. Sherds of Blue Willow china were also found. In attempting to further

WESTERN CANADIAN PICTORIAL INDEX / WCPI I5

identify the manufacturer, archaeologist Sid Kroker was told that the pattern is described in the following folklore verse:

Three little birds flying high
A little vessel sailing by
A bridge with three and not with four
A weeping willow hanging o'er
An apple tree with apples on
A great long fence to end my song.

The dinnerware and ornamental ceramics were produced by a wide variety of manufacturers, often British, but also French, Belgian, Bavarian and, particularly for later samples, even Canadian.

In addition to ceramics, large quantities of glass, bottles and containers were found in many places on the site. Together, they painted a picture of the evolution of commercial glassmaking over the twentieth century. The amethyst color of some specimens made it clear that they were produced before 1914; the color is due to the presence of manganese, which causes glass to turn a rich amethyst colour when exposed to light for a prolonged period. Since Germany controlled most of the world's supply of manganese, the outbreak of World War I caused manufacturers to cease using it. Of the specimens found, seven complete amethyst bottles bore the Hudson's Bay Company crest.

Other early bottles were often aqua in colour, with a turned lip, into which a cork stopper was usually placed. Milk bottles, however, were invariably clear, sometimes with

ribbed "panelling" and embossing that usually identified the dairy. One unbroken specimen was embossed with "CITY DAIRY", which operated in Winnipeg between 1915 and 1952. Other sherds came from Crescent Creamery.

A vast variety of other items were also found as the excavations progressed, including stoneware, earthenware, metal and wire. Among these were handwrought nails, all manufactured before 1885, shoes with lace hooks and household goods of every conceivable item. All these things – commonplace reminders of everyday life – said much about the business of railway travel. For most of their combined history, the various railway companies located at the East Yards served average Canadians engaged in normal pursuits. Sometimes, in fact, those

*This elaborately decorated plate and blue and white pitcher were among thousands of pieces of china, dinnerware and ornamental ceramics that were found among a myriad of other castoffs among the tracks and buildings when reclamation activities were undertaken in the late 1980s.*

*Found in 1996 under Main Street in a cellar of Upper Fort Garry, the multi-coloured plate was manufactured by Spode prior to 1850. The design, known as King Sheet, was identified by the curator of the Spode Museum in England. The elaborate colour indicates that it was an expensive item. It probably belonged to the wife of the Governor of the HBC.*

*Streetcar tracks, rather than railway tracks led to the front door of Union Station for many years. This is the view looking east on Broadway in 1938.*

normalcies were pursued with such intensity that they became extraordinary. Winnipeggers' passion for their beaches was one example.

Canadian Northern began running passenger trains to Grand Beach on the east side of Lake Winnipeg in June 1916 – in the midst of the Great War. By war's end, the company was providing daily service except on Sundays and in the late 1920s, Union Station handled as many as 8,000 passengers in a single day. Fares in 1934 were a dollar for a day's round trip, $2.20 on weekends and for the romantically inclined, there was a Moonlight service, just as the CPR provided for visitors to beaches on the west side of the lake.

There were dramatic times, too. Between 1939 and 1945, CN again played a key role, ferrying troops both east and west during the Second World War. Again, the huge rotunda of Union Station reverberated with military bands as soldiers departed for war and again it echoed with tears when far too many failed to return.

In 1947, a steam plant was built to supply power to the East Yards as well as to Union Station, the Hotel Fort Garry, and the Manitoba Club. Today the quaint building, which survived several demolition plans, houses the A-Channel television studios. And three years later, heavy snow and warm April temperatures combined to create an event that is almost synonymous with the Red River Valley – a spring flood.

**W**innipeggers had seen floods before; in1882 the first Broadway bridge, christened just days before, was swept away on the flood waters of the Red. But this was unlike anything any living person had seen, the worst inundation since 1826, when almost everything at The Forks had washed away or been grievously damaged.

Now, the waters rose over the yards, covering the tracks and halting operations. Union Station, on high ground, was untouched, but the lower Flats – despite the metre-and-a-half of fill that covered them – were submerged. The worst hit building was the historic NP&M engine house; there water levels reached a quarter of the height of the building.

The clean-up took time, but nothing could stop the slow slide into irrelevance. Even before amalgamation, the Grand Trunk had built yards in Transcona. The CNR also had yards in Fort Rouge. When CN opened its colossal, fully automated Symington Yard in north St. Boniface in the 1960s, the writing was on the wall for its old downtown yard, which couldn't compete with the new facility's efficiencies.

By the 1980s then, the East Yards seemed superfluous. But anyone who took an opportunity to walk among the tracks along the Red River on a warm summer day might have realized that this was not only the starting point for so much of Western Canada's history, it was also where the future lay. Other cities were rediscovering their urban hearts, and few had more to work with. The railyards, after all, were only an interlude. It was time to reclaim the junction of the Red and the Assiniboine for the people of Winnipeg.

*Crossroads of the Continent*

PETER ST. JOHN

THESE TAN TILES REPRESENT THE
HIGH-WATER MARK OF THE 1950 FLOOD.
THE UPPER ROW OF TAN TILES REPRESENTS
THE HIGH-WATER MARK OF THE 1826
FLOOD - THE GREATEST FLOOD IN
MANITOBA'S RECORDED HISTORY.

WESTERN CANADIAN PICTORIAL INDEX / WCPI 10

*The great flood of 1950 left Union Station (seen in the foreground) high and dry, but drowned the rest of the East Yards. The river's edge is marked by an arch of willows at the top of the photograph. As we have seen (pages 44-45), there have been bigger floods. The tiled poles in The Forks plaza, inset, compare the levels of the 1950 flood (bottom ring) with the 1826 flood (top ring).*

# The Forks

*This is The Forks as we all know it today, a place of gatherings, with lights twinkling over the water, lovers walking by the river, friends dining in the warm summer air. But really, has it changed all that much? A thousand years ago, the people who met here at the confluence of the rivers very likely did much the same things.*

# Today

By Peter St. John

On an average summer Sunday, The Forks draws more than 28,000 people to its markets, shops, restaurants, historic features and plazas. In the winter, the concourse is packed at lunchtime and the plaza hums with activity all week long. People arrive on foot, by water taxi, by bus or by car; some skate to The Forks during the winter months, others come by train from far beyond Manitoba's borders.

Behind the news

# Dream of the rivers can be achieved

Concerts at The Forks have drawn 60,000 people; events during the 1999 Pan American Games attracted crowds of 50,000. Visiting The Forks National Historic Site, the market and the plaza, walking the river walks, climbing the tower to gaze out over the river confluence – these activities rank as No.1 when city-dwellers are showing Winnipeg off to visitors. In short, Winnipeggers are mad about The Forks. But it wasn't always so.

*The view from the mouth of the Assiniboine in 1985, with its riverside undergrowth and the Hotel Fort Garry beyond, gave little hint of what was soon to come.*

FOR A CENTURY, BETWEEN 1888 AND 1988, the confluence of the Red and Assiniboine Rivers was almost completely out of sight and out of mind. Apart from those who worked for Canadian National Railways at what were known as the East Yards, this continental crossroads had disappeared from public consciousness. Crisscrossed by railway tracks, littered with heaps of debris, edged by rivers that had become little more than sewers, this once-bountiful meeting place had all but vanished, as far as most Winnipeggers were concerned.

Winnipeg was not alone in this neglect of its riverbanks and waterways. Many other cities – London, St. Louis and Minneapolis among them – had done the same. All over the Western world, the development of paved roads had diverted attention away from the rivers and the development of industry had lowered both air and water quality. Winnipeg had been aware of the state of its rivers since the late nineteenth century, when river-borne typhoid had repeatedly swept through the city, killing hundreds of people, many of them the elderly and the very young. For the "Chicago of the North", it was a grim reminder that development had a price tag. The city's response was to pipe potable water, via an aquaduct, west from Shoal Lake, but raw sewage and industrial waste continued to pour into the rivers.

The next warning came with the flood of 1950; the sludge that remained when the water receded appalled many. Still, little was done. But public attitudes were changing, both abroad and in Canada. When the fish all died in the Thames River in the 1960s, it not only spurred changes in Britain, but provided fodder for the fledgling environmental movement and encouraged a growing consciousness of the opportunities and values suggested by historic waterways. London was built to be seen from the river and Winnipeg had been settled from the rivers; people began to wonder what had been lost.

Columnist Val Werier was one of these. As early as 1968, he and his close friend D.I. Macdonald, the first commissioner of the newly-unified City of Winnipeg, used to tromp through

THE FORKS NORTH PORTAGE PARTNERSHIP

*Crossroads of the Continent*

the East Yards, talking and dreaming about what could be done to reclaim the heart of Winnipeg's heritage. By 1973, Werier was writing about his dream in *The Winnipeg Tribune*: "the 65 acres of East Yards cradled in a loop of the Assiniboine and Red Rivers", he called it. He and Macdonald were now convinced of its historic significance and of the need to liberate it from a century of enslavement to the railways. They reasoned that the era of the railways would inevitably end and knew the junction of the rivers might easily fall into commercial hands. They also believed there were better options.

Others were thinking about the land at the historic confluence, for different reasons and with different ends in view. One was the federal government, which had responsibility for nationally significant historic sites and rivers Canada-wide. It was pursuing an obligation to preserve the crucial fur trade routes and sites that had created Canada; among these were the Red and Assiniboine and the various forts that had stood at their confluence.

Not surprisingly CNR, an empire builder in its own right, was also interested. It owned the East Yards, but realized the facilities there were dated and, after the creation of Symington Yards, all but obsolete. Yet the land itself was a rare commodity indeed – undeveloped real estate at the heart of a large city. The company could be expected to hold out for a good price.

Both the provincial and civic governments were interested in The Forks. Not only could they expect to either lose or gain from whatever developed there, but should the development create public space, they would likely be administratively responsible for the result. Moreover, both governments were responsible to the citizens of Manitoba and Winnipeg for the creation of public spaces for leisure and enjoyment.

Finally, there were the visionaries, those citizens, whether history buffs, environmentalists, landscape planners or poets, who saw the enormous potential for public recreation at The Forks. They envisioned a magical green space emerging phoenix-like from the cinders and steel track. It would take imagination, but they had it in spades.

Through the 1970s, the interaction between these groups led in the 1980s and '90s to something quite unprecedented: the creation of a forty-five hectare green space for public recreation and entertainment, parachuted by a tri-level government agreement into the centre of a city – a place for gatherings and celebrations.

*This aerial view of the CN East Yards, taken from the north, shows the B & B Building in the left foreground, Johnston Terminal in the centre and what are now the two wings of The Forks Market – originally built as stables for the Canadian National Cartage Company and the Grand Trunk Pacific Railway – in the upper right.*

*Inspired by Prime Minister Trudeau's Byways Program, the redevelopment of The Forks was nudged along by many who believed it was the "pearl of the [Red River rejuvenation] project".*

**P**inpointing the precise beginning of this remarkable process isn't easy, but perhaps a good place to start is on August 1, 1972, when Prime Minister Pierre Trudeau announced his Byways and Special Places Program in Winnipeg, "to commemorate historic communication routes in Canada by preserving and adapting them for recreational use."

The Red River from the American border to Lower Fort Garry National Historic Site, a river distance of 160 kilometres, was immediately identified as a principal historic route in Western Canada. It had not only serviced the fur trade and subsequent settlement, but had been an artery for travel for centuries before. Trudeau's announcement led to the Red and Assiniboine Rivers Tourism and Recreation Study in 1974, overseen by Manitoba's assistant deputy minister of Tourism and Recreation, Mary Liz Bayer, and implemented by the landscape architecture firm of Garry Hilderman and Associates. The firm identified seventeen sites of significance along the Red River, including the river confluence. For Hilderman it was the beginning of a long love affair with The Forks.

Meanwhile, in November 1973, columnist Val Werier wrote, "There's a magnificent stretch of land in the centre of the city that offers an unparalleled opportunity for Winnipeg. [It's] a great place for a park." Because of the historic and scenic

Behind the news

By Val Werier

## It's Winnipeg's move on river-junction project

NOV 2 0 1974

significance of the junction of the rivers, Werier reported, CN was firmly committed to working with all three levels of

government to achieve a mutually acceptable solution for all. He went on to quote CN vice-president N. J. MacMillan, a former Winnipegger:

"The acreage between the present CN station and the Red and Assiniboine Rivers is the most historic land site in Western Canada. I've had a dream for years to liberate the area for a more suitable use than railyards."

Still nothing happened. Undaunted, in 1975 Werier called the site "this most glamorous stretch of land" and enthused, "the city and CN have an unusual opportunity to do something exciting at the historic junction of the rivers." He also pointed out that Mayor Steven Juba was on side, and particularly interested in including restaurants and other facilities to attract people down to the site.

While ideas were thus percolating, Trudeau's original Byways Program evolved into the Agreements for Recreation and Culture or ARC program. Under general manager Ian Dickson, the agreement developed seventeen sites along the Red River with $14.1 million in federal funding. Among the sites were the Trappist Monastery in St. Norbert, St. Boniface Cathedral and nearby docks, Twin Oaks and Kennedy House on River Road and the Selkirk Marine Museum. Professor Jean Friesen, later to be minister of culture and heritage for the province, played a leading role in the sites along River Road and later became deeply involved in The Forks project. But until The Forks was part of the chain of sites, Dickson felt the rejuvenation of the historic Red River was incomplete. "The Forks," he said, "would be the pearl in the whole project."

Others agreed. In May 1986, a second agreement was signed, earmarking $3.5 million for the creation of a national historic site, owned and operated by Parks Canada.

It would stretch from the river confluence to Provencher Bridge and would "commemorate the junction as a place of national historic significance in the development ... of the West."

Encompassing just 5.5 hectares of riverside land, it would include a multi-use open area for festivities, events and heritage programs, an amphitheatre, a river promenade, a boat dock, an interpretive area and a pedestrian link to Juba Park. With initial plans by Ross McGowan's Lombard North firm and detailed design by Hilderman, Witty, Crosby, Hanna and Associates, work began in 1987.

IMAGES THIS PAGE: THE FORKS NORTH PORTAGE PARTNERSHIP

*The Forks National Historic Site, seen at left in more recent years, and the initial stretch of the riverwalk were undertaken in 1987. The following year, inset, it seemed that the ring park might be "an island of renewal", in a sea of railway tracks.*

*Landscape architect Garry Hilderman recalls that during construction of the riverwalk "we couldn't keep the people off the construction site on weekends. It was the first time Winnipeggers had been able to walk the riverbanks at river level."*

151

IMAGES THIS PAGE: THE FORKS NORTH PORTAGE PARTNERSHIP

minister Lloyd Axworthy, the initiator of the CAI and the man who "broke the mold on urban renewal", the parties could not reach an agreement with CN over the East Yards. The price was simply too high; in addition to payment for the land, the railway wanted assistance with rail relocation.

*It took imagination, talent and more than a little faith to transform the B & B Building, above and Johnston Terminal, at right.*

Almost immediately, however, the flow of federal funds began to dry up and soon it seemed that, when completed, the national site might be an island of renewal in a sea of abandoned railway tracks. A beachhead had been created, but would it be enough to reclaim The Forks as a whole? In the meantime, CN was playing hardball and the bottom line was money. To outsiders, prospects for The Forks looked dim.

But The Forks had several guardian angels waiting in the wings. Among them were those involved with the Core Area Initiative (CAI), a tri-level funding agreement aimed at revitalizing Winnipeg's urban core. Its key sites were the north Logan industrial area, the north Portage retail and commercial area and the CN East Yards. In the first five years of the agreement, between 1980 and 1985, progress was made on the first two areas, but despite the substantial efforts of federal cabinet

Years later, Al Baronas, secretary to the tri-level East Yards task force, recalled, "Lloyd Axworthy's role was critical in creating and driving the Core Area Initiative, which was ultimately the mechanism that created The Forks. But Lloyd could not reach an agreement with CN."

By 1985, when the Core Area agreement came up for renewal, the federal Liberals had been replaced by Brian Mulroney's Conservatives and Jake Epp was minister in charge of the CAI. Winnipeg's chief commissioner, Nick Diakiw, met with Epp. "I remember," Daikiw says, "that Jake Epp asked me:

*Crossroads of the Continent*

'What federal project would be of the greatest service to Winnipeg? What would be an enduring legacy?' And I replied, "The Forks: something entirely new and yet old and historic."

The response gave Epp a focus that brought back important family memories. Decades before, his grandfather had made the three-day journey from Steinbach with horse and buggy to sell vegetables at The Forks. Now, though more than sixty per cent of Manitoba's population lived in Winnipeg, no one had any access to the province's place of birth.

"I believe that events work together for a purpose," Epp says in retrospect, recalling how he watched the Skydome being built in Toronto, and the Granville Island project developing in Vancouver. These projects, as well as the riverbank development in Saskatoon, gave him ammunition to pressure Industry and Transport Minister Don Mazankowski for cabinet support over The Forks. It's no different than Vancouver's Stanley Park, he told his cabinet colleagues; it's a wonderful potential green space at the heart of Winnipeg.

"Lloyd Axworthy had tried earlier, and given us the vision of what could be done," Epp muses. "The river gives Paris its personality; why not celebrate Winnipeg with its two rivers?"

But celebration is one thing, cutting a deal is another. In the end it was land and not money that made an agreement possible; the federal government turned over a twelve-million-dollar office tower in downtown Vancouver in exchange for fifty-eight acres, or 23.7 hectares, at The Forks. CN retained seven hectares along the tracks.

Epp is modest about his contribution. "It's the sparks that light the fire," he says. "[Mayor] Bill Norrie, Cam MacLean [chair of the interim Board of Directors] and Nick Diakiw all promoted The Forks. They were visionary people. I was simply

the one who got the land through cabinet."

But Diakiw believes Epp deserves more credit. "If any one person was responsible for The Forks, it was Jake Epp. He was the one who brought the land to the table."

With the logjam broken, development at The Forks could continue and in 1988, as the work was near completion on the national historic site, the physical transformation from rail yards to No. 1 attraction began, under the aegis of the Core Area Initiative. Though there were undoubtedly differing visions for The Forks, the passion to see it reclaimed for the people of Winnipeg was shared by all. The people took command of the process, Diakiw says.

In fact, a small corps of them had been at work since at least 1986, when the tri-level East Yards Task Force was established, with Tony Reynolds representing the federal government, Peter Diamant the province and Diakiw and Dave Henderson the city of Winnipeg. Supported by architect Etienne Gaboury, financial planner Cam Osler, city planner Ross McGowan and a trio of

*In 1988 four of the major players met to discuss The Forks development. From left, MLA Larry Desjardins, Core Area Initiative CEO Jim August, MP Jake Epp and Mayor Bill Norrie.*

IMAGES THIS PAGE: THE FORKS NORTH PORTAGE PARTNERSHIP

enthusiasts – Jim August, Janet Walker and Al Baronas – in the office, the task force was ordered to come up with the first five-year plan in just eight months.

To do the plan justice, the task force not only had to collect information on the long history of The Forks, as well as the structures that sat on the property, but also to discover what had been done elsewhere in similar reclamation projects – including, of course, the mistakes that had been made. Then, the group had to develop a plan that would create an all-season recreational facility with an emphasis on the past and a view to the future. It should have a riverfront focus and open views and sight lines, yet still be part of Winnipeg's downtown. It sounds well-nigh impossible, but remarkably, the task force achieved it, and indeed went farther.

Looking over the plan, one can see the influence of Gaboury, who as a French-speaking resident of St. Boniface believed his community had been cut off, psychologically speaking, from Winnipeg by the creation of the East Yards and the closure of the Broadway Bridge in 1912. As had the original planners of the city, who had meant Broadway to flow right across the river, in a straight line, to join Provencher, Gaboury envisioned strong links between the rivers and the urban centre. He wanted to celebrate the environment and work with it, not against it. He urged the group to insist on a year-round facility, to be used by all cultures, all ages and all levels of interest. Throughout, he said, the plan must emphasize heritage protection and interpretation.

After visiting Vancouver's Granville Island, as well as projects in Detroit, Toronto, Minneapolis and Washington, the task force spent several weekends brainstorming at Shoal Lake and submitted its report late in 1986. It recommended the establishment of The Forks Renewal Corporation, to be run by a board of ten appointed members. Armed with a budget of $20.1 million for the first five-year phase, the board would oversee a public development corporation that would make decisions at arm's length from government, always with a focus on the mandate of The Forks. And always working toward an ultimate goal of self-sufficiency.

*Construction of the Market Courtyard, which linked the two stable or storage buildings, at right, began early in 1988. Just over a year later, opposite, the courtyard was attracting throngs of people.*

IMAGES THIS PAGE : THE FORKS NORTH PORTAGE PARTNERSHIP

*Crossroads of the Continent*

An interim board of directors was appointed in May of 1987. Chaired by Cam MacLean, and including representatives of all three levels of government, it was instructed to finalize the plan for The Forks following – and here's the challenge – public hearings. Even before embarking, the board realized the public consultation process would be a crucial element in the planning process. "We had been very active about the whole Forks project and its potential," recalls Nick Diakiw, "yet it seemed ninety-nine per cent of Winnipeggers knew nothing about it. So we asked for and received 150 written and oral submissions."

For the veteran city manager, the public consultations were among the hardest things he had ever done. They were

THE FORKS NORTH PORTAGE PARTNERSHIP

## BLANKET FLOWER (*Gaillardia aristata*)

Though named for a French botanist, Gaillard de Marentonneau, gaillardia is a North American flower and one of the signal plants of the tall grass prairies that once stretched from southeastern Manitoba to Texas. With its ray of yellowy-orange florets set in a reddish-purple centre, it has long brightened the prairies in early summer. Another popular name for it is "firewheel".

The flowers branch from a stalk anywhere between twenty and sixty centimetres high, which in turn grows from a slender taproot. This hardy perennial of the daisy family is not only widely cultivated in gardens today, but has been used in many places as part of a campaign to reintroduce indigenous plants to the verges of highways. It grows at The Forks in the Tall Grass Prairie Garden and the Native Species Garden near the entrance sculpture at The Forks NHS.

often tense, with high – and sometimes diametrically opposed – expectations. Paul Jordan, operations manager at The Forks today, laughs at how Diakiw, who had managed a staff of 10,000, would shake at the prospect of each new public confrontation. By the end of the process, however, the people of Winnipeg had taken ownership of The Forks, and changed the original plans. "It was the people who drove the process," Diakiw reflected later. "For instance, originally there was to be a residential component to the plan, yet seventy per cent of the people were against housing."

By December 1987, the interim board had confirmed the Phase I plan, approved the land transfer and completed the search for a first CEO. To no one's surprise, that person was Nick Diakiw, a man with a reputation for getting things done.

The Forks National Historic Site opened in the summer

One of the reasons – or perhaps that should be twenty-one of the reasons – The Forks works as well as it does is its coterie of volunteers, the members of its Ambassador Program operated jointly by The Forks and Parks Canada. These devoted Winnipeggers assist at special events, meet VIA Rail trains, accompany school and seniors tours, guide tour buses and patrol the site every

# FORKS AMBASSADORS

day, answering questions, offering information and assistance – and generally making a visit to The Forks that much more special.

Led by Visitor Services Coordinator Leesa Carter, who spent several years as a volunteer herself before taking the position, the Ambassadors share a passion for the place and a desire to make it memorable for others. Like the group from southern China, for example, who arrived during winter and, having never experienced snow before, wanted to go tobogganing. "So I got them a toboggan and sent them up the slide ..." Carter says, recalling. "It's really steep, and it was quite cold ... you should have seen their faces as they came down. But you know, they wanted to do it all over again. And this time, they wanted their picture taken."

When it was over, she exchanged cards with them, wondering if she'd ever hear from them again. A few weeks later, a photograph arrived in the mail, along with a letter telling her that the tobogganing episode had been one of the highlights of their trip – something none of them would ever forget.

It's the kind of thing that brings the volunteers back year after year. Though they're required to sign on for a minimum of six months, some of her crew have been Ambassadors for six years or more. Carter herself has seven years experience.

The number of volunteers at The Forks on a given day varies, of course. There are always at least two working out of the Information Caboose on the site; special events, like Parks Day, can triple that number.

The caboose itself is of interest to many Forks visitors, and the Ambassadors are happy to give conducted tours. These are likely somewhat more leisurely than the tours offered to east–bound VIA rail passengers when their train arrives twice a week at Union Station.

"The stop is supposed to be a half-hour," Carter says, "but it rarely is. And you'd be surprised how much you can cram into twenty minutes. A dash to the market, some fresh baked goods, a quick look at the harbour and back – all before the train leaves."

It's clear she finds the work rewarding, and still believes, as she did when The Forks was just a dream, that "this is the jewel in the crown of our city."

of 1989, just as The Forks corporation began Phase I of the transformation. It says much for the architects involved in all the phases of The Forks – Garry Hilderman, Etienne Gaboury and Steve and Cynthia Cohlmeyer, who designed the Forks historic port and public square, as well as the Tall Grass Prairie Garden, that there is such continuity in the original planning. To this day, it is impossible to distinguish the boundaries between the national historic site and the larger public space.

Of course, nothing could be done until the rail lines, heaps of debris, layers of cinders and thousands of cobblestones had been removed. Not all of this was refuse. The piles of debris provided an archive of sorts for site archaeologist Sid Kroker, and the cobblestones proved to be historical treasures. They were real paving stones, not unlike the sort that create the surface of some of Britain's oldest streets – though these are sandstone, not granite – thick, heavy and all but indestructible. In London, many survived the bombing of World War II; in Winnipeg, they easily handle Winnipeg's almost as destructive winters. Today they give the main Forks parking area and the lanes around the market an authentically historic feel.

By 1989 the site had been cleared and The Forks, as we know it today, began to rise from the cinders. Steve and Cynthia Cohlmeyer, architect and landscape architect respectively, were responsible – in consultation with Gaboury – for many of the elements that Winnipeggers immediately associate with The Forks. They designed the plaza and the boat marina, the

IMAGES THIS PAGE: THE FORKS NORTH PORTAGE PARTNERSHIP

lighthouse and the viewing tower, the streets, the landscaping and the low glare lighting. The marina, says Steve Cohlmeyer, was very much a joint effort, for Gaboury continually pushed him over the design.

**T**hroughout the process, each area was first investigated by site archaeologist Sid Kroker and his team, aided by hundreds of interested volunteers (see Crossroads of the Continent on page 46). Beneath what is now the terraced approach to the marina, as well as other areas to the northeast toward Johnston Terminal, the archaeologists found the remains of fishing camps some 3,000 years old. A large section of this area was designated an archaeological preserve; to help people understand the long history of The Forks and "pique their curiosity", Cohlmeyer designed the Wall Through Time, which curves in an S-shape around the preserve from the plaza down to the riverwalk. The wall, with various levels clearly delineated by an intricate blend of brick and tile, was a gift to The Forks from the International

Union of Bricklayers and Allied Craftsmen, Local One, to commemorate 100 years of service in 1990. Drawing on a similar creation in London, it relates the history of The Forks in panels worked into the stone masonry.

Steve Cohlmeyer has studied the creation of public spaces since the early 1970s and was particularly influenced by sociological literature that focused on what attracts people to a space, makes them comfortable and gives them an incentive to return. A key to this process, he believes, is to intrigue people, and perhaps lead them to self-discovery. This may well account for the enduring attraction of the Forks plaza and boat basin. With its many levels, including the tall glass tower (which is particularly popular during periods of flooding), and its varied materials, the plaza seems to be at the heart of The Forks experience, and serves to emphasize the whole market concept.

The riverfront quay, or Forks Historic Port, was at first a modest scheme, until the instability of the riverbank – and the demands of the public – combined to make it urgently necessary to develop a well-anchored harbour with extensively layered landscaping. The project was held up

*From the Wall Through Time, background photo, to the harbour, left, as well as Oodena and the riverwalk itself, the design of The Forks imitates nature in that there are few hard edges and many curves.*

IMAGES THIS PAGE: THE FORKS NORTH PORTAGE PARTNERSHIP

*A tray full of cinnamon buns, hot from the oven, top, draws shoppers like flies.*

*Customers at the market, above, come in all sizes and every age range.*

for more than a year by a legal challenge, but Winnipeggers made it clear during the winter of 1989-90 that they intended to use the harbour, development or no development. As soon as the ice froze, they descended on The Forks from the river, quickly wearing deep channels into the bank as they scrambled from the ice surface to the plaza above.

With its deep piling and substrate pinning, the boat basin opened in 1991. Brightened at night by a lighthouse, the quay became an instant success, not only among Winnipeggers, but also those who visit the city. It's not uncommon to find tourists wandering near Portage and Main, plaintively asking passers-by for directions to "the Winnipeg harbour".

Just as popular, in every season of the year, is the riverwalk. Initially designed by Garry Hilderman as part of The Forks National Historic Site, by 1989 a second stretch had been completed by Steve Cohlmeyer from the river junction to the Main Street railway bridge. People thronged to it, immediately demonstrating its popularity. Believing the walk should continue along the north bank of the Assiniboine, provincial cabinet minister Larry Desjardins insisted on setting aside another three million dollars to extend it to the Manitoba legislature. Though it has been plagued in recent years by summer flooding, the walkway is used in all four seasons by Winnipeggers. It is so popular that following a spring or summer inundation, crews find they have only hours to clean up the debris before people are themselves flooding onto the walk.

As we will see later in this chapter, the problems with high water in summer could potentially be a thing of the past, for the province, realizing the passion that Winnipeggers have for their riverwalks (and their more recently introduced water taxi system), is looking into whether it might make better use of the floodways in future, when high water threatens.

While all this work was going on along the rivers, the buildings on the site were being assessed, stabilized and renovated. As indicated in Gateway to the West, our chapter on the railway period (see page 126), some of these buildings had long and colourful histories and one was, at least by Winnipeg standards, very old. The brick buildings that now constitute The Forks Marketplace were built in 1909 and 1910 as stables for a cartage company that worked for Canadian Northern Railway, CN's predecessor. Gazing upward, visitors to the market can still see the arched entries that marked each stable and imagine the haylofts that once occupied the second floor. Today, joined by a glass atrium, the stables shelter a busy marketplace, with dozens of shops and restaurants and several offices.

Opened in 1989, the market has been a huge success. Not only is it a consistent money-maker, but it draws people to The Forks like a magnet. And as Winnipeggers have become increasingly food conscious, its shops and stalls are increasingly popular. Here, for example, is one of the few places in the city to buy bison roasts and cuts, to purchase organic vegetables, or an array of products made from beeswax. Pop in any morning and the smell of freshly-baked cinnamon buns is all but irresistible. Here, too, are specialty goods such as handmade jewelry, native crafts and a huge variety of cards and paper goods.

Nearby Johnston Terminal, built between 1928 and '30, was initially slated to be redeveloped as a hotel, but a failure of private financing led to its current development as

*Crossroads of the Continent*

THE FORKS NORTH PORTAGE PARTNERSHIP

PETER ST.JOHN

*Whether dining on the plaza on a summer evening or shopping on a winter afternoon, people find the attractions of The Forks Market almost irresistible.*

came to mean Bridges and Building Department). After several years of community fundraising driven by then-Winnipegger Linda Isitt, in 1994 the Manitoba Children's Museum moved from its original home in the Exchange District into the completely renovated space. For Winnipeg's youngest citizens, it has proved to be immensely popular.

The pavilion skating oval and canopy was created in 1990 and has become a focal point for hundreds of events at The Forks, from the boxing events of the 1990 Western Canada Summer Games to Christmas at The Forks and performances during royal visits. In between, it serves as a public skating rink – one of several on the site – in winter and a canopied multipurpose space in spring, summer and fall.

Predictably, both at the national historic site and The Forks Market, heritage events and activities have played an important part in the whole development process. Sid Kroker saw his role as site archaeologist as part of the bigger picture. "I was in charge of the recognition of The Forks as a repository of cultural knowledge," he says, looking back. And, as the previous chapters have outlined, there was culture from at least 6,000 years to acknowledge. It included the long human history at The Forks and the recognition of its role as an important gathering and trading site. Different cultures have come together here for thousands of years, at times, it seems, for agricultural and diplomatic reasons as well as to fish and trade. This role as a gathering and trading place continued through the fur trade and immigration eras and it seemed from the beginning that Winnipeggers

*It's fitting, perhaps, that the oldest building on the site now houses attractions for the youngest visitors.*

commercial space; the Travel Idea Centre, with shelves of information on Manitoba attractions, was added to the northwest end. At Johnston Terminal, visitors can celebrate Christmas all year long, gossip with friends at one of the best coffee bars in town – incidentally a favorite of Bono, lead singer of U2 – or dine with a view of North America's endangered tall grass prairie.

Farther northeast, the B&B Building was the oldest on the site and indeed one of the oldest structures in Winnipeg. Built in 1889, it originally had a roundhouse with a turntable on one end, and was used for engine maintenance and repair. (The initials originally stood for Brakes and Boilers; later they

BOTH IMAGES: THE FORKS NORTH PORTAGE PARTNERSHIP

*Crossroads of the Continent*

understood the intrinsic importance of the history of The Forks.

Between 1989 and 1994, a series of archaeological digs, funded to the tune of $100,000 annually, took place under Kroker's direction. Invited to participate, the public swamped the program, filling every spot, even in inclement weather, and queuing in long lines to view the progress. In the first year, the program had 25,000 visitors. For three years, the digs continued at Fort Gibraltar II and Fort Garry I, then moved for another two years to the 3,000-year-old campsite near the Johnston Terminal. The latter sparked the public's imagination; sadly, however, the recession of the early 1990s brought the program to an end after the 1994 season. But Kroker has continued to be involved in every excavation since and has created a series of detailed and fascinating reports.

There were others who understood the importance of the site's long history. Some of them have served on The Forks Heritage Advisory Committee, which was established in 1988. Tireless in their enthusiasm and concern for the development of the site, the committee has met well over 100 times since, and has included distinguished archaeologists Leo Pettipas and Leigh Syms of the Manitoba Museum; historians Jean Friesen, later deputy premier, and David McDowell; Aboriginal activists Mary Richard and Clarence Nepinak; representatives of Parks Canada and St. Boniface's francophone community and others with a passion for preserving Winnipeg's past.

On the advice of these and others, a Heritage Interpretive Plan was developed in 1993. It established seven heritage themes, which identified key periods in the site's long past and recommended that renewal should be based on four underlying principles, The Forks as: Canada's crossroads,

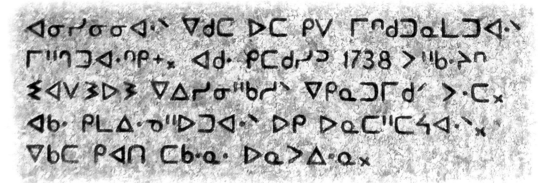

PETER ST. JOHN

a meeting place for old and new, and the meeting of diverse cultures. The final principle saw The Forks as a place for people to meet, work and play. The Forks National Historic Site has a similar mandate: to recognize, protect and present the significant stories of the people, the land and the rivers that flow through it. As Barbara Ford, operations manager at the national historic site, wrote in 1996:

> Some have viewed The Forks as a home, a place of still waters; others have seen it as a whirlpool, a place of challenge and change, while still others have used it as a stepping stone, to get to another place.

In addition, the 1993 interpretive plan ensured that there would be an Aboriginal presence, later identified as South Point. Finally, the plan emphasized that heritage development should attract visitors to this ancient meeting place, provide all-season recreation and educate the public in the long history of The Forks. It should instill in Winnipeggers a "pride of place" and emphasize the city's role as the gateway to the West.

Over the years, many developments have met these goals in whole or in part. Among them are the Wall Through Time (1990), the Archaeological Preserve (1990), Oodena Celebration Circle (1993) and The Forks National Historic Site's heritage sculptures, including the Gambling Sticks (2000).

The wall, which was described earlier, contains the

*The long history of The Forks is told in Cree, shown above, as well as French and English on the Wall Through Time.*

**P**erhaps nothing encapsulates the history of The Forks National Historic Site better than the award-winning sculpture that graces its entrance. Created by sculptor Marcel Gosselin, and titled The Path of Time, it includes two parts, two bronze shells, each weighing more than 1500 kilograms, and a limestone centrepiece. Together, they create a giant timepiece of sorts.

# THE PATH OF TIME

The bronze shells, each a quarter sphere, are made of melted down parts of railway cars; each carries a large cutwork ribbon of symbols depicting the tools that have been used at The Forks during its long history. This remarkable story moves from east to west — as does the sun and as did the European influence on Canada. The upper band of tools traces the path of the summer sun, while the lower traces the path of the sun during the spring and fall.

The symbols begin with a hand, man's fundamental tool, and continue with, among others, depictions of a tipi, a fish spear, a canoe and paddle, a bow and spear point. Here too, are a musket, the wheel of a Red River cart, a powder horn, a spinning wheel and a railway lantern.

On the other shell, among many other symbols, can be found a cobbler's last, a fire hydrant, a hammer and crescent wrench, a tractor, an automobile and a satellite. Cradling the sculpture is a circular limestone structure that symbolizes both the Earth and the sundance circle, the meeting place for many Aboriginal cultures. Other sculptures can be found throughout the site.

Marcel Gosselin is a native of St. Boniface and a graduate of the University of Manitoba. His work has been displayed from Alberta to Newfoundland.

PETER ST. JOHN

archaeological preserve located just east of Johnston Terminal. Reached by a series of ramps and stairs from the plaza, the preserve ensures that nothing is built on an area that is particularly rich in archaeological remains. Appropriately, the site is now covered by the Tall Grass Prairie Garden, a recreation of the magnificently diverse grasslands that once stretched from southern Manitoba to Texas. Planned by Cynthia Cohlmeyer, with help from volunteers, in 1999, it has been tenderly nurtured by Gina Nickle. With grasses stretching two metres or more into the air, and dozens of flowering plants and herbs that were used for medicinal and spiritual purposes for millennia, the prairie garden gives visitors a glimpse of the remarkable and now endangered grasslands that once covered southeastern Manitoba. To enhance awareness of this rich ecosystem, signs identify many plants and The Forks is partnering with the Nature Conservancy to tell the story of Winnipeg's prairie past through interactive displays.

Adjacent to the tall grass prairie is Oodena Celebration Circle. Oodena, which means "heart of the community" in Ojibwe, was created by landscape architect Hilderman and his associates at Hilderman Thomas Frank Cram in 1993. HTFC had been commissioned to create a physical entity that would create a spiritual and ceremonial "heart" for The Forks. It was a tall order, but as many have discovered in the past decade, Oodena has succeeded admirably.

**O**val and concave in shape, constructed of cobblestones with huge buttress surrounds, it is open to the elements and was designed to put those who gathered there in touch with the Earth's natural forces – air and water, earth and sky. Open to seasonal change and the movement of the stars, Oodena has about it something of the feel of an ancient stone ring. Yet the buttresses are fitted with laser lights and a sound system, which dance on the clouds and echo through the circle in ways the ancients never knew.

"Oodena was created to remind us of how man related to the elements before technology came along," says Hilderman, "but it also has to serve today's needs." He has also, only half in jest, called the circle "a Star-trekkian

Stonehenge". In the same vein, the multitalented Roy Mason, an Oji-Cree spiritual leader, university lecturer and school

THE FORKS NORTH PORTAGE PARTNERSHIP

PETER ST. JOHN

counsellor, who was consulted during the planning process, said the circular design and buttresses speak of the traditional Aboriginal wheel of life, and the four directions of life.

Oodena has gathered momentum over the years as a centre of activity at The Forks. More and more groups use it as a gathering and theatre space; those who have attended events there often say there is something almost mystical about the place. Roy Mason wouldn't be surprised.

Near the walking bridge to South Point stands Natalie Rostad's Healing Rock, a large block of granite that serves

*The Tall Grass Prairie, opposite, recalls the seemingly-endless grass-lands that once covered the eastern prairies from Manitoba to Texas, while Oodena, this page, was created as a spiritual and ceremonial heart for The Forks.*

*The Healing Rock, with one of the faces "released" from the stone.*

PETER ST. JOHN

as a canvas for spiritual openness and artistic inspiration. Rostad is a Winnipeg Aboriginal artist who studies rocks – the ancient bones of the Earth – seeking to interpret and release their spirituality. Her two-metre, one-tonne oblong balances on three points, which Rostad says represent the body, the mind and the spirit. At least a hundred visions – some highlighted by Rostad's remarkably nuanced painting – can be seen in the rock. And for two weeks every year, visitors may even encounter the artist herself as Rostad camps nearby to work on the monument, guarded by her enormous dog.

A step or two south of the Healing Rock is a steel bridge across the Assiniboine River. Built in 1912 for CN Rail, partially restored in the 1960s and recreated as a walking bridge and link to South Point as a 1999 Pan American Games project, the bridge was a Carnegie original. Its cement counterweight, designed to allow the bridge to lift to permit the passage of ships up the Assiniboine, was considered revolutionary in its time. Alas, it never worked, and to this day no ships of any size can enter the smaller river. Trains, however, used it for decades, rumbling over the steel spans to the East Yards for repair or storage.

Today, it serves as a popular and much-used link to South Point and vantage point over the plaza.

South Point is a remarkably unspoiled six-hectare tract of land at the true confluence of the rivers. Designated for Winnipeg's Aboriginal community, this peaceful, treed green space, crisscrossed by paths and backed by the Bridge of the Old Forts, is a counterpoint to the developments occurring on the north side of the Assiniboine. Its value, both to Aboriginal Manitobans and others should not be underestimated. On a visit to Winnipeg in the mid-1990s, Montreal Mayor Pierre Bourque climbed to the top of the tower. Looking out over South Point, he exclaimed, "I can't believe you still have all this wonderful green space, right here in the heart of the city." Many in Winnipeg concur.

Which is not to say that South Point may not, one day, be developed. Over the past fifteen years, several ideas have been contemplated; in 1997, Douglas Cardinal, the celebrated architect of the Museum of Civilization in Hull, Quebec, spent a day with Manitoba elders, seeking a vision for South Point. They developed the concept of "Spirit Island", which would include an interpretive centre and multi-use facility, a place of gathering and celebration, learning and communication, forgiveness and healing. For now, however, the focus of many members of the Native community is on Thunderbird House, the Aboriginal Centre of Winnipeg at Main and Higgins. Moreover, as Mary Richard points out, the community is deeply divided over the future of South Point.

By 1994, then, The Forks had emerged with a basic plan that combined a degree of very popular commercial development anchoring a larger, landscaped green space ringing the north side of the river confluence. There are many who believe

*Crossroads of the Continent*

a continuation of this kind of mixed-use development is both desirable and necessary, particularly if The Forks is ever to pay for itself, as it was initially intended to do. On the other side of the debate are those – both numerous and vocal – who believe that there is already entirely too much development at The Forks.

Jim August, current CEO of The Forks, says this dichotomy has always existed. "There was always a tension between the commercial proponents and the public park advocates." Steve Cohlmeyer believes the two positions are not irreconcilable. He is convinced that only the fear of change and a misunderstanding of what "public space" really means are inhibiting the proper development of the site.

Garry Hilderman, however, feels that there is always a tendency to move too quickly. "Open space is the most valuable commodity a city has. [The city] should guard and keep it." The angry discourse that accompanied two recent developments at The Forks – the creation of a hotel and the erection of a parkade – is proof that many Winnipeggers agree.

Phase II of The Forks began in 1995, with a new board under chair Ernie Keller and employing CEO Kent Smith. Despite its immediate and evident popularity, the site was not paying its way and the new board was faced with finding a road to financial viability as the federal and provincial governments began to withdraw their financial support. To facilitate this, in 1995 the Forks Renewal Corporation was merged with the North Portage Development Corporation, allowing annual shortfalls to be absorbed by the newly created Forks North Portage Development Corporation, and allow North Portage parking revenue to flow to The Forks.

The new entity also focused on creating private-public partnerships; since 1995 these agreements have significantly

added to the attractions at The Forks. In 1995 and '96, the old steam plant was converted into studios for A-Channel Television, with financial assistance from the Craig family of Brandon. In 1998, CanWest Global Park, a baseball stadium championed by Winnipeg entrepreneur Sam Katz, opened on the northwest corner of The Forks, north of Water Street. Home to the Winnipeg Goldeyes, the ball park has been a huge success, selling out its 7,000 seats for most games.

In 1999, the Theatre for Young People, pioneered by Leslie Silverman, spearheaded by Ruth Asper and sponsored by CanWest Global opened opposite the market. Today, its busy schedule of plays and festivals draw crowds year round.

The 1999 Pan American Games left a significant footprint at The Forks and created a whole new level of public expectation. Fifteen nights of free evening concerts drew thousands of people every evening to the newly-constructed Royal Bank Stage (later renamed, when Scotiabank took over the lease) in what is now known as Festival Park, at the heart of The Forks.

The huge, enthusiastic crowds sat on lawns that stretched for hundreds of metres in all directions; the grass, in turn, was

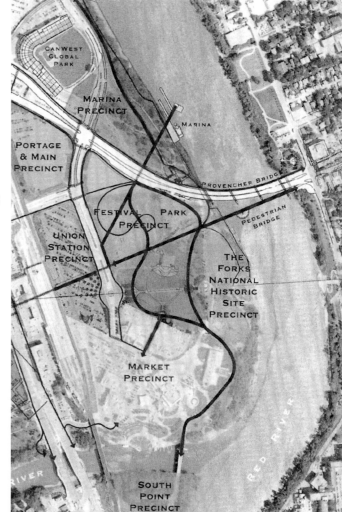

*The new master plan for The Forks, above, divides the site into seven "precincts".*

DENNIS FAST

THE FORKS NORTH PORTAGE PARTNERSHIP

*Perhaps more than anything else, The Forks is for celebrations. It's a place where people can come together to listen to the Winnipeg Symphony Orchestra, watch the sky light up with fireworks, or simply spend a memorable evening with a special someone.*

a legacy of other crowds, just as enthusiastic, who were involved with the 1990 Western Canada Summer Games. In 1989, with much of the site still just rubble and cinders, the organizers of the regional games convinced The Forks board to allow them to hold a series of events there. Turning the cinders into lawn was a must, but neither organization had money to spare and estimates of the cost of having the job done professionally ranged from $195,000 to $205,000. The solution: volunteers and cooperation on an impressive scale. Summer Games board member Don MacKenzie managed to obtain 8,000 square metres of sod for just $20,000, The Forks leveled the site and on three consecutive Saturdays hundreds of volunteers came out and laid sod in exchange for breakfast and a T-shirt proclaiming their contribution.

This remarkable donation of time and effort had several longterm impacts on The Forks. One was a realization that The Forks really could become the heart of the community. Another was a passion for green space; many of those who laid the sod and watched what had been a wasteland of debris turn into an expanse of lush lawn the following spring became committed to the Greening of The Forks.

Other cities have apparently experienced the same reaction.

Touring the Renaissance Centre project in Detroit with the interim board in 1987, former MP Dorothy Dobbie recalls being warned: "Don't leave the site green," said a director, "or people will think the place belongs to them."

In recent years, reconciling the gap between advocates of development and champions of open space has required a delicate balancing act and sometimes drawn a storm of protest. To attempt to draw crowds twenty-four hours a day, the board approved construction of a hotel in 2002, though not without considerable criticism. Parking has also been a constant concern, created by a simple and quite contradictory reality; nobody wants the site covered by asphalt, but everyone wants to park right in front of the market.

As Nick Diakiw recalls, following a public presentation on developments at The Forks during his term as CEO, he was startled by a member of the audience who stood up to say: "You must have misheard us, Mr. Diakiw. We were asking for more park, not more parking."

There are also those who question the underlying doctrine of self-sufficiency. In recent years, for example, the annual shortfall at The Forks has been under a million dollars. Many feel that's an entirely reasonable sum given the site's intense, year-round public use and significant tourism and marketing power; they believe it should be factored into the provincial and municipal budgets.

Both senior levels of government recognize the impact

THE FORKS NORTH PORTAGE PARTNERSHIP

of The Forks and regularly stage events there; despite certain well advertised boat problems and less than perfect weather, the federal government was delighted with the almost overwhelming response of Winnipeggers, who filled every available space when Queen Elizabeth II toured the site, listening to music, watching performances and receiving, as Prince Philip later put it, "every flower in Winnipeg" in October 2002.

From the beginning, the province has also made considerable efforts to organize events at The Forks. Premier Gary

Filmon put hundreds of hours into the bid for the Pan Am Games, always with The Forks in mind as one of the key venues. And as chair of the Festival Committee, his wife, Janice Filmon, was ultimately responsible for the enormously successful nightly entertainment during the games. Premier Gary Doer has been a passionate supporter of The Forks in a variety of roles for many years and continues to direct key events there. In 2001, all of Canada's premiers spent an evening at The Forks, beginning with a reception on the bridge to South Point and

*A sunny summer afternoon at The Forks: when not covered by water, the terraced harbourfront is usually awash with people.*

THE FORKS NORTH PORTAGE
PARTNERSHIP

*From concerts in Festival Park, to the jubilee visit of Queen Elizabeth II, every year more than 150 special events and festivals are held at The Forks.*

*Opposite page: Winter is no time for hibernation; from dawn to long after dusk, curling, hockey, tobogganing, snowboarding and endless skating make this a "happening" place, no matter what the weatherman says.*

ending with dancing under the canopy.

Indeed, special events and The Forks are now almost synonymous for Winnipeggers. In addition to two popular annual events – the New Year's Eve Celebration and the Canada Day Concert – special celebrations and fundraisers draw huge crowds. In June 1997, a Guess Who concert to raise money for flood relief drew 60,000, most of whom stayed despite heavy rain. Filmed by CBC, and replayed on more than one occasion, the event typified the best of Winnipeg, a passionate sense of community and a tremendous commitment to charity. In September 2000, a similar concert, initiated by Lloyd Axworthy to raise money for Children of War, drew 50,000 to listen to the Tragically Hip.

The success of such events led to the development of the Spiritfest Concerts for Causes, which occur during the summer months and solicit donations from those who attend. Based on a similar program in Boston, they raise about $75,000 in voluntary contributions each year. In 2002, the program won the International Downtown Association award, one of seven major awards won by The Forks.

Of the 150 or so events that take place at The Forks every year, about a tenth use the Festival Stage. Among the most memorable were the elegant opening and closing ceremonies of the 2002 North American Indigenous Games. The ceremonies, which drew thousands of Aboriginal athletes and cultural competitors from all parts of the continent, were a particularly appropriate use of The Forks, given its long history.

In part thanks to the special events, a parade of celebrities has passed through The Forks, including British royalty, Canadian prime ministers, American rock and film stars and even a former United States president. Jimmy Carter was in the midst of an impassioned speech on behalf of Habitat for Humanity one spring day, when the rising floodwaters actually began to swirl around his shoes.

The visit of Queen Elizabeth and the Duke of Edinburgh in 2002 caused a great commotion in the British press when the motor on the queen's water taxi suddenly stalled in mid-stream when crossing the Red River. Though slightly embarrassing at the time, in retrospect the incident has turned out to be almost priceless in terms of international awareness. There is, it's said, no such thing as bad publicity. Other notables who have visited include Rob Lowe, late of television's West Wing, actors Shirley Maclaine, Keanu Reeves and William Hurt, and Garth Brooks – via helicopter.

In winter, the festivities are quite literally put on ice. Skating and walking trails meander for more than four kilometres along the Assiniboine, decorated with evergreens and punctuated at regular intervals by warming

IAN WARD

*Crossroads of the Continent*

WINTER IMAGES: THE FORKS NORTH PORTAGE PARTNERSHIP

shack. As well, a skating trail winds through The Forks itself, from the frozen pond in Festival Park, behind the Children's Museum, around Oodena and over the railway bridge. Indeed, quite a number of people employed at The Forks and elsewhere downtown skate to work, some all the way from Crescentwood. Plans for the future include an extension of the river ice trails down the Red River to Point Douglas, which will make them longer than their Ottawa equivalent, on the Rideau Canal.

Winter facilities at The Forks also include a toboggan slide, snowboard park and hockey pond. On the river, curling rinks and an enormous hockey rink draw dozens of teams, particularly during February's hugely popular Festival du Voyageur. And a dogsled classic is run along the river out to the University of Manitoba, echoing the dog trains of old that connected The Forks with places north, south and west.

Some are regulars at The Forks; one of the most celebrated

*T*here are few who know the business of The Forks Market better than Mo Razik. He was there even before either of his retail establishments - Fenton's Gourmet Foods and Fenton's Wine Merchants — were. In fact, as he recalls with some relish, when he began mapping out the stores, what is now the central market area was nothing but a gravel road. "I drove right up," he says, "and parked my car right in front of the store."

# THE MARKET

Things have changed in the past decade and a half. Today, there are fifty businesses in The Forks Market and another twenty in Johnston Terminal.

Like most of the other business owners — not to mention their tens of thousands of customers — Razik believes an outing at The Forks should be a unique experience. Whether shoppers are looking for fine wines, Manitoba-grown squash and berries or Canadian-made gifts, Razik and his colleagues have worked hard to make the market feel like the real thing — with a little help from their friends in government.

It's hard to imagine, for example, the Golden Boy gracing the aisles of your local supermarket. Yet there he was, in all his increasingly golden glory, during the summer of 2002. It's unlikely Manitobans will have another opportunity to view the province's best-known symbol at such close proximity for decades, perhaps even centuries.

Summer is not a time that the merchants at The Forks ever contemplate holidays, for the market and the adjoining shops at Johnston Terminal are packed seven days a week. Other times of the year are not quite as busy, though weekends buzz with shoppers year round. But if there is one wish the merchants share, one shop owner confides, its that Manitobans would quit thinking of The Forks as a place just for specialty items and realize they could do almost all their shopping there. With the place ever more popular, that might happen sooner than he realizes. And then when would holidays be scheduled?

THE FORKS
MARKET
COURTYARD

PETER ST. JOHN

is a skater who turns up most days to figure skate at the small rink on the plaza. Occasionally, he brings out a small stuffed monkey and places it at the centre of the ice. When this happens, word goes around the market and people stream out to watch; once the audience is in place, he puts on a demonstration of skating for several minutes, then whirls and heads straight for the monkey, soaring over it to a roar of appreciation from the assembled throng.

*The new pedestrian bridge over the Red will greatly enhance access to the east side of the river, allowing visitors to easily tour the magnificent facade of St. Boniface Cathedral, below.*

**T**wo of the most popular recent additions to The Forks are the pedestrian bridge to St. Boniface and the Splash Dash water taxi service. After nearly a century, the footbridge will right an historic wrong, by restoring the original linear connection between Broadway and Provencher. This is, in fact,

the third Broadway Bridge. The first, an obviously fragile wooden construction, opened in April 1882, only to be swept away just days later by the floodwaters of the Red. A year later, its much anticipated replacement provided a link that served the French and English communities for three decades, though by 1910 there were concerns about its ability to handle the vastly increased vehicular and streetcar traffic that marked the burgeoning city.

But it was traffic of another kind that closed the bridge for good. In 1912, following the construction of Union Station, and the development of the East Yards, motor traffic was barred from the bridge. Residents of St. Boniface felt cut off, humiliated, excluded from Winnipeg. Those feelings remained, even after the first Provencher Bridge opened in 1917. The new bridge will not only allow St. Boniface residents direct access to The Forks, but give visitors to The Forks easy communication with Winnipeg's beautiful and historic francophone community. It should also be considerably more versatile than its utilitarian predecessors; with a bridge house midstream. And salvaged components of the old Broadway Bridge will be featured in the east and west landings and central plaza.

The water taxi service has proven to be tremendously popular with Winnipeggers. Working from a growing series of docks from Crescentwood down the Assiniboine to The Forks, St. Boniface and beyond, the speedy, canopied taxis run on a regular daily

COURTESY OF GABOURY PRÉFONTAINE PERRY

IAN WARD

*Crossroads of the Continent*

IMAGES THIS PAGE BY DENNIS FAST

schedule that provides increased morning and evening rush hour service and regular transport dozens of times a day from late spring to mid-autumn. Winnipeggers love it; many put their cars away and take the taxis to work every day. Others plan evenings at The Forks with no concerns about designated drivers or finding a parking spot. The Splash Dash service also provides tours of the rivers, and a larger boat for corporate and family outings.

The only drawback to the entire exercise has been the unexpected series of summer floods that have drowned both the riverwalks and the harbour in recent years. In each case,

the owners of the taxi service have operated as long as they can, then fretted – as do thousands of Winnipeggers – until the water receded. At last, however, the province has stepped in with a promise to study the impact of summer use of the floodways on both rivers, attempting to balance the financial and tourism impact on Winnipegers against the financial impact of allowing low-lying rural fields to be flooded. If a solution can be found, both the partnership that operates the taxi service and the thousands that enjoy it will be grateful.

A new hotel, a parkade and the footbridge to St. Boniface are all part of Phase III of The Forks development plan,

*In addition to its permanent features, the Manitoba Children's Museum offers a multitude of activities and programs including after-school crafts, holiday festivities and theme-based summer day camps.*

THE FORKS NORTH PORTAGE PARTNERSHIP

*Also for young visitors is the Manitoba Theatre for Young People, which showcases a wide variety of theatrical productions between October and mid-April; the summer months are devoted to a series of week-long day camps.*

which began in 2001 under a board chaired by Bill Norrie and a staff headed by Jim August. Both have been involved, in one capacity or another, with The Forks since the beginning.

The 116-bed hotel, which was approved after considerable controversy, will incorporate a large fireplace at the entrance and house some of the nearly 5,000-year-old artifacts unearthed at The Forks. The parkade, though backed by a number of the merchants at The Forks was also controversial and a second similar structure was put on hold to examine other parking alternatives.

While the new hotel and parkade are located in the "Market Precinct", as the Phase III plan calls it, the main focus for the future is likely to be on the site's other areas. As Parks Canada's Barbara Ford points out, "Everyone wants to leave their footprints [here], but there is much more to The Forks than meets the eye. The current Forks is only a snapshot in time."

Certainly, there are plans aplenty. For example, Festival Park, which circles the outdoor stage between The Forks National Historic Site and Union Station, will include a meandering pedestrian path with themed sculpture gardens and water features, as well as a greenhouse and pond. And treed and landscaped, the path leading to the new bridge may remind some of a miniature Champs Elysée as it passes through Festival Park. Throughout, there will be an emphasis on the area's long and significant history, for it was here, archaeologist Sid Kroker believes, that the remarkable Peace Meeting took place about 650 years ago (see page 62).

It may be here that a new human rights museum, a project that has been strongly supported by Winnipeg's Asper family, will be located. With a focus on the history of human rights, it would tell the stories of many communities that have experienced and overcome racial prejudice, including Native North Americans, as well as Canada's Jewish, Chinese, Japanese and Islamic communities. A museum truly national in scope would be a significant attraction, potentially drawing thousands to The Forks every year.

Farther north are the "Marina Precinct", which runs along the river from Provencher Bridge to the Exchange District and the "Portage and Main Precinct", from York almost to Winnipeg's famously windy corner.

Plans for The Forks include more than landscaping or construction, and reach beyond the site's boundaries to include connections to the Exchange District, the downtown business core, Union Station and one the oldest pieces of Forks history, the Upper Fort Garry Governor's Gate. In recent years, the staff at both The Forks National Historic Site and The Forks itself have expanded their interpretive programming to emphasize these links. Five days a week during the summer months, live, bilingual theatrical walking tours, conducted by costumed actors, tour The Forks.

Recently, in addition to partnering with ethnic and heritage groups, staff members at both the national historic site and The Forks have also created liaisons with downtown business firms, as well as those in St. Boniface; the latter will only be strengthened by the new pedestrian bridge. Their joint aim is to celebrate Winnipeg's remarkable and historic central green space, to strengthen business ties with this historic meeting place and ultimately to create economic self-sufficiency.

There are those, including Steve Cohlmeyer and many of the merchants at The Forks, who believe that self-sufficiency will never be achieved without a residential component. Yet from the outset, Winnipeggers have made it clear they oppose private housing at The Forks. Cohlmeyer argues that a discreet residential neighbourhood would complement the commercial and recreational opportunities The Forks offers. "A park," he says, "need not consist of grass only. It could also include plazas and developed areas where people feel comfortable, and return again and again."

Critics of Forks development believe this philosophy is nothing more than creeping commercialism, which will ultimately make the site indistinguishable from the rest of the city, leaving only The Forks National Historic Site as green space. They contend that the original vision for The Forks is slipping away, pressured by City Hall and the need for financial independence. And they believe that like New York's Central Park, open space at The Forks will increase housing in adjacent areas, like Waterfront Drive.

Yet there may be a middle road between these positions. Even a glance at the map of Winnipeg shows The Forks as the true hub of the city, with tremendous potential as a catalyst. The division of the site into regions or precincts may well be the way to preserve green space in some areas and encourage discreet development in others, creating a flow of people and business from the adjacent business communities and benefiting all. To employ a parallel, the United Nations is only as effective as the states who use it; in the same way, The Forks

may succeed to the degree that the adjoining regions cooperate with and work through it. Greatly simplified then, the role of The Forks is to be available for use, hanging on to its historical and cultural mandate and building bridges – both concrete and abstract – to the rest of the city.

Those bridges could include enhanced transportation links. The skating trails to the park, as well as the riverwalk and water taxis, have overwhelmingly demonstrated that when the links are made, people will use them. More links would undoubtedly mean more use and more people. That is why The Forks is currently examining several possibilities, including a downtown streetcar system extending along York Avenue through The Forks Arrival Square to St. Boniface, and connecting with Waterfront Drive and the Exchange District.

For those who prefer to walk, paths along the Red River to the Exchange District and Point Douglas are planned, as are connections from the last remnant of Upper Fort Garry, the Governor's Gate. This window on Winnipeg's fur trade past, though located on Main Street across from Union Station, is unknown to most Winnipeggers. In fact, Main Street runs right through what was once its southeast corner; the fort was dismantled in the early 1880s to straighten the street. This grand emporium of the trade also fronted on the Assiniboine River and there are plans to recapture that river view, giving Main Street some much needed green space and reestablishing the historic connections between the fort and The Forks.

All in all, The Forks is a work in progress and, just as its creation was the work of visionaries and cooperating levels of government, so its future will depend on good leadership to maintain and strengthen this magnificent vision – The Forks as a heritage centre and meeting place for future generations.

*One of the annual winter highlights is Festival du Voyageur, which spills over from its base in St. Boniface to include activities, including educational snow sculptures and dogsled races on the rivers and at The Forks.*

PETER ST. JOHN

DOGSLED AND RIVERTRAIL IMAGES: THE FORKS
NORTH PORTAGE PARTNERSHIP

# BIBLIOGRAPHY

### CHAPTER ONE  The Foundation of The Forks

*Geological History of Saskatchewan*, by Dr. John Storer, Saskatchewan Museum of Natural History, Regina, 1989

*Minnesota's Geology*, by Richard W. Ojakangas and Charles L. Matsch, University of Minnesota Press, Minneapolis, 1982

*Natural Heritage of Manitoba: Legacy of the Ice Age*, James Teller, ed., Winnipeg

*The Land Before Us: The Making of Ancient Alberta*, by The Royal Tyrrell Museum of Palaeontology, Red Deer College Press, 1994

### CHAPTER TWO  Laying Down the Landscape

*The Face of North Dakota*, by John P. Bluemle, North Dakota Geological Survey, Educational Series 21, 1991

*The Geography of Manitoba: Its Land and Its People*, John Welsted, John Everitt and Christof Staedel, eds, University of Manitoba Press, 1996

*The Great Lake: The Beauty and the Treachery of Lake Winnipeg*, by Frances Russell, Heartland Associates, Winnipeg, 2000

"Holocene evolution of the Assiniboine River paleochannels and Portage la Prairie alluvial fan", in *The Canadian Journal of Earth Sciences*, Vol 26, 1989

### CHAPTER THREE  A Continental Crossroads

*A 3,000 Year Old Native Campsite and Trade Centre at The Forks*, compiled by Sid Kroker and Pam Goundry, published with the assistance of The Forks Renewal Corporation, Canadian Parks Service and Manitoba Culture, Heritage and Citizenship, 1993

*Archaeological Monitoring and Mitigation of the Assiniboine Riverfront Quay*, by Sid Kroker and Pamela Goundry, The Forks Renewal Corporation, 1989

*Archaeological Monitoring of the Stage I Construction Program*, by Sid Kroker and Pamela Goundry, The Forks Renewal Corporation, 1990

*North Assiniboine Node Archaeological Impact Assessment*, by Sid Kroker, The Forks Renewal Corporation, 1989

### CHAPTER FOUR  A Hub of the Fur Trade

*Exploring the Fur Trade Routes of North America*, second edition, by Barbara Huck et. al., Heartland Associates, Winnipeg, 2002

"Fort Douglas", by Martha McCarthy, a report prepared for Manitoba Historic Resources Branch, 1990

*Fur Trade Wars*, by Jack Bumstead, Great Plains Publications, Winnipeg, 1999

*Indians and the Fur Trade*, by A.J. Ray, University of Toronto Press, Toronto, 1974

*In Search of the Western Sea: Selected Journals of La Verendrye*, by Denis Combet, Great Plains Publications, Winnipeg, 2001

*The Canadian Prairies: A History*, by Gerald Friesen, University of Toronto Press, 1984

"The Hudson's Bay Company and the Fur Trade: 1670 – 1870", by Glyndwr Williams, in *The Beaver*, special edition, 1983

### CHAPTER FIVE  By Water to Winnipeg

*Backwater to Park: The Forks in Relation to Downtown Winnipeg*, by R.R. Rostecki

*The Forks and the Battle of Seven Oaks in Manitoba History,* Robert Coutts and Richard Stuart, editors, Manitoba Historical Society, 1994

*Fire Canoe: Prairie Steamboat Days Revisited*, by Ted Barris, Toronto, McClelland and Stewart, 1977

*My First Flatboat Trip Down the Red River and Incidents Connected Therewith*, by George Winship, manuscript, PAM, MG3 B15

*My Canadian Journal, 1872-1878*, by Hariot Georgina Hamilton-Temple-Blackwood, Marchioness of Dufferin and Ava, London, 1891

"Notes of a Journey to the North West Land", *The Sunday at Home*, January 20, 1883, PAM, MG1B28, 1950–9

*Red River*, by J. J. Hargrave, Montreal, 1871

"Steamboating on the Red River", by Marion Herriott, *Minnesota History*, September 1940

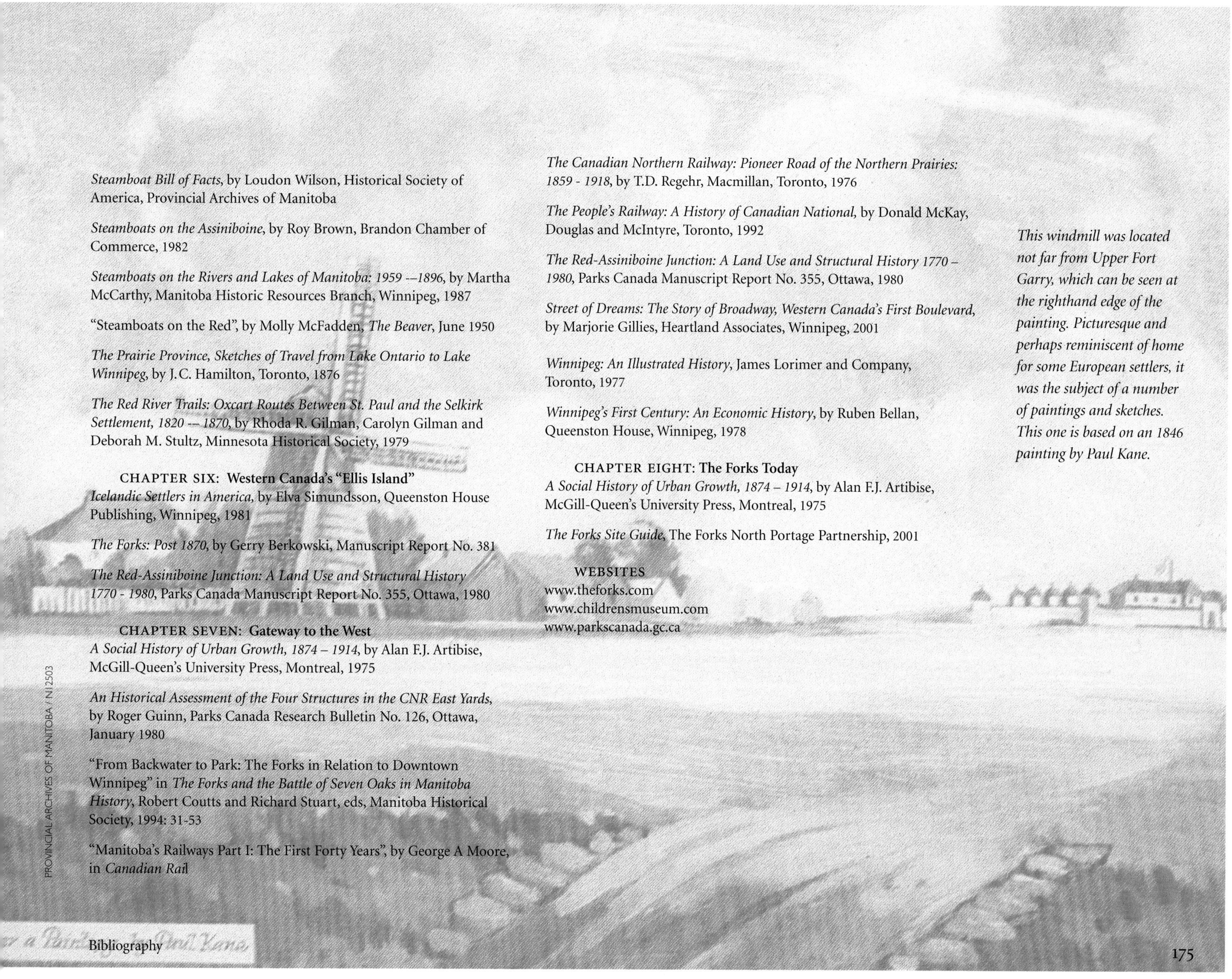

*Steamboat Bill of Facts*, by Loudon Wilson, Historical Society of America, Provincial Archives of Manitoba

*Steamboats on the Assiniboine*, by Roy Brown, Brandon Chamber of Commerce, 1982

*Steamboats on the Rivers and Lakes of Manitoba: 1959 -–1896*, by Martha McCarthy, Manitoba Historic Resources Branch, Winnipeg, 1987

"Steamboats on the Red", by Molly McFadden, *The Beaver*, June 1950

*The Prairie Province, Sketches of Travel from Lake Ontario to Lake Winnipeg*, by J. C. Hamilton, Toronto, 1876

*The Red River Trails: Oxcart Routes Between St. Paul and the Selkirk Settlement, 1820 -– 1870*, by Rhoda R. Gilman, Carolyn Gilman and Deborah M. Stultz, Minnesota Historical Society, 1979

**CHAPTER SIX: Western Canada's "Ellis Island"**
*Icelandic Settlers in America*, by Elva Simundsson, Queenston House Publishing, Winnipeg, 1981

*The Forks: Post 1870*, by Gerry Berkowski, Manuscript Report No. 381

*The Red-Assiniboine Junction: A Land Use and Structural History 1770 - 1980*, Parks Canada Manuscript Report No. 355, Ottawa, 1980

**CHAPTER SEVEN: Gateway to the West**
*A Social History of Urban Growth, 1874 – 1914*, by Alan F.J. Artibise, McGill-Queen's University Press, Montreal, 1975

*An Historical Assessment of the Four Structures in the CNR East Yards*, by Roger Guinn, Parks Canada Research Bulletin No. 126, Ottawa, January 1980

"From Backwater to Park: The Forks in Relation to Downtown Winnipeg" in *The Forks and the Battle of Seven Oaks in Manitoba History*, Robert Coutts and Richard Stuart, eds, Manitoba Historical Society, 1994: 31-53

"Manitoba's Railways Part I: The First Forty Years", by George A Moore, in *Canadian Rail*

*The Canadian Northern Railway: Pioneer Road of the Northern Prairies: 1859 - 1918*, by T.D. Regehr, Macmillan, Toronto, 1976

*The People's Railway: A History of Canadian National*, by Donald McKay, Douglas and McIntyre, Toronto, 1992

*The Red-Assiniboine Junction: A Land Use and Structural History 1770 – 1980*, Parks Canada Manuscript Report No. 355, Ottawa, 1980

*Street of Dreams: The Story of Broadway, Western Canada's First Boulevard*, by Marjorie Gillies, Heartland Associates, Winnipeg, 2001

*Winnipeg: An Illustrated History*, James Lorimer and Company, Toronto, 1977

*Winnipeg's First Century: An Economic History*, by Ruben Bellan, Queenston House, Winnipeg, 1978

**CHAPTER EIGHT: The Forks Today**
*A Social History of Urban Growth, 1874 – 1914*, by Alan F.J. Artibise, McGill-Queen's University Press, Montreal, 1975

*The Forks Site Guide*, The Forks North Portage Partnership, 2001

**WEBSITES**
www.theforks.com
www.childrensmuseum.com
www.parkscanada.gc.ca

This windmill was located not far from Upper Fort Garry, which can be seen at the righthand edge of the painting. Picturesque and perhaps reminiscent of home for some European settlers, it was the subject of a number of paintings and sketches. This one is based on an 1846 painting by Paul Kane.

PROVINCIAL ARCHIVES OF MANITOBA / N12503

Bibliography

# TIMELINE

## MODERN ERA

2003 Third Broadway Bridge opens
      Publication of *Crossroads of the Continent*
2002 Royal Jubilee visit
      North American Indigenous Games
2001 Phase III Forks plan
1999 Pan Am Games
1997 Red River flood
1995 Phase II Forks plan
      The Forks North Portage Partnership created
1990 Union Station awarded heritage designation
      Western Canada Summer Games
1989–93 Forks public archaeology program
1989 Forks National Historic Site opens
1988 Forks Heritage Advisory Committee created
1987–90 Riverwalk created
1987 Forks Renewal Corporation, Phase I
1986 Tri-level East Yards Task Force
1980 Agreements for Recreation and Culture (ARC)
1974 Red and Assiniboine Rivers Tourism and Recreation study
1950 Red River flood
1939–45 World War II
1919 Winnipeg General Strike
1917 Canadian National Railways created
1914–18 World War I
1911 Union Station opens
      Second Broadway Bridge closed
1909-10 Construction of stables (now The Forks Market)
1908 St. Boniface Cathedral opens
1891–95 Fort Garry Park at The Forks
1898 Canadian Northern and Grand Trunk Pacific Railway
1889 Construction of the B & B Building (now Children's Museum)
1888 Northern Pacific and Manitoba Railroad
1882–3 First and second Broadway Bridges built
1877 First railway engine – *Countess of Dufferin* – arrives at The Forks
1872–84 Forks used as Western Canada's immigration centre
1873 City of Winnipeg created
1870 Province of Manitoba created
      Louis Riel elected to head provisional Manitoba government

1859 First steamboat – *Anson Northup* – arrives at The Forks
1852 Red River flood
1835 Upper Fort Garry completed
1826 Red River flood – worst in 350 years
1821 Hudson's Bay Company and North West Company merge
      Fort Gibraltar II becomes Garry I
1817 Fort Gibraltar II built
1816 Fort Gibraltar I destroyed by HBC
      Battle of Seven Oaks
      Métis seize Fort Douglas
1812 Selkirk settlers arrive at The Forks
      Fort Douglas built just downstream
1810 Fort Gibraltar I built
1790 NWC traders at Forks
      Métis community begins to grow on east side of the river
1762 Red River flood
1747 Red River flood
1738 Fort Rouge – the first fur post – built at The Forks
1400 Ancestral Cree, Anishinabe and Dakota all using The Forks
      First farming at The Forks?
1325 Great Peace Meeting at The Forks
1250 Assiniboine River floods – Flood of the Millennium?

## ANCIENT EVENTS AT THE FORKS – YEARS BEFORE PRESENT (BP)

1,300 – 2000 BP Assiniboine River returns to channel at The Forks
6,000 – 125 BP First Nations use Forks regularly to fish and trade
7,000 BP Ancestral Assiniboine moves to flow into Lake Manitoba
7,500 BP Ancestral Assiniboine flows to The Forks
8,000 BP Lake Agassiz retreats from The Forks
11,000 – 8,000 BP Lake Agassiz covers The Forks
22,000 – 11,000 BP Late Wisconsinan glaciation
2 mya to 22,000 BP North America experiences between 17 and 20 glaciations. Mammoths, mastodons and other mammals at The Forks during interglacial periods
2 mya Ice Age begins
65–2 mya Forks populated by early mammals
65 mya Extinction event—dinosaurs die
460 mya – 60 mya Forks intermittently covered by North American seaway